Sexy

Sexy

The Quest for Erotic Virtue in Perplexing Times

By Jeff Mallinson

An imprint of New Reformation Publications

Sexy: The Quest for Erotic Virtue in Perplexing Times

Unless otherwise noted, all Scripture quotations are taken from the Revised Standard Version of the Bible, copyright 1952 (2nd edition, 1971) by the Division of Christian Education of the National Council of the Churches of Christ in the USA. Used by permission. All rights reserved.

Hallelujah
Words and Music by Leonard Cohen
Copyright © 1985 Sony/ATV Music Publishing LLC
All Rights Administered by Sony/ATV Music Publishing LLC, 424 Church Street, Suite 1200, Nashville, TN 37219
International Copyright Secured All Rights Reserved
Reprinted by Permission of Hal Leonard LLC

Anthem
Words and Music by Leonard Cohen
Copyright © 1992 Sony/ATV Music Publishing LLC and Stranger Music Inc.
All Rights Administered by Sony/ATV Music Publishing LLC, 424 Church Street, Suite 1200, Nashville, TN 37219
International Copyright Secured All Rights Reserved
Reprinted by Permission of Hal Leonard LLC

Bird On The Wire (Bird On A Wire)
Words and Music by Leonard Cohen
Copyright © 1968 Sony/ATV Music Publishing LLC
Copyright Renewed
All Rights Administered by Sony/ATV Music Publishing LLC, 424 Church Street, Suite 1200, Nashville, TN 37219
International Copyright Secured All Rights Reserved
Reprinted by Permission of Hal Leonard LLC

Published by:
Virtue in the Wasteland Books
PO Box 54032
Irvine, CA 92619-4032

Publisher's Cataloging-In-Publication Data
(Prepared by The Donohue Group, Inc.)

Names: Mallinson, Jeffrey.
Title: Sexy : the quest for erotic virtue in perplexing times / by Jeff Mallinson.
Description: Irvine, CA : Virtue in the Wasteland Books, an imprint of New Reformation Publications, [2017] | Includes bibliographical references.
Identifiers: ISBN 978-1-945500-81-7 (hardcover) | ISBN 978-1-945500-79-4 (softcover) | ISBN 978-1-945500-80-0 (ebook)
Subjects: LCSH: Sex—Religious aspects—Christianity. | Love—Religious aspects—Christianity. | Intimacy (Psychology)—Religious aspects—Christianity. | Man–woman relationships—Religious aspects—Christianity.
Classification: LCC BT708 .M35 2017 (print) | LCC BT708 (ebook) | DDC 248.4—dc23

Virtue in the Wasteland Books is an imprint of New Reformation Publications, exploring goodness, truth and beauty in our complex culture.

Printed in the United States of America

Contents

To Stacie

The Religious and Philosophical Perspective of This Book

It is foolhardy to pretend that any author approaches his or her subject from a completely neutral vantage point. It is also rarely the case that an author is perfectly consistent. I'm a Lutheran Christian, albeit relatively untamed. Because of my relatively traditional context and background, and I will often use language and concepts familiar to that community. Having taught world religions and philosophy over the years, I will also introduce concepts and themes drawn from various cultures. This is not to assume that all religions are saying the same thing but to draw wisdom wherever it is found.[1] Classically, Christians have often enjoyed the spoils of Greco-Roman philosophy—say, from Seneca or Plato—without fear of syncretism (the amalgamation of two different religions into a new synthesis). I believe we Western Christians are free to do the same with the great philosophers of the East, among other rich cultures. In this, I don't mean to engage in some goofy cultural appropriation; rather, it is in the spirit of charitable *appreciation* of insights from near and far. Even if you don't share my Christian commitment, therefore, you just might gain life-changing insights for personal healing and the healing of romantic relationships. I have a hunch that it works best with a deep rootedness in the core message of Jesus, and if you are not now religious, you might want to explore some of the best Christian ideas down the line. But for now, let's sit back, rest easy, know that we are in friendly company, and get down to the business of being honest about ourselves and our loves.

---

[1] See the introduction to Stephen Prothero, *God Is Not One: The Eight Rival Religions That Run the World* (New York: HarperOne, 2010), to understand this point in depth.

How to Read This Book

I tend to start my classes and writing with attention to methodological and background ideas. This means that often the easier-to-understand parts are in the middle and end. Some readers will want to skip to the chapter or chapters that apply best to their life circumstances and circle back to other chapters as needed. I sometimes get playful or anecdotal in the book. Sometimes I invite you to go along with me on more theoretical and complicated academic matters. Try to wrestle through that stuff, but if it isn't working for you, it won't hurt to skip a section here or there. Note also that I'm trying to throw out ideas for discussion and contemplation. I'm not trying to be overly prescriptive here; rather, I'm inviting readers to consider Christian sexual ethics not as a burdensome list of prohibitions but as an invitation to a beautiful experience of embodied love. Christian love makes a certain kind of romantic relationship possible. That's the good message we explore in this book. Therefore, even if you disagree with my conclusions, perhaps you will at least find value in applying the *perspective* and background assumptions set forth. The perspective—the New Logic of the Gospel—is what I'm most interested in promoting.

Readers should be wary of trying to justify their own misdeeds through these pages. I find some of the chapters to be sort of like a Rorschach test. Readers get what they want to find. For instance, I've had one person say that he never really considered divorce until reading my chapter about it. Another person read the same chapter and determined that she should remain in her marriage. The good news here is that I do indeed intend not to tell you precisely what to do in each situation but instead to give you tools for developing certain values and character, and thinking about relationships along the lines of virtue rather than legalism. That said, if you think that what I'm doing in this book is meant to encourage permissiveness or moral laxity, that's simply not the case. I'm intent on inviting people to a life of radical commitment, unconditional love, and marital fidelity. I just don't think shouting rules at people is how we get there. It needs to be an internalized, virtue-based way of living rather than a blind obedience to a set of codes. In the end, I hope you and I share at least one common goal: creating and sustaining healthy erotic lives.

Sexual Identity and Other Debated Topics

This book focuses on big-picture issues related to sexuality, relationships, and embodiment. I hope its principles will be helpful for people who find themselves connected to an identity contained under the letters LGBT. However, the main focus *here* is the old boy meets girl, boy marries girl, both struggle, contemplate divorce, patch things up, and grow old. I'm indeed interested in the ways in which Christians can better address perplexing issues related to gender, sexual orientation, celibacy, asexuality, androgyny, remarriage, and polyamory. And perhaps I'll write about such topics in a future book. For this particular book, though, I needed to limit the scope of our exploration.

That said, if you don't find the hope, positive possibilities, or the answers you're looking for after reading this book, don't give up. Instead, find wiser or more applicable authors, but in the meantime, please feel free to contact me directly online (virtueinthewasteland .com). Let me know what issues still need to be addressed. What pains might I have accidentally caused you? What do you think I'm missing? Or if you have further questions, ask them. I'm notoriously slow in responding, even to close friends, but I usually get to everything eventually.

Glossary

The following phrases and terms occur throughout this book, and if you aren't familiar with the way I use them, you might be thrown off, offended, or confused. To avoid that, keep these definitions handy. Note that some definitions involve reference to other definitions in this glossary.

Agape. Unconditional love that draws on the infinite grace of God. It is the kind of love one might dare to have even for an enemy, since it is unconcerned about transaction. It does not expect something in return; that is to say, it is not an investment. It is pure gift, no strings attached.

Eros. Desire for unity with something beyond our own egos. Though sometimes associated with sexual desire, it is much deeper than that. It is the drive for life and connection in the universe. It is not about lust but rather about intimacy. It can be applied to a desire for God, for connection with nature, and for unity with a sexual partner. When paired with *agape*, it ignites what this book will refer to as true *sexiness*.

Mysticism. Experience and awareness of divine reality, a partial glimpse or foretaste of what the medieval theologians called the beatific (blessed) vision. Consciousness of how things truly are, accompanied by a moment of ecstasy and inner peace that all is well despite the pain and doom we see around us. This is a difficult, possibly distracting term, since people use it in various ways. I myself have written about false mysticisms of the church, wherein I was referring to claims that God gave some guy down the road a special revelation never before revealed. I remain exceedingly skeptical about those who claim to have received some wild new teaching, and I remain allergic to culty leaders of all brands. I remain uncomfortable with those expressions of religion that rely on or cultivate spectacular spiritual signs. I take with a grain of salt even the pronouncements of church leaders like the pope if they claim to infallibly speak for the Almighty. One might call those things "mysticisms," since the term often means direct, *unmediated* access to God. This sort of thing is closer to what should be called *magic*, since magic is about harnessing or conjuring supernatural forces to do one's bidding. Healthy mysticism of the cross is rooted in the grace of God, which we seek in, with, and under tangible *means*. For instance, I encounter an experience of God's grace both intellectually and emotionally in the sacrament of Holy Communion. There, I hear, taste, and see that the Lord is good. I do this alongside others, many of whom I otherwise might not like, and experience vertical restoration (the relationship between me and God) and horizontal restoration (the relationships between me and other people).[2]

New Logic, the.   Living a life of love that has been set free and is empowered by the astounding good news of divine grace given on account of Christ. It is Christian enlightenment born out of

---

[2] For a full account of this concept, check out Bengt Hoffman, *Theology of the Heart: The Role of Mysticism in the Theology of Martin Luther* (Minneapolis: Kirk House, 2003).

repentance—which involves a radical change of mind or spiritual enlightenment—that occurs when we recognize the seriousness of holy judgment on our false beliefs and practices. It playfully shrugs off the seemingly unrelenting logic of nature, which only knows law, self-interest, violence, competition, and death; it takes seriously the ways in which grace can transform our relationships, even with the most unlovable and broken people among us. It is a state of mind that chooses empathy over scorn; it believes in the hope of redemption and transformation for all, even if we aren't the ones to do the healing. It is the Tao of Jesus. It produces a peace that transcends understanding, but a peace that—when we rest in its comforting light—turns out to be the true, deeper magic (not an illusion or wishful thinking) in, with, and under all things. From this peace, we discover the security necessary for healthy romantic and sexual lives.

Old Logic, the. Karmic thinking. Spiritual bean counting. It is transactional and falsely assumes relationships are best when governed by hope of reward and fear of punishment. It is legalistic. It looks like the safe choice for romantic well-being, but it is its greatest threat. Now, in some forms of Buddhism, *karma* refers not to a law of retribution but has more to do with inertia. If we create momentum in an unhealthy way, we find ourselves moving, even against our wills, away from goodness, truth, and beauty. There's something true in this way of thinking. Nonetheless, the New Logic is deeper than this and works miracles, even when our inertia has us dangerously close to the edge of the abyss.

Penultimate, the. Literally, "the second to last." It refers to the existence we experience in this life. German theologian Dietrich Bonhoeffer uses it to describe how we ought to live in this world of imperfection, suffering, and uncertainty. Saint Paul writes that we see now in a glass darkly but will someday see God face-to-face (1 Cor. 13:12). Likewise, Martin Luther treats the life of faith as being an "already-but-not-yet" sort of reality. From this perspective, we free ourselves from having all the answers when we confront perplexing questions, especially complex situations related to our sexuality. By recognizing the penultimate nature of our current reality, which exists before God's new heavens and earth are established, we can be more compassionate toward others who see things differently than we. We can mourn with those who mourn (and even struggle with those who struggle in their sexual lives) without making the mistakes committed by Job's counselors, who thought in terms of the karmic Old Logic. We are able to live with many tensions and paradoxes of this life—not because we doubt the promises of the ultimate but precisely because our hope in the ultimate allows us to relax a little, have a little fun, release our need to control our world and others, and rest assured that everything will be OK in the end. When understood, it teaches us to "care and not to care," as T. S. Eliot says in "Ash Wednesday."

Sexy/sexiness. The drive for life; the meeting point between *eros* and *agape*, hope rather than despair, life rather than shrinking into death. It creates a desire in us to share that kind of unconditional love with all those around us, including our romantic partners. Its opposite is despair, or the cardinal sin of

ссhia — sloth. Now, sloth is not laziness or fatigue; it is the vice people develop when they have no sense of meaning or hope left. Sexiness causes us not to retreat from relationships, which threaten to cause us pain; instead, it drives us toward others in love.

Surfing the Tao. This is the way I describe the joy of being *sexy*, effortlessly relating to others in light of the *New Logic*, hanging "loose" through an awareness that we are living in the *penultimate* world, which we cherish and enjoy but don't grasp too tightly. Since the *Tao* is the ultimate reality, "surfing" it means to realize the flow of the world and learn not just to passively drift with the flow but to use the way of things to create, play, love, and move to where we truly want to be without frantic effort or flailing about. Perhaps the most eloquent expression of Tao surfing comes from Zhuang Zhou: "On the Tao there is ease and comfort. Drifting easily through life. The spirit remains intact. Virtue is unsullied."[1]

Tao. This ancient Chinese term means something like "the way." I appropriate it, as C. S. Lewis felt free to do, to refer to ultimate reality (though in a slightly different way: Lewis' concept has more to do with natural law, and mine includes the intersection of Law and Gospel). It is a handy term because, though some Westerners might associate it only with religious Taoism or with Eastern religions in general, I use it simply to mean the deep truth we are all seeking. According to the opening line of the *Tao Te Ching*, "The Tao that can be defined is not the eternal Tao." There is something important to consider there. Christians like me contend that God was born a baby and that his creation goes on forever. Jesus is the Tao incarnate, the one who allows us to taste and see what the

---

[1] Chuang Tzu, *Chuang Tzu* (Chicago: Cloud Hands Press, 2015), Kindle Loc. 4191–94. Note that there are various spellings of the name of the one Chinese philosopher.

Tao looks like in this world. I'm intentionally making this connection between a Christian concept and a foreign term in a way similar to that of the second-century Church father and philosopher Justin Martyr, who explained that Jesus is the *Nomos* (the Torah of ancient Israel) *and* the *Logos* (divine creative reason, as discussed by the Stoic and Neoplatonic philosophers). In other words, we might say that Jesus is the door to the *Nomos*, *Logos*, and *Tao*. Jesus himself said he is "the way [Tao], the truth and the life" (John 14:6). I take liberties like I just did here because while we must respect the fact that various religions explain the way to the way (the religious path to the Tao) in diverse and often doctrinally contradictory ways, they are in fact all trying to provide a map to an ultimate reality.

Virtue. The art of understanding who you are and fulfilling your purpose with excellence. It is about striving to be the best you that you can be. It is not about nitpicking moralism. It's not prudishness. It's not self-righteousness. Indeed, it sometimes looks odd to an outside observer. It is about having the strength of character, rooted in God's grace, to avoid worrying about looking pure and instead get one's hands dirty in the process of *working to be good toward those we encounter.* In philosophical ethics, in addition to virtue theory (sometimes called personalism), which considers the *character of a person performing an act*, there are two other approaches to moral decision making: (1) *consequentialism*, which considers the *outcomes of an act*, and (2) *deontology*, which considers one's unchanging, rational duty and judges the *quality of an act itself.* A virtuous person practices habits of virtue in order to respond nimbly to perplexing, urgent situations as they arise. This becomes valuable when we encounter new dilemmas (cases when we have two competing values at stake and can't do justice to both) that have yet to be confronted to our satisfaction.

Acknowledgments

I must thank my wife, Stacie Lynn, above all for being part of the process. I'd say more, but the love that can be written in the acknowledgments page is not the eternal love. Love is in the history, and for that, I raise a toast to my lady. Earlier versions forced us to work through some past and ongoing relationship issues, but it was well worth it. I thank my son Augustine for the conversations we had leading up to this book and for constantly allowing me to bounce these ideas off of him. It was great to have his girlfriend, Sydnie, join the life of our family and allow us to run ideas by her and test out some of those ideas. Thanks to my son Aidan, who was about as important to my ability to survive the last few years, emotionally, as any human on earth. He's a guy who has an amazing ability to feel people's pain and was one of the most important supports during difficult career or relationship patches over the years. Thanks to our dear Mana Nikjou for bringing light to our family, of which she is an honorary member, even when times were tough. Thanks to my father, Rick, for frequent conversations about spirituality, life, and sexuality. Thanks to my mother, Chris, for sacrificially taking care of her many children without letting us ever think that we were loved conditionally.

Thanks to the many friends who were there throughout the process and the conversations they had about these ideas. Thanks especially to my friend and podcast cohost, Daniel van Voorhis. His book, *Monsters*, and mine are really two parts of the same strange conversation we've been having about the intersections among addiction, music, mysticism, and God. Thanks to those who read and edited manuscripts of the book (in addition to Stacie and Dan): Scott Keith, Sam Leanza, and Beth Anne van Voorhis. Thanks to Kurt and Debi

Winrich for their edits, contributions, and overall support of a group of folks who want to contribute to a bigger legacy than themselves or even some particular institution. Thanks to Steve Byrnes at New Reformation Publications for taking care of the important logistics and for reviewing the manuscript. Thanks to the listeners of the podcast, Virtue in the Wasteland, who have supported us over the years, and thanks to you, dear reader, for supposing I have anything worthy to contribute.

Finally, thanks be to God, the source of infinite, unconditional love. Without that love, there wouldn't be anything too sexy about this existence in the first place

Introduction

Sexiness at the Intersection of Goodness, Truth, and Beauty

There is no aphrodisiac like innocence.

—Jean Baudrillard

They say novice poets should stick to ordinary topics like dry riverbeds, cracks in teacups, or salty banjo players. Such advisers warn against taking on grandiose subjects like sunsets, death, and—especially—romantic love. A clever young poet *might*, so their wisdom goes, discover hidden beauty in a mundane experience and thereby offer a modest artistic insight into daily existence. Those fools, however, who attempt to capture something resplendent risk having their words fall embarrassingly short of their subject's glory. There's no better example of this awkward naïveté than the gushing verses about love written by aspiring young poets who have not yet loved, lost, and regained love again.

Why, then, would I be so foolish as to write about erotic love, having written only academic prose to this point? First off, I'm no poet. Granted, to my (dis)credit, I've committed more than enough fouls in the game of love to have learned some hard but important lessons. I remain perplexed in many ways: perplexed both by the issues faced within the changing landscape of contemporary Western culture and by the persistent conflicts and disappointments within my own romantic life. With respect to the cultural situation, perplexity often arises from the incongruity between what most traditional cultures and religious codes say about dating, sex, and marriage and what we humans tend to do in practice, whether or not we're proud of our behavior. Many today no longer assume that traditional Christian sexual values even *can* be integrated. With respect to my personal situation, I've come to understand the profundity of divine love and its call for unconditional giving. And yet, as I meditate, teach, and write about this idea, I find myself constantly falling back into a logic of conditions, bean counting, law, and transactionalism in my own marriage.

For these reasons and others, addressing the topic of erotic virtue has been agonizing at times. I'm a relatively speedy writer, but this book took a while. More than once, when I would sit down to write, a life episode would arise and abruptly challenge the ideas I had been trying to articulate. For instance, one night, while I was writing about how my gracious parenting style seemed to produce surprisingly well-behaved kids whose dating lives didn't need intrusive policing, I got a late-night call from "Officer Sanchez." He asked if I knew that my boy was with his girlfriend in the local mall's parking structure past curfew. I set that chapter aside for a time. A week later, when I was trying to write about how loving the unlovable was humanly possible when we understand the New Logic of gracious love, I slammed my laptop shut in order to quarrel with my wife about a trifle. Distractions like these sidetracked my attempts at writing more often than I can count. It wasn't that each little incident occupied too much of my time. It was that these episodes made me feel like a fraud. They caused me to think I should abandon this project altogether because whatever wisdom I thought I had discovered, it didn't seem to be working consistently within the embodied world.

What rescued me, and this project, was the last book on a reading list I created for myself in preparation for writing: Søren Kierkegaard's *Works of Love* (1847). There I encountered a writer who caught a glimpse of something I had also seen: that there is a vast difference between the infinite love of God that inspires us to love the whole world—every one of our neighbors—and the type of romantic love described by pagan poets. Kierkegaard insists that when poets sing about love, they are really singing about self-love. He explains that conventional romantic love *selectively* focuses an individual's love on one object of desire, and this object is one that he or she chooses to enhance reputation and ego. In such cases, the beloved provides the lover with some emotional reward, such as physical pleasure, status, security, or comforting affection. Christian love, however, is indiscriminate. That is, it isn't preferential. It's based not on admiration for the beloved but on the eternal love of God. For this reason, according to Kierkegaard, poetic love and Christian love differ *essentially*:

> The poet and Christianity are diametrically opposite in their explanations. The poet idolizes inclination and therefore is quite right, since he always has only erotic love in mind, in saying that to command love is . . . the most preposterous talk; Christianity, which always has only Christian love in mind, is also quite right when it dethrones inclination and sets this *shall* [the command to love regardless of reward] in its place. The poet and Christianity explain diametrically opposite things, or, more accurately expressed, the poet really explains nothing, because he explains erotic love and friendship—in riddles. He explains erotic love and friendship as riddles, but Christianity explains love eternally.[1]

So while I'm neither a poet, nor a psychologist, nor a pastoral counselor, I do know a little bit about theology and philosophy. What's more, in teaching these subjects to college students for a decade and a half, I've had a chance to hear firsthand accounts of erotic perplexity in our times. Thus, to finish writing this book, I eventually had to realize that I wasn't even *supposed* to mimic the poet and describe the riddles of passion in creative ways. Rather, I needed to re-center myself and my readers.

So what *is* this center? The center is the divine source of love itself. If we can figure out this business about the center, the rest will almost seem simple. Not easy to execute, mind you, but easy to identify as a new erotic logic. We must remember that the simplicity of Christian love is precisely what many find offensive. Indeed, Kierkegaard writes that unconditional love for all neighbors "seems both too little and too much."[2] It is too little in that it is too simple. It sounds cliché: *the answer is love*. It might be described eloquently by Paul in 1 Corinthians 13, but love—pure and simple—is *the* answer

---

[1] Søren Kierkegaard, *Works of Love* (Princeton, NJ: Princeton University Press, 2013), 50.

[2] Ibid., 81.

to the perplexity of what we mortals think of as the problem of love. On the one hand, it has none of the strange mystery of a romantic drama, where characters discover some secret connection and find themselves connected to *the one*—the one they were meant to be with, their soul mate. It isn't a puzzle to be solved. It's right there: *love!* On the other hand, it is too much because neither we nor any moral heroes we know seem to have perfected the art of loving all other humans indiscriminately.

Something else Kierkegaard suggested helped me finish this book. He once asked his readers to imagine two artists. The first traveled the world extensively and yet complained, "I have sought in vain to find a man worth painting. I have found no face with such perfection of beauty that I could make up my mind to paint it." The second stayed close to home and yet happily said, "I have not found a face so insignificant or so full of faults that I still could not discern in it a more beautiful side and discover something glorious. Therefore, I am happy in the art I practice." As you might guess, Kierkegaard identifies the second fellow as the true artist, someone who could look closely enough to find beauty between the cracks in our world.[3] In a similar way, I hope to write about love not in order to cage it within printed words but instead to speak of love in a manner that seeks to point the way to beauty, even within the seemingly unpleasant and unlovable experiences of romantic relationships. I will speak of it even in the embarrassment of dating, the trials of married life, and the rubble of divorce. I'm on the hunt here for romantic diamonds in the roughest rough. I think I've found a few gems. Therefore, I am happy in the art I practice.

The whole formula—or perhaps I should say *emergency instructions*—for our journey together is rather simple: *Find healing, then heal others.* Stop worrying about the symptoms of your erotic turmoil and let the spiritual healing affect other areas of your physical life. We need to remember the advice of the flight attendants: put the oxygen mask on your face first, *then* help children and others around you with theirs. In other words, just as it is impossible to help someone near you when you are passed out unconscious in a decompressed cabin, it is impossible to cultivate a healthy, loving

---

[3] Ibid., 156.

relationship if you yourself are suffocating, lacking the life-giving breath of God's Spirit.

Those Who Can't Do, Teach

Perhaps, with the help of Kierkegaard, I have convinced you (and perhaps myself) that if I stick to theological and ethical discourse, I can be bold enough to proceed with this book. Fair enough, but shouldn't I get my act together before I start to play the sage?

When I start worrying about *this* question, I turn to the Stoics. They famously set out on a quest to cultivate *apathy*, or distance from passions. Passion and emotion cloud one's reason, they thought. Eliminating passion would thus keep one's senses working properly. In this way, they believed they could remain virtuous and dignified in even the most chaotic of worlds. In any case, we tend to use the term *stoical* these days to describe someone who is emotionally aloof and perhaps grumpy. Upon closer inspection, however, many Stoic writers seem to have been shouting at their own inner monsters. I suspect that many of them struggled more than the average person with fear, anxiety, melancholy, and rage. Their philosophy was meant to reduce such feelings. I bet they talked so often about suppressing emotions because their particular emotions (such as anxiety or dread) posed the greatest threats to their own happiness, not because they had defeated them once and for all. After all, what would be the point of teaching people how to foster personal tranquility if they didn't think there was something unsettling and disturbing about life in the first place?

It's worth noting that I'm a fan of the Stoics in many ways. Concerning our topic, however, I'm at odds with these old sages. I will contend that though philosophies like Buddhism and Stoicism rightly understand that the elimination of desire can produce practical benefits, Christian philosophy runs in the opposite direction. Or at least it should. It desires, and in desiring, it suffers. Strangely, despite this, it *welcomes* passion. (It is interesting that the root of this English word *passion* relates back to *passio*, the Latin word for suffering.) So while I won't mimic the Stoics' philosophy, I will follow their example by approaching a topic that is vexing *to me*. In other words, if they were threatened by emotion and yet wrote about how to eliminate it, I will be bold to write about erotic virtue even though I have failed in this arena.

At the risk of protesting too much, I should also note that it's been strange to observe, as an academic, how many of my colleagues in various fields and at multiple universities comically lack personal mastery over subjects in which they've held PhDs. I've met neurotic psychology professors, theologians who lost faith in God's existence long ago, boring public speaking instructors, education professors who taught mind-numbing theory with text-heavy PowerPoints, and business deans who had trouble managing departmental budgets. I am not the first to notice this, of course. Western stories frequently employ the archetype of a scandalous ethicist who uses moral philosophy to break the rules. Check out, for instance, the character of Thomas Square in Henry Fielding's novel *Tom Jones* (1749), the Alfred Hitchcock film *Rope* (1948), and Woody Allen's *Irrational Man* (2015) and you'll catch my drift.

But this incongruity between teaching and doing isn't always a case of hypocrisy. It often has more to do with our deeply personal quests. Academics are people on a hunt for something just beyond their grasp. They often have an insatiable, private need to succeed in this hunt. I mention all this because I don't claim to have mastered the art of erotic virtue, let alone spiritual tranquility. Rather, I've caught a glimpse or two of a map—a map that I believe points accurately to erotic virtue. If you're old enough to remember the days when people used paper maps instead of a GPS to get around town, you know that following a map isn't always as straightforward as one would wish. But that doesn't mean we should toss out the map altogether.

I'm a guy who studies, teaches, and writes about theology and ethics, drawing heavily from intellectual history. This book examines the intersections of sexuality, the sacred, and virtue ethics. It seeks out wise advice from great minds regarding how we might reconnect spirituality, ethics, and sexuality in our own age. So if you understand that I'm not an MD, or a therapist, or a representative of some denomination's official magisterium,[4] welcome to the expedition. We have important ground to cover.

---

[4] A *magisterium* is a church body's official authority for establishing doctrines and practices.

Folks today, especially young adults, are definitely in a difficult place when it comes to navigating sexuality. They are marinating, on the whole, in lives of sexual tragedy. I wish it were otherwise. I wish it were simply a matter of our decadent age embracing loose codes of conduct. Alas, it's much more ominous than that. Most of them are mired in erotic despair, unaware that fearless and infinite love is even possible in principle. Few know anyone from the older generations who even have a framework for understanding the situation and how to find healing. Few have any good role models for healthy relationships in their lives. Thus they have lost access to something vital: they've lost the art of being sexy.

What Is Sexy?

If you react negatively to this word *sexy*, you are not alone. I've received a few angry e-mails recently, merely because I used this adjective to describe a concept. Note that I'm using the word colloquially here: I'm referring to something that's attractive, exciting, and alluring, or the energy within a person toward life rather than despair and death. In a broader sense, *sexy* points to a desire for something outside of one's self, to connectedness, intimacy, and something profoundly spiritual.

Nonetheless, the meaning and relative offensiveness of a word can fluctuate rapidly these days. For instance, I remember an age when to say something or someone "sucked" was to utter an extreme obscenity. Today, I've heard it on the lips of pious Sunday school teachers, and no one blushes. It just doesn't mean what it once did. Similarly, the word *sexy* only worked its way into English vocabularies in the last fifty years.[5] New, scandalous words have a way of becoming boring old words, and *sexy* is relatively new. Perhaps it may someday become, ironically, *unsexy*. For now, I think we're in the sweet spot when we employ it, linguistically speaking. Granted, it might seem cocky, but know that I'm only trying to be playful.

The first time I encountered sexiness was when I was in second grade. I had a crush on a sweet girl named Olivia. She worked

---

[5] This can be illustrated by consulting a tool in Google Books that tracks the frequency of any given word.

in the lunch line. Sometimes after she scooped some sloppy-joe meat onto my plate, she would pat my head with her little plastic-gloved hand. I think that ruined the spirit of the health code, but it was a delightful and age-appropriate way of expressing warm feelings. That pat on the head was nothing, however, like the feeling I got when she gently poked the back of my neck, just beneath my skull, with a freshly sharpened number-two pencil. It awakened an electrical system in me that I had not noticed before. It was pure. It was not at all overtly sexual as we would think of sexual energy today. That was about the extent of our relationship. And it was good. A little emotional connection coupled with a little loving touch. That is just as much what sexy is about as is the time I slow-danced with my wife at a Sam Outlaw concert, a bit tipsy from the bourbon.

We should, of course, reject any move to overly sexualize childhood and adolescence. We should not encourage folks to engage in risky behaviors, nor should we approve of advertisements that commodify sexuality in order to sell clothing. If you're worried about any of that, then we're comrades in the battle for wholesome love. All that cultural junk is symptomatic of a larger problem: none of it is sexy, though it gets mislabeled as such. To confuse sexiness and obscenity is either a misunderstanding of the deep beauty and sanctity of real sexiness or a reaction against those vicious folks who deliberately misuse the term in their discussions of how to grab profit and power. It doesn't take a saint to recognize this.

Most people know that throwing oneself desperately at a potential partner isn't sexy. Philosopher Slavoj Žižek aptly explains this:

> Until recently, hardcore pornography respected certain prohibitions: although it showed "everything," including real sex, the narrative providing the frame for these sexual encounters was, as a rule, ridiculously non-realistic, stereotypical, stupidly comical, staging a kind of return to the eighteenth-century *commedia del'arte* in which the actors do not play "real" individuals, but one-dimensional types—the Miser, the Cuckolded Husband, the Promiscuous Wife. Is not this strange compulsion to make the narrative ridiculous, a kind of negative gesture of respect:

yes, we show everything, but precisely for that reason we want to
make it clear that it is all a great joke, that the actors are not really
engaged?[6]

What's missing from antierotic "erotica" is intimacy. My podcast
cohost, Dan, tells me that for recovering alcoholics, the opposite of
drunkenness is not sobriety but intimacy. That's important for our
expedition because, according to the proper erotic arithmetic, *no
intimacy = no sexy*. Furthermore, without unconditional love, there's
no intimacy. Thus *no love = no intimacy*, and accordingly, *no love =
no sexy*. This goes for people of all religions as well as for atheists and
for lovers on the political right and the political left. It's about reality.

Sexiness is what drives us to continue to pursue life itself,
especially when others might give up, shrivel up, and fade out. Like
salmon relentlessly struggling upstream to spawn, real sexiness fuels
heroism and hope for the future. But unlike those tragic salmon that
die soon after they spawn, sexiness can be a reality throughout the
human life cycle. We encounter it in the courtship dance, in which
young people learn whom to love and how to love. It remains present
when an aged couple holds hands and walks along the beach, remi-
niscing about their lives together.

But unfortunately, we're living in an age in which we have too
much smut and not enough intimacy. We want to reignite it with
little blue pills, spicy lingerie, or what have you, all to no avail. If we
want to do something about this, if we want to rescue the next generation from their erotic despair, we need to radically rethink how
we talk about sexual ethics. We can't just put the sexual genie back in
Granddad's old bottle. As Robert Capon explains in relation to the
concept of romance, "We have always been called *forward*; it is only
religion that pretends there is a way of going back."[7]

I can imagine folks wringing their hands, worrying that I've just
tipped my hand regarding how I'm going to throw the whole system
out to accommodate cultural changes. Don't go there just yet, please.
Remember that I'm devastated by much that I hear regarding young

---

[6] Slavoj Žižek, *Living in the End Times* (London: Verso, 2011), 122.

[7] Robert Farrar Capon, *Health, Money, and Love: And Why We Don't Enjoy Them* (Grand
Rapids, MI: Eerdmans, 1990), 137.

adults' sexual lives. Almost every generation bemoans the subsequent generation's behavior, but this time, I think it's different. For one thing, this time it's our collective fault. We have allowed a secular, reductionistic, transactional narrative about the purpose and promise of sex to lure us away from something far more beautiful. We've let a lackluster clone of sexiness usurp the real deal. Too many today experience sexuality devoid of both *agape* (unconditional love) and wholesome *eros* (desire). Therefore, they don't realize the importance of seeking sex within the context of marriage and instead see marriage as an old-fashioned hassle.

There are some signs that young people seem to be making positive moves *away* from the risky practices of previous generations. Nonetheless, many in our time know only a bleak sexuality that seeks mere biological gratification. Some young adults might boast of several sexual encounters, but they often can't overcome loneliness. It's not that most folks wouldn't like something more beautiful; it's that they have no reason to believe an authentic, spiritually mature eroticism—rooted in *agape*—is possible. Maybe they've never had a chance to see such love modeled by adults in their lives. Perhaps they've never even heard the rumor that such love is possible.

Now, I'm not primarily worried that young people today are doing naughty things. Many are, and what's going on is sometimes more unsettling than many want to admit. This isn't just about young people from "bad" families; it also holds true for those who grew up in conservative churches. I'm sure my generational distance creates blind spots for me too. For this reason, the high school graduation of my son Augustine was originally what prompted my desire to write this book. I wanted to unload as much wisdom as I could before he set off into this strange world. Of course, I hoped that my second son, Aidan, would also find it useful when the time was right. But it has become a broader quest than that. I also write at the request of several students with whom I've shared these ideas over the years. I tend to ramble in person. So here I'm writing things down and editing out at least a few rabbit trails to get the overall concept on paper. Finally, I'm writing for my many friends whose romantic lives, like mine, often become as frustrating as they are rewarding.

So this book is about sexuality throughout the span of human development, but a main fear of mine remains tied to today's youth.

The younger generation's sexual despair ironically has led to the loss of seduction, in Jean Baudrillard's sense of the term. For Baudrillard, contemporary culture's consumeristic and pornographic tendencies are problematic because they substitute a parody of eroticism for true romantic play. He writes, "When desire is entirely on the side of demand, when it is operationalized without restrictions, it loses its imaginary and, therefore, its reality; it appears everywhere, but in generalized simulation. It is the ghost of desire that haunts the defunct reality of sex."[8] This ghost of virtuous desire floats through our cultural wasteland but now serves only to mock us. There may have been a time when we could hope for true love. But often we only catch a glimpse of love's shadow. At its root, this erotic problem is a byproduct of our failure to understand and promote *agape*, or unconditional, divine love. For instance, *agape* gives a couple the confidence to unveil ourselves before each other in more ways than one. It says not only "I'd cross the desert for you!" and "I'd endure a thousand trials for our love!" but also "I'll be by your side when you suffer with clinical depression" and "I love you so much, I'll cuddle you when we are old and you have to wear adult diapers." The loss of *agape* is likely behind many middle-age divorces. Without the astonishing commitment of *agape*, marriages die out when the flame of *eros* flickers and fades.

Of course, some married couples learn to fake a loving relationship. Modern technology and pharmaceuticals can help somewhat. After a while, though, young people are able to sniff out the nihilism in our sexual lives and reasonably conclude that they might as well just dispense with the pipe dream of deep, romantic *eros* from the outset and get busy ensuring their own financial and emotional happiness. Hoping for such a fairy tale is foolish, they reason. So they cut right to the sexual chase, if they have embodied (nonvirtual) sex at all. And the consequences are tragic. Too few of us realize how many are in a living hell these days. But I think those hellions know it better than anyone. And they aren't demons; they're just lost in the little loops in which they've become trapped.

Moreover, many don't seem to me to be having as much fun anymore. When it comes to sex, I hear a lot about sorrow and very

---

[8] Jean Baudrillard, *Seduction* (New York: Palgrave Macmillan, 1991), 5.

little about fulfillment. Seduction, holding hands, flirting—these are lost arts for far too many. The seductive dance in the Song of Solomon demonstrates the mutual love and deep affection these people lack. The true lover doesn't manipulate, overpower, or bribe the beloved into intercourse. Rather, the lover entices the beloved, beckons the other to a holy connectedness, with a love beyond measure in order to attract the beloved into something of a mystical experience, one of passion and connectedness.

The practical application of this is important. Instead of telling people in their sexual prime to be chaste *or else*, we might ask them some important questions instead: Who are you? What kind of person do you want to be? When you look into the eyes of your beloved, how do you want to treat that person? Who is the sort of person who will help you be your true self? Who is more enviable: the person who chases an orgasm at the expense of love or the person who chases love itself only to discover that superior orgasms come as a bonus in such relationships? Such thinking encourages us to stop asking what our private parts are allowed to touch and start remembering that if we get our hearts in the right place, our private parts just might follow on the path of goodness, truth, and beauty.

If Hollywood has taught us anything, it's that prostitutes often refuse to kiss on the mouth. Why? Because they, more than most, know that *eros* can't really be for sale. And, by definition, *agape* was never for sale in the first place. Only a parody of true love can ever be for sale. The real deal is free. It flows from a Gospel that promises that all is well and all shall be well. If we have a firm grasp on the true Gospel, we can't help but love everyone around us. In the romantic context, this means that we are free to express special love for another individual. If we are lucky, this results in commitment, romance, and vows. We could love anyone, but we are called to love the one who, for love's sake, stands vulnerable before us. So look into another's eyes with passion. Be enlivened by the joy that streams from reconciling love. Kiss delicately. Flirt playfully. Love. Be sexy. But don't let our nihilist age pull you down into the hellish world of sexual dissolution.

How True Beauty Can Seduce Us Back to Holy Love

Both philosophy and theology share something in common: they seek to answer the biggest questions of life. Though they approach their material in various ways, both areas of investigation try to understand how to think and live responsibly in light of goodness, truth, and beauty. What do we mean when we call an action *good* or *bad*? Philosophers spend a lot of time and effort trying to answer this question, but children tend to have a quicker and more genuine response. No one has to explain to a child that the villain in a fairy story is vicious, and admiration for virtuous heroes in folklore usually seems self-evident. For this reason, our ancestors—prior to the rise of Greek philosophy—rarely tried to legitimize their ethics through rational proofs. Rather, they told stories. Young people who valued virtue would strive to become the hero of future tales. For ancient children, virtue was received as they listened in wonderment on a grandfather's knee. The rest of us these days find locating such things as goodness, truth, and beauty far more problematic.

Philosophers have described goodness, truth, and beauty as the *transcendentals*, or what Aristotle called the *huperbainein* (ὑπερβαίνειν), which means "to cause to go beyond" and indicates that these ideas transcend all his other categories of being.[9] Sexiness is about going beyond ourselves, even our own life span, both biologically and spiritually. By choosing life, we procreate to ensure that the human story continues after we are gone.

The Neoplatonist philosopher Plotinus spoke of beauty, goodness, and *the virtues* this way:

> This [the vision of an authentic person who has cultivated virtue] is the only eye that sees the mighty Beauty. If the eye that adventures the vision be dimmed by vice, impure, or weak, and unable in its cowardly blenching to see the uttermost brightness, then it sees nothing even though another point to what lies plain to sight before it. To any vision must be brought an eye adapted to what is to be seen, and having some likeness to it. Never did eye see the sun unless it had first become sunlike,

---

[9] Interestingly, the only time this Greek word shows up in the New Testament is 1 Thessalonians 4:6, where it means to transgress ethical boundaries or to sin. But that is, of course, not what I'm after.

and never can the soul have vision of the First Beauty unless itself be beautiful.

Therefore, first let each become godlike and each beautiful who cares to see God and Beauty. So, mounting, the Soul will come first to the Intellectual-Principle and survey all the beautiful Ideas in the Supreme and will avow that this is Beauty, that the Ideas are Beauty. For by their efficacy comes all Beauty else, but the offspring and essence of the Intellectual-Being. What is beyond the Intellectual-Principle we affirm to be the nature of Good radiating Beauty before it. So that, treating the Intellectual-Kosmos as one, the first is the Beautiful: if we make distinction there, the Realm of Ideas constitutes the Beauty of the Intellectual Sphere; and The Good, which lies beyond, is the Fountain at once and Principle of Beauty: the Primal Good and the Primal Beauty have the one dwelling-place and, thus, always, Beauty's seat is There.[10]

The ancient philosophers were not consistent with their enumeration or ordering of the transcendentals. For simplicity's sake, we might think of these transcendental goals as the three great quests of philosophy:

1. The good: ethics
2. The true: epistemology and logic
3. The beautiful: aesthetics

It's hard to ignore the relationship between these transcendentals and a theological framework. For Christians, the great transcendentals are in God and revealed in Jesus Christ. This was the perspective of Augustine, who writes in his *Confessions*, "You stir man to take pleasure in praising you, because you have made us for yourself, and our heart is restless until it rests in you."[11]

Sexiness is not its biological manifestation alone. It is rather the desire of the heart for what transcends—though it does not

---

[10] *Enneads* 1.6.9.

[11] Augustine, *Confessions*, trans. Henry Chadwick (Oxford: Oxford University Press, 1991), 4.

disdain—all the things of life that we tend to use to try to fill the
God-shaped vacuum within us. When we are perplexed—something
the great Socrates was famous for instigating in his students—we are
forced to recognize that our earthly idols cannot accomplish what
ultimate truth, goodness, and beauty *can*. Thus I find hope in the perplexity of our current age, since it opens the door for a deeper exploration. The Chinese philosopher Zhuang Zhou also realized this:

> Perhaps the one who confesses
> To being confused
> Is not lacking in clarity.
> While the ones who believe themselves
> To be wise
> Will end their days
> As consummate fools
> Without ever having seen things in the
> Clarity of the light.[12]

I contend that beyond perplexity lies Jesus, the *Logos* who inte-
grates our selves with others and our selves with God. John 14:5–21
is important to consider in this matter:

> Thomas said to him, "Lord, we do not know where you are
> going. How can we know the way?" Jesus said to him, *"I am the
> way, and the truth, and the life. No one comes to the Father except
> through me. If you had known me, you would have known my
> Father also. From now on you do know him and have seen him."*
> Philip said to him, "Lord, show us the Father, and it is enough
> for us." Jesus said to him, "Have I been with you so long, and
> you still do not know me, Philip? Whoever has seen me has
> seen the Father. *How can you say, 'Show us the Father'? Do you
> not believe that I am in the Father and the Father is in me?* The
> words that I say to you I do not speak on my own authority, but
> the Father who dwells in me does his works. Believe me that
> I am in the Father and the Father is in me, or else believe on
> account of the works themselves.
> "Truly, truly, I say to you, whoever believes in me will also
> do the works that I do; and greater works than these will he

---

[12] Chuang Tzu, *Chuang Tzu* (Chicago: Cloud Hands Press, 2015), Kindle Loc. 4012–18.

do, because I am going to the Father. Whatever you ask in my name, this I will do, that the Father may be glorified in the Son. If you ask me anything in my name, I will do it.

"If you love me, you will keep my commandments. And I will ask the Father, and he will give you another Helper, to be with you forever, even the Spirit of truth, whom *the world* cannot receive, because *it neither sees him nor knows him.* You know him, for he dwells with you and will be in you.

"I will not leave you as orphans; I will come to you. Yet a little while and the world will see me no more, but you will see me. *Because I live, you also will live.* In that day you will know that I am in my Father, and you in me, and I in you. Whoever has my commandments and keeps them, he it is who loves me. And he who loves me will be loved by my Father, and I will love him and manifest myself to him."[13]

Here all the answers to life's big questions are embedded: beauty draws us to truth, truth leads to goodness, and goodness draws the world back into God's beauty. We encounter beauty when we get a glimpse of the world from the perspective of the beatific vision. It is just a glimpse, but only from this perspective can we see the truth: how things *truly are* in light of the Gospel. When (and only when) we have the truth, we can begin to be good, albeit imperfectly. When we are good, the lost and broken can catch a glimpse of the divine light borne by the kingdom of God and its means of grace. By becoming citizens of this kingdom, we can begin to see things from God's beautiful perspective. Then we will see the truth, and hence goodness will push back against the ugliness in our fallen world.

How do I draw all this out of this passage from John? Let me suggest that we can make the following connections here.

The Way: This is the beauty we behold as incarnate in Jesus. The Greek *hodos* (ὁδὸς) indicates a road or journey. Thus it is already but not yet a reality. It is incremental. We see in a glass darkly but

---

[13] Unless otherwise noted, all biblical citations will be from the Revised Standard Version because I find it the most aesthetically pleasing and because, being old but not archaic, it strikes most readers anew. I apologize to both those who take offense at the gender-exclusive pronouns it uses and those who would have preferred I use a version ideologically aligned with conservative Christianity. I offer my love humbly to all parties and hope you will indulge me here in not letting this matter distract us for the moment.

soon will see face-to-face (1 Cor. 13:12). Is truth in the eye of the beholder? Yes, in a sense, but it is not arbitrary subjectivity we are talking about here. For who is the ultimate beholder? God.

I don't think the *way* is identical to ethics for Christians: the way is not the way of merit and ascent, for it comes only through the Gospel, through the revelation of God's salvation in Christ. This is the context of John 14, where Thomas confesses in verse 5 that with respect to the way, he and his pals *don't know it*. They are well acquainted with the Ten Commandments but are unclear as to how to find salvation in this kingdom of heaven about which Jesus speaks. No, it is not ethics but a way of finding beauty in places where legalistic Christians fail to look. Other traditions have terms that relate to a way (like the Chinese *Tao* or Hindu *Dharma*). Though these traditions understand the actual directions for the way differently, it remains interesting that a "way" seems to suggest something like a world view or a religious perspective. We need Jesus' perspective, and that perspective helps us see genuine beauty.

The Truth: The truth, *aletheia* (ἀλήθεια), is revealed in the person of Jesus, according to Christianity. The philosopher Charles Sanders Peirce suggested, "Logic follows Ethics and both follow Aesthetics."[14] I think there's something helpful in this idea. If our hearts are in the wrong place, our heads are pretty good at concocting self-justifying theories and self-serving ideologies. Goodness and beauty are often helpful signposts that direct us to truth.

Martin Luther notes the connection between what Jesus reveals through his suffering on the cross and seeing things truly. In his Heidelberg Disputation (1518), theses 19 through 21, he states:

> 19 That person does not deserve to be called a theologian who looks upon the invisible things of God as though they were clearly perceptible in those things that have actually occurred,
> 20 he deserves to be called a theologian, however, who comprehends the visible and manifest things of God seen through suffering and the cross.

---

[14] *Collected Papers of Charles Sanders Peirce*, vol. 1 (Cambridge, MA: Harvard University Press, 1931), 311.

21 A theologian of glory calls evil good and good evil. A theologian of the cross calls that thing what it truly is.[15]

We find this truth vindicated in practical issues of life. For instance, if I'm an addict, I won't be able to clean up my act without first experiencing a "moment of clarity" about my brokenness. Likewise, if I'm only interested in winning arguments, I will be unable to experience a harmonious marriage, which can only emerge when we examine the root causes of relationship disputes. Likewise, what we often seek to defend in our radical sexual liberation (or, for that matter, our stubborn traditionalism) is often that we don't have the guts to see things as they truly are. Our cognitive biases, political agendas, and community mores sometimes obstruct our view of how things ought to be.

The Life: I connect goodness with this true life, *zoe* (ζωή), because John 13:35 records Jesus as saying, "By this all men will know that you are my disciples, if you have love for one another." This isn't to say that we expect to become entirely pure. But if our neighbors don't see any real love in us (again, not perfected works but sincere love for the world), then they are right to wonder if we've gotten hold of the real deal, if we ever tasted the beautiful truth in the first place. Incidentally, if your particular community of faith is not marked by love, then you should rightly worry that your congregation is on the wrong track concerning the beauty of the Gospel.

So what's the point of all this?

The truth is often hidden under its apparent opposite in Jesus' way of thinking. For Him, the world's losers are the true winners, the meek will inherit the earth, prostitutes will process into the kingdom of heaven before the religious leaders, and we must lose our lives in order to gain them back in full.

Consider this example of Christian irony: Christians have an important day in the church calendar that is oddly called *Good* Friday. It is the precise historical culmination of the good, the true, and the beautiful in human history.[16] But we must ask, isn't it ugly

---

[15] My translation from the Latin.

[16] I suppose there may be a clear etymological reason I should already know about and one that has nothing to do with goodness. I suspect it has something to do with holiness.

and painful? Yes, it is. And yet, from God's angle, we can call it good. At the moment when everything *seemed* overwhelmed by evil, false allegations, and ugliness, God's goodness, truth, and beauty were *in fact* powerfully active. Most Romans couldn't see it because they valued power and glory, but Jesus submitted to humiliation. The Greeks thought of resurrected bodies as we might think of zombies: tragically reborn to endure this evil, material existence. Many Jews in the first century expected an anointed one, or *messiah*, to overthrow the tyranny of Rome, but Jesus seemed to have failed; they assumed that a dying messiah would be cursed (Deut. 21:23; Gal. 3:13). In other words, during the first century, whichever culture you embraced in the Mediterranean world, Jesus looked like a loser. Nonetheless, the followers of His Tao insisted that He was the most beautiful loser of all.

Thus that God reconciled the world to Himself through the cross of Christ is the truth that unlocks other profound truths. It is unexpectedly beautiful. It is good because it sets us free from sin, death, and hell, freeing us to love our neighbors not because we have to but because those who have truly tasted the uncut Gospel can't help but be transformed by what they've encountered. Such people are uncomfortable living by the karmic Old Logic. They can't help but embrace the wounded or console those broken by abusive churches or those crushed by the world. Love marks out the true church because, through Word and sacrament, we are invited to marinate in God's love each week, and—no matter what we Christians do—the holy marinade of Christ's blood can overcome our blandness and fetidness.

So in our expedition together, I invite you to behold God's beauty by turning your eyes to Christ, even if it isn't something you normally do. Let the light of Christ's beauty enlighten your view of the true state of things even when the horizon looks bleak, and live as beacons of love. Learn to see those around you as Christ sees them. Learn to appreciate the wisdom that appears foolish, the strength that seems weak, the inner riches of the spiritually poor. Rejoice that the Incarnate One has unlocked the most important questions of this life in His own person. As C. S. Lewis noted, "I believe in Christianity as

---

Nonetheless, if it is a happy accident, I am content to enjoy my good fortune and press on without digging into linguistic fine points.

I believe that the Sun has risen not only because I see it but because by it I see everything else."[17] He was on to something—the idea that there is a vital connection between the New Logic of the Christian message and freedom from erotic illness—and I think this will help us recover sexiness.

---

[17] From a talk called "Is Theology Poetry?," originally delivered in 1944 to the Socratic Club, Oxford University. Since then, it has been widely distributed in the public domain.

A Secret Chord (The Relationship between Divine and Human Love)

I heard there was a secret chord that David played and it pleased
   the Lord
But you don't really care for music, do you?

—Leonard Cohen, "Hallelujah"

The chord that can be transcribed on paper is not the eternal chord.
Its secret sometimes flitters right in front of us. But alas, to capture it
is like grasping a salmon in a cold stream. Likewise, the romantic love that can be cultivated merely through a list of practical
steps is not eternal love. This love involves a total conversion of
the mind to the New Logic of grace. True love heals because it
returns us to the fundamental music of the universe. We must get
in tune with this music if we are to find the healing that eternal
love offers.

I've struggled with episodes of melancholy throughout my life.
Fortunately, I encounter it less often these days, but the darkness
still threatens to drag me down to despair from time to time. When
it does, I wrestle with what Continental philosophers describe as
dread, angst, and insomnia. These relate to the inner trials and affliction Martin Luther called *Anfechtung*. This is the inward struggle to
make sense of our own freedom, seek meaning, connect with God,
and overcome despair. It's a struggle not for practical optimism but
rather for hope. Recovering what I'm calling *sexiness* is indispensable for this quest. When we lose hope, we lose our desire for living,
for those around us, and for reconnection to God. Sexiness is about
reawakening that holy desire for existence itself. Fortunately, it also
can have a healing effect on our biological sexuality.

The opposite of hope, a theological virtue, is the deadly vice called *sloth*. Sloth isn't laziness, something born of physical fatigue. Sloth is a phenomenon experienced by those who have lost all hope and therefore fail to live, love, and press on. Sloth, when it comes to love, is a result of being so traumatized by failed relationships that we close the door to all forms of intimacy, whether divine or human. Indeed, according to my friend Betsi Little-VanFossen, one of the most common symptoms of mental health disorders, according to the *Diagnostic and Statistical Manual of Mental Disorders* (*DSM-5*) used by psychotherapists, is a deadened or dramatically decreased libido.

The psychologist Viktor Frankl, reflecting on his experience of Nazi concentration camps in his book *Man's Search for Meaning* (originally published 1946), asserts that though one might expect to find an increase in same-sex and masturbatory behavior in a conventional prison, the hopelessness of the concentration camps he endured during the holocaust was so extreme that the overall ethos was starkly sexless. Similarly, he noted that when a prisoner abandoned all desire—for instance, if he refused to even smoke his cigarettes—he usually died physically within a few days.

A cheap and swift way to quell our inner turmoil and sloth is to self-medicate, to so inebriate ourselves that we can't remember our regrets and our minds become too foggy to dwell on our immediate, desperate realities. Even the chronically debauched can see that this is only a temporary solution, for when we awaken from our stupor, we remember that we still have to face the problems we had before we knocked ourselves out. Moreover, we often rub our eyes to realize we made things worse. Sexiness, as we shall see, requires freedom from this self-destructive inebriation. It's about staying awake, moving forward, and choosing life.

If you don't have a substance abuse problem, you're not yet off the hook. Maybe you're a teetotaler who is on a perpetual health kick. Perhaps you exercise vigorously so that by the time you crawl into bed, you fall fast asleep, never wondering if your existence matters, never reflecting on the fact that you have a broken heart. Or maybe your career is your obsession, to the extent that you take it home with you, falling asleep with papers strewn around your bed. Or perhaps you're the sort of person who fills the void with pornography, compulsive masturbation, or random, casual sex. None of this is sexy. Rather, these things are usually symptoms of erotic sloth.

Whatever your favorite diversions, they are frail attempts to subdue your terrifying inner silence with a parody of frivolity. Maybe you don't want to think too much about the past, your current romantic situation, or your ultimate doom. Maybe you're flooding your inner silence with a din of triviality: you are so busy with the kids' after-school lessons, sports talk with the cousins, and gossip with coworkers that it leaves no time for silent reflection. Maybe you're afraid to be present in the moment and aware of your embodiment, afraid to recognize your need for touch and for connection to others.

I know it's terrifying to be honest with ourselves and others. We are naked and afraid in this life. So we stitch together security blankets of moral purity. That's nothing new for us mortals. But in the process, do we close the door to intimacy? You bet we do.

Nonetheless, I'm convinced that there's a good reason to stay on the quest for erotic virtue: there's a wonder to the universe—a sexiness, if you will—that pours out more goodness, truth, and beauty than we can notice at first glance. This sexiness helps us make sense of our spiritual *and* erotic lives. If this way of speaking sounds too weird, it's probably because we've carefully separated the erotic from the divine to the extent that neither the topic of sexuality nor that of God are much fun for us anymore. I'll explain the connections in due course. But to get started, let's explore the relationships among our erotic drives, God, and music.

A Sexy Playlist

In his song "Hallelujah," the poet-songwriter Leonard Cohen sings about a secret chord that David strummed, and this sublime sound pleased God. Cohen (whose name means "priest," incidentally) here alludes to a biblical story in which David—the kid with the slingshot, who became the second king of Israel—soothed an ill-tempered King Saul with music. First Samuel 16:23 describes this odd phenomenon as follows: "And whenever the harmful spirit from God was upon Saul, David took the lyre and played it with his hand. So Saul was refreshed and was well, and the harmful spirit departed from him."

Not only can music console us emotionally and spiritually, but music is one of the best analogs to a genuine mystical experience we've got in this life. Music is simultaneously measurable (we can analyze it in a music theory classroom, for instance) and beyond explanation. Its composition comes from a mysterious place that corporations would bottle and patent if they could. It soothes the soul and carries our minds to realms of transcendent beauty. It forces us to encounter the sublime. When it resonates with something inside us, it stirs emotions, inspires bravery, and calms anxious hearts. When we are despondent, a sad song reminds us that we are not alone. When we are ready to rejoice, it offers up a suitable track. It can transport us to a timeless place from which we can get a healthy perspective on reality. It is ultimate and empty simultaneously. It relies on the spaces between notes and beats to unveil something resplendent.

This has been my experience, at least. One of the best gifts my father ever gave me was a Sam Cooke Gospel record. He handed it to me when I was in one of my melancholic emotional valleys. When I played the album on my rented car's stereo, it was hard to miss the echoes of the secret chord in Cooke's "Pilgrim of Sorrow" or "Touch the Hem of His Garment." My dad shared this music with me because he thought it might help cast out my existential demons. And, at least that day, it worked wonders.

Music can be an outlet for, an expression of, and a way of connecting with the reality sought by mystics. This reality is described as *ineffable*, which means it is not something we can perfectly express with words. Try as we might, our finite language never can do justice to the infinite reality we've encountered. According to Evelyn Underhill: "The mystery of music is seldom realized by those who so easily accept its gifts. Yet of all the arts music alone shares with great mystical literature the power of waking in us a response to the life-movement of the universe: brings us—we know not how—news of its exultant passions and its incomparable peace."[1] Life-movement and exultant passions? That sounds like sex, right? But as with sex, no matter how close music comes to the divine reality itself, one cannot merely memorize the notes and play, hoping to capture something

---

[1] Evelyn Underhill, *Mysticism: A Study in the Nature and Development of Spiritual Consciousness*, 12th ed. (Mineola, NY: Dover, 2002), 76.

sublime. Instead, music is *good* music only when a deep resonance abides in, with, and under the music. Likewise, *making* love is only *good* love when a *deep* love abides in, with, and under the lovemaking.

Consider this analogy: even if you happened to know the precise fingering on a guitar's fretboard that would be required to play the secret chord, you would be unable to *play* this secret chord without first actually *hearing* the secret chord. Cohen seems to fool his listeners when he casually reveals to them how to make the musical magic happen. In the second stanza of "Hallelujah," he sings,

> Well it goes like this, the fourth, the fifth, the minor fall, the
>   major lift

That's that, right? So it's not just a special chord but a chord that must be strummed within a particular formula. If we play *that* chord progression, or those particular tones in unison, then we've got the secret chord, right?

Not so fast.

What Cohen describes here is little more than the basic structure of most pop songs: it's something we find in the ear candy played by radio stations and personal playlists. These three clean, major chords sound swell and are the stuff of hit rock ballads. I dig them, and cosmic beauty may indeed be conveyed in their skillful execution. But formulaic composition isn't enough to get us to the sexy secret chord.

We come closer to the secret chord when we consider "the minor fall" and "the major lift." In such a moment, art awakens something profound within us. The "minor fall" recognizes and laments the sorrow brought about by the cosmic Fall. The "major lift" points to a cosmic reconciliation of even the bluest of our notes. In other words, the magic of the secret chord involves the way it catches us when we are musically and spiritually falling. It is like J. R. R. Tolkien's concept of *eucatastrophe*: "the sudden happy turn in a story which pierces you with a joy that brings tears."[2] It is a movement unexpected but most welcome.

---

[2] For a detailed explanation of this concept, see my entry "Eucatastrophe," in *Encyclopedia of Religion and Film*, ed. Eric Mazur (Santa Barbara, CA: ABL-CLIO, 2011).

This business of "minor" chords reminds me of a scene from a "mockumentary" about a has-been hair metal band titled *This Is Spinal Tap* (1984), which includes the following dialogue between Nigel Tufnel, a rocker, and Marty DiBergi, a documentarian. Nigel plays a melancholic tune beneath the following dialogue:

Marty. It's pretty.

Nigel. Yeah, I like it. I've just been fooling about with it for a few months now. Real delicate.

Marty. It's a bit of a departure from the kind of thing you normally play.

Nigel. Yeah, well it's part of a trilogy really, a musical trilogy of what I'm doing, in D minor, which I always find is really the saddest of all keys. Really, I don't know why but it makes people weep instantly when I play it . . .

Marty. It's very pretty.

Nigel. Yeah, just simple lines intertwining, you know, very much like—I'm really influenced by Mozart and Bach—it's sort of in between those, really. It's a Mach piece, really. It's sort of . . .

Marty. What do you call this?

Nigel. Well, this piece is called "Lick My Love Pump."

If we can look past the crass joke here, it's uncanny that Nigel associates sexuality with a spontaneous emotional response to D minor.[3] The relationship among sex, spirituality, and music—as we shall see—is not as absurd as this comedic scene suggests. In fact, a recent study of brain scans of Mormons contemplating religious texts suggests that the same reward circuits in the brain become

---

[3] I've heard evangelical Christian church musicians say something similar to this: they say that a rightly placed minor chord followed by a powerful major chord can produce a physiological experience that is quasi-orgasmic. In this way, the experience of church can be triggered with the right technique. In some charismatic churches, this translates to hands flying into the air as a signal of spiritual ecstasy.

active during spiritual experiences that are active while using drugs, listening to great music, or having sex.[4] Don't get me wrong: music and sex are not identical to the great cosmic reality the best sages tried to chase down. But they are most certainly analogs to that reality. They point to a bridge between the earthy and physical resonances in this world and the wavelength of eternity.

But if Cohen's secret chord isn't the simplistic formula for the basic structure of a pop song, what is it? I think I have an answer, but I'm afraid to share it. I want to say that there's a beauty that is so beautiful that when one glimpses it, all the ugliness and pain of the world become worth the trouble. To even think this seems unjust—maybe even blasphemous—given the severity of suffering in our world. Moreover, the fact that I'm a white dude who's lived a relatively comfortable life in Southern California suggests I have no right to think that someone else's life traumas are a price worth paying for the cosmic joy I've glimpsed. Yet the idea that there's an infinite beauty so exquisite that it vindicates all suffering and ugliness is a notion I can't abandon.

I must continue with this seemingly insensitive line of thinking. Please understand, however, that I'm not talking merely about my personal experience of joy here. I'm talking about the astounding beauty of reality itself. In such reality, God's loving presence is enfolded within the fabric of our existence, though it remains hidden. We glimpse this reality not in power and glory, but as if under a veil. When we get a peek at this reality, everything starts to make sense. I wish I could give you more empirical proof, but you'll have to accept that I have no reason to lie to you, at least for now. This sense of a peace that surpasses all understanding is often frustratingly ephemeral—that is, it escapes us as quickly as it appears. Nonetheless, I believe that there's a special kind of beauty that emerges out of healed discord and pain. And I believe it's more beautiful than the type of beauty that has never needed to overcome life's ugliness. It's the beauty of the monstrous crucifix; the beauty behind wood, sweat, blood, nails, and splinters; the beauty of a happy final

---

[4] Michael A. Ferguson et al., "Reward, Salience, and Attentional Networks Are Activated by Religious Experience in Devout Mormons," *Social Neuroscience*, Nov. 29, 2016.

chapter that caps off a string of sad chapters. (See the actual final chapter of this book for more on the related idea of *recapitulation*.)

I admit this way of thinking sounds strange today, but it has a long history in the Christian tradition. Again, it makes me nervous to admit these ideas. If I believe anything beyond what's right before my eyes, I believe that ultimately *everything is going to be OK*. But I confess that it's usually hard to see how this assertion is possible given the mess we've made of things. As I write, for instance, a jihadist decapitated a priest in Paris. My country's political parties are in disarray. Racial tensions are acute. Death, destruction, distrust: these are becoming the norm. But I still believe things shall be well.

Why? Because—forgive me for jumping so quickly to what I think the last chapter of human history holds for us—God's most amazing work of art was His ability to transform our fall, sin, and evil into something good, true, and beautiful. I'm not even a heretic within my religious tribe for saying this, despite our usual talking points these days. Here's how the idea of a fortunate fall shows up within the music of the Western church's Holy Week: "*O felix culpa quae talem et tantum meruit habere redemptorem*" (O happy fault that earned for us so great, so glorious a Redeemer). Several respected—and orthodox—figures in the history of Christianity have expressed similar thoughts. For instance, Augustine said, "For God judged it better to bring good out of evil than not to permit any evil to exist."[5] In other words, the fact that there is so much brokenheartedness in the world is not proof that hearts won't experience a future happily ever after. It might mean that we will rejoice all the more when broken hearts are mended. And if they *are* mended, the love will be even more magnificent. I know that this sounds too good to be true. But if it happened to be true, would it sound otherwise?

Remember that almost everything Jesus did overturned what people expected of a religious sage or military hero. He rode in for his "triumphal entry" on a donkey's back rather than on a war-horse (Mark 11:7). He was born in a stable (Luke 2:1–7). He hung out with tax collectors and sinners but chided the religious leaders. The point

---

[5] Augustine, *Enchiridion: On Faith, Hope, and Love*, chapter 8, from Albert Outler's 1955 translation, now widely available in the public domain.

is, God doesn't seem to work in ways that immediately make sense to us.

I would outright resist the idea that there is a way to redeem suffering had I not noticed something interesting about the devil's chord, or the *diabolus in musica*. In music theory, this refers to the tritone interval, or the flattened fifth, also known as the augmented fourth. It represents the distance of three whole tones on the Western musical scale, which means it's dissonant and distressing, and it sounds evil. Church music historically avoided this combination on the assumption that harmony, rather than discord, was appropriate for music in God's house. Still, if there is a secret chord to be discerned, it promises to address the dread aroused by the devil's chord. If you want an audible example of the devil's interval and are near a computer or smartphone, you can track it down by listening to Jimi Hendrix's "Purple Haze" or Metallica's "Enter Sandman." I suspect you'll recognize it when you hear it.

Now, some say the Roman Catholic Church banned the devil's interval and would even execute a medieval composer for using it, since it had the power to conjure evil, but I'm not aware of any historical evidence for this. Even so, it's a fun but terrifying idea that such a policy existed. In any case, it's true that churchmen discouraged the use of the devil's interval, along with certain modes and rhythms that seemed to induce rebellion or unrestrained sexuality. Concern for appropriate music is nothing new. After all, Plato himself warned against bad modes of music in *The Republic*, book 3. This isn't simply a matter of Christians being uptight.

Despite the medieval church's apprehension about it, the devil's interval turned up in at least one interesting place. According to Jimmy Veith, in a July 27, 2011, guest blog on *Cranach: Christianity, Culture, Vocation*, we hear it beneath two famous lines from Luther's hymn "A Mighty Fortress Is Our God," where Luther mentions the devil:

> For still our ancient foe
> does seek to work us woe
> His wrath and power are great
> and armed with cruel hate
> On earth is not his equal.

Luther enjoyed taunting the devil, at least after he discovered
the New Logic of the Gospel, something he encountered during his
famed "tower experience," which may have occurred when he was
contemplating Romans 1 on the toilet. When he wasn't throwing
inkwells at demonic apparitions, he used baser means: "I resist the
devil," he wrote, "and it is with a fart that I chase him away. When
he tempts me with silly sins I say, 'Devil, yesterday I broke wind too.
Have you written it down on your list?'"[6] We see here that Luther
learned to play the blue notes without despair and the devil's interval without embracing evil once he knew something important: that
all is and will be well when the secret chord resounds in earnest.
What, for Luther, was the way to resist our ancient foe? "One little
word shall fell him," says his hymn. What's that word? *The* Word.
More on that in due course.

For the person who has ears to hear the ultimate harmony of the
universe, even the devil's interval can be made to serve divine beauty.
To get a sense of how this works, consider Tolkien's "Ainulindalë," the
first story contained in the *Silmarillion*. It's a story that serves as a
creation myth for the elves of Middle Earth. In it, a creator crafts
a beautiful "mighty theme." Then an evil god introduces a dissonant
theme. The creator, instead of simply eliminating all demonic dissonance, takes celestial music to an even more beautiful moment. He
does this by composing a *third theme* that brings everything back
together. This third theme is the secret chord. The secret chord is
thus the Gospel, or "good message." It's the New Logic that helps us
learn to surf the Tao and repent of our law-based transactional relationships. It's a preview of the beatific vision, the sublime unveiling
of God's ultimate reality.

Whatever we call it, awareness of God's ability to incorpo-
rate and reframe evil into the cosmic story is at the core of all
great theological, philosophical, and spiritual teaching. It helps us
make sense of odd expressions in the Bible itself, such as the dark
"antiwisdom" texts of Psalm 39, Job, and Ecclesiastes. Such writings existentially crush us in order to demonstrate the limits of
our own power and the vanity of our best intentions and efforts.

---

[6] Martin Luther, *Luther's Works*, vol. 54, ed. Theodore Tappert (Philadelphia: Fortress Press, 1967), 105.

This prepares us for the "wisdom of the counterorder," which is Incarnate Wisdom.

In this life, no one even gets a peek at the beatific vision without passing through this leveling process. The deathblow of the Law must come before the life-giving Gospel can make sense. Luther wrote of this mortification this way: "It is through truly living—or better yet through dying and being damned that one will become a proper theologian, not through intellectual effort, research, or speculation."[7]

Thus we aren't being naïvely optimistic when we seek true love as if we had some easy formula. We are hopeful because we have a promise that the symphony ends beautifully. In the meantime, we can find healing by noticing the intimate connection between the Greek words *eros* and *agape*. For this reason, the old Chinese philosopher Zhuang Zhou likened the depths of his philosophy to an ability not to be clever but to hear the true music of the universe: "The people whistle the popular tunes and sing of 'pretty flowers' and go about contentedly. They do not care to listen to the great chorus."[8]

Jesus Is My Boyfriend

The connection between music and sexuality used to freak me out. I remember once, when I was a student at Wycliffe Hall, Oxford, I was too arrogant for my own good. I was infatuated with the old liturgy, and especially the quality of its execution at a university town in the United Kingdom. I didn't have much time for the contemporary praise songs they wanted to sing at Wycliffe. For one thing, I found them too reminiscent of the American evangelical aesthetic I was trying to escape. For another thing, I worried that the songs they were adopting fell into the old trap of conflating erotic and divine love.

A few friends came to visit, one of whom had been in my high school rock band. We had a good time out on the town, shutting down the pub and drinking a bit too much. When we returned to

---

[7] *D. Martin Luthers Werke: kritische Gesammtausgabe*, vol. 5 (Weimar, 1892), 163, lines 29–30. This is my loose translation of the Latin: "Vivendo, immo moriendo et damnando fit theologus, non intelligendo, legendo aut speculando."

[8] Chuang Tzu, *Chuang Tzu* (Chicago: Cloud Hands Press, 2015), Kindle Loc. 4027–30.

the hall, we went into the chapel and did a parody rendition of a song that I found excruciatingly full of sublimated sexuality. I played drums and sang while my friend played guitar. We were too loud and didn't know that a bishop was sleeping in a guest room near enough to hear our clamor and become roused from his slumber.

Though the next morning I was apologetic for my lack of decorum, I felt justified in lampooning what we used to call "Jesus Is My Boyfriend" songs. One might find these songs in contemporary praise music or in contemporary Christian pop music. The latter got a comedic shellacking in a *South Park* episode in which Cartman forms a band called Faith+1 and sells a bunch of albums by substituting "Jesus" for "baby" in stereotypical boy-band songs.

Now, I think I was misguided. I was right, over the years, to note the latent sexual energy in contemporary worship songs and old monastic writings, such as the homoerotic work of Saint John of the Cross, "Stanzas on the Soul," from which we get the phrase "dark night of the soul." But I was wrong to think that sexual metaphors were *in principle* off limits for spiritual writing. To be sure, there are times when that might be an off-putting way to go and other times when we confuse the need for physical intimacy with divine reconciliation.

Nonetheless, the more I've researched sexuality and spirituality, the more I've realized the similarities among musical ecstasy, spiritual bliss, and orgasms. Moreover, I've come to realize that there is nothing unholy, in principle, about orgasms. Therefore, it seems that I was the one in error, to the extent that I criticized church music for using romantic imagery. (That said, I still stand by the idea that church music should be of high quality, regardless of the genre, and that soft rock and synth pop are not as conducive to prayer and worship as is chanting the ancient liturgy. So I still can be a musical snob at times, but sexuality or instrumentation per se is no longer a primary consideration.)

Uniting *Eros* and *Agape*

There are at least four Greek words for love, and each involves important nuances, which C. S. Lewis explores in his book *The Four Loves*. *Storgē*, or affectionate love is associated with familiarity and familial ties. *Philia* is the strong and vital bond of friendship. *Eros* is romantic love, rooted in a desire to unite with another. Finally, *agape* is unconditional, selfless love; it is the love of the great love hymn in 1 Corinthians 13, especially verses 4–6: "Love is patient and kind; love is not jealous or boastful; it is not arrogant or rude. Love does not insist on its own way; it is not irritable or resentful; it does not rejoice at wrong, but rejoices in the right. Love bears all things, believes all things, hopes all things, endures all things." The last time I heard this passage read—and I've heard it more times than I could even begin to count—it was by my friend Dan. I was particularly frustrated with the universe that day. Nonetheless, he decided this was a good text to share in a devotional talk he gave to a group of English teachers that he, my wife, and I were leading in China. We were in a foreign country, and it felt hotter than hell. I was frustrated with our situation for a hundred reasons that day. I was pissed at my wife, Stacie. The workload was too heavy because some of our Chinese colleagues who we thought would be there abruptly resigned before we arrived. Dan knew all this, yet he read this shopworn text to us. It was infuriating: he knew damned well what quoting Paul's love hymn meant; it meant I had to maintain my cool or else forsake my thesis about the power of sexiness.

I was working on this book in the evenings. How could I fail to heed the idea that love is patient and kind and keeps no record of wrongs, especially while I was writing about love? Who the heck did he think he was throwing this high-minded, unpractical teaching in my face?

His reading of this passage from 1 Corinthians 13 slew me. If I wanted to heed Paul's words, I had to hope all things, believe all things. I had to hope not out of obligation but because, though it sounds cliché, it's one of the coolest passages you can find in the Bible. It's got the ring of truth. It's the core of Jesus' way, and it's why I remain in the church even when it gets uncomfortable. Track the passage down now if you can. Read it as if for the first time. Ignore the fact that you've heard it cited during too many sappy wedding sermons. Just absorb its simple beauty and radical call. For an even stronger effect, track down the graphic novel version of *The Walking Dead*. Somebody reads it at a wedding while zombies are outside the door; this scene demonstrates how astounding the Christian call to love is. Love doesn't seek its own interest? But it's the end of the world out there. There are cannibals and hordes of brain eaters outside; how can we help other humans in need without endangering ourselves? These are the sorts of questions Christian love should instigate. If we don't ask them or hear them enough, we are likely doing it wrong.[9] Perhaps veteran pastors know it is the right text for a wedding because *agape* is the only reliable power source for the other forms of love. It's essential for surviving the turbulent times of any relationship. It is the sort of love that emerges from a timeless place, the center of the universe from which goodness, truth, and beauty flow.

If we can reconnect these two loves—*eros* and *agape*—in our culture and in our relationships, we will be able to discover erotic virtue and sexual healing. As for *eros*, if we want to get serious, we must resist the temptation to equate this concept with lust or *erotica*. There is a legitimate linguistic connection, but for our purposes, remember that *eros* is not identical with lust, unless you mean something like "lust for life." Lewis explains this well: "Lust is a poor, weak, whimpering, whispering thing compared with that richness and energy of desire which will arise when lust has been killed."[10]

Thus when I mention *eros* in *this* book, I'm referring to a powerful desire to move toward the source of life itself, not to turn from the source to vacuous carnal pleasure. *Eros* is about more than mere biological sexuality. This is not some novel approach on my part. Plato expanded the concept of *eros* beyond the colloquial understanding of his day. You've probably heard of *Platonic love*. Its meaning has become cheapened today by its association with the infamous "friend zone," and colloquially it indicates a bond between two individuals who do not plan to sexualize their relationship.

Plato's original concept, however, had to do with divine *eros*. He suggested that two people, mutually pursuing the good, true, and beautiful, could inspire one another to turn their attention from

---

[9] I find it vitally important for Christian educators and theologians to consider that if we were to treat all our theology as if we were living amid a zombie apocalypse and keep a straight face, we'd be sages indeed. The apocalypse renders all the petty church and culture debates obsolete. It brings us starkly to a choice between good and evil but offers no clean path to the good. It requires hope for divine rescue, virtue, and love *that endures all things*.

[10] C. S. Lewis, *The Great Divorce* (New York: HarperOne, 2001), 104.

carnal desire to a desire for the transcendent world of ideas or forms. The inner—and possibly outer, but not *necessarily* outer—beauty of another person can awaken a desire within our hearts to unite profoundly with that other person. In special cases, the purity of this love and the beauty of the other person is able to inspire us to turn our attention toward the source of beauty in the heavenly realm. Thus beauty in another person reminds us of ideal beauty itself. In this way, *eros* has the power to turn our attention from petty, fleeting things toward ultimate truth and goodness.

Consider the old concept of courtly love, or—if you're the sort whose preferred mythology is that of the fantasy genre crafted by Tolkien—the love Gimli the dwarf had for Galadriel, an enthralling elf queen. In the narrative, there is absolutely no expectation that the palpable *eros* present would result in physical intercourse between the dwarf and the elf. Rather, Gimli became overwhelmed by a holy desire to behold true beauty. Prior to leaving the elf realm, Galadriel asks Gimli which gift he desired for his journey. His response is cool: "There is nothing, Lady Galadriel. . . . Nothing, unless it might be—unless it is permitted to ask, nay, to name a single strand of your hair, which surpasses the gold of the earth as the stars surpass the gems of the mine. I do not ask for such a gift. But you commanded me to name my desire."[11] As Tolkien knew, this theme of divine-human love can be found throughout ancient mythology. Even in Plato's nonmythological use of this phenomenon, *eros* serves as a bridge between divine and human realms, and it inflames a mortal's desire for immortality. In his *Symposium*, Plato identifies *Eros* as a *daemon*, which can mean a nature spirit, a force of nature, or even a deity. This shouldn't be surprising, since Eros is the name for the god the Romans called Cupid. This is the same being who shoots arrows into the hearts of men and women, arousing earthly love. Eros kindles human hearts with sparks of divine love, which translates to something ecstatic lovers often express to one another: "You make me want to be a better person" (as seen in the movie *As Good as It Gets*). *Eros* is, according to one interlocutor in Plato's *Symposium*, the only force capable of empowering a human to overcome the fear

---

[11] J. R. R. Tolkien, "Farewell to Lórien," *The Fellowship of the Ring*, in *The Lord of the Rings* (London: Unwin Paperbacks, 1983), 396.

of death: "Love will make men dare to die for their beloved—love alone; and women as well as men."[12]

Nevertheless, there's no need to prudishly divorce physical touch from this idea of divine eroticism. If Plato is right that *eros* can exist even when a partner isn't physically beautiful, and the form of beauty is beyond all our temporal experience and thus of little ultimate concern, we can see that *agape* and *eros* together could be a glue that binds people together, even when bodily impulses fade. Menopause, low testosterone, and wrinkles can hardly diminish true love, therefore. They are external, temporary matters. Plato was looking for something timeless, something untouchable by life's contingencies.[13]

Before Plato, Eros was considered a god or spirit, a life-force that connected humans and seduced them toward a deeper reality: to *divine love itself*. According to Hesiod's Greek cosmogony, Eros was the oldest of the gods, the offspring of Chaos and Earth (Gaia). Our modern age tamed this divinity, divorced it from its seductive power, and ultimately tempted us to become idolaters, worshiping the gyrations that were originally supposed to be a dance in honor of divine love. But now, alas, we are left with little more than the husk of love. We are no longer sexy. And this makes us sad. Or numb.

The philosopher Slavoj Žižek might be of help here. Concerning Western pseudoeroticism, which naïvely assumes that sexual liberation symbolized human liberation in general, he writes, "Eroticization relies on the inversion-into-itself of movement directed at an external goal: the movement itself becomes its own goal. . . . Therein resides the difference between the goal and the aim of a drive: say, with regard to the oral drive, its goal may be to eliminate hunger, but its aim is the satisfaction provided by the activity of eating itself (sucking, swallowing)."[14] In other words, our disordered modern approach to sexuality mistakenly makes the act of sexual intercourse *the purpose* of our otherwise meaningless existence. The

---

[12] Plato, *The Dialogues of Plato*, vol. 1, trans. B. Jowett (Oxford, 1892), 549.

[13] Make no mistake: Plato wouldn't make a good traditional erotic saint. Folks have dug his philosophical ideas for centuries, but they often fail to mention that he also thought a sublime form of human sexuality involved sexual intimacy between men and boys.

[14] Slavoj Žižek, *Living in the End Times* (London: Verso, 2011), 72–73.

toxic result is that we end up despairing of ultimate purpose altogether. And the gyrations start to bore us. Thus we fall into nihilism:
the idea that there is no end, meaning, or purpose to any of this life.
Cupid's arrows fall short of our hearts in such cases. What's worse,
many have already *lost heart* altogether. Consequently, the arrows
pass through a tragic vacuum in our modern chests.

Christianity, despite its many historical failures in understanding sacred eroticism, possesses a key to the romantic cage in which
we've imprisoned ourselves. In this regard, Lutheran virtue ethicist
Gilbert Meilaender explains the connection between *eros* and *agape*
well:

> If romantic love, fickle as it is, promises faithfulness, Christians
> were bold enough to claim that *eros* could be fulfilled—could
> be what it claimed to be—only when brought within the trans-
> forming power of *agape*. To be sure, such a combination must
> always be unstable; either love can threaten to absorb or extin-
> guish the other. On the one hand, if *eros* does not submit to
> transformation and correction, we will conclude that, since fall-
> ing in love was a good reason to marry, falling out of love (or
> into love with someone else) must be a good reason to break
> the marital bond. But on the other hand, if the call for fidel-
> ity extinguishes our appreciation for the power and beauty of
> erotic love, we will not see how great a sacrifice we sometimes
> ask—albeit rightly—when we grant *agape* governance in our
> understanding of marriage. . . . *Eros* is continually transformed
> by *agape* even while the attempt to be faithful to one's spouse
> is constantly instructed by the passion and power of romantic
> love. This is the way the Christian life is, in fact, lived as theo-
> logically grounded worldliness.[15]

We'll get into the struggles of putting all this together and weather-
ing romantic storms in coming chapters. Make no mistake: none of
this is easy. As Meilaender admits, many obstacles, tripwires, temptations, and frustrations lie before us. But the map is the map. And
the map is accurate.

---

[15] Gilbert Meilaender, *Faith and Faithfulness: Basic Themes in Christian Ethics* (Notre
Dame, IN: University of Notre Dame Press, 1992), 14–15.

Why Leonard Cohen's Song "Hallelujah"
Keeps Turning Up in This Book

A quick glance at the table of contents reveals that each of the titles come from the lyrics of Leonard Cohen's oft-covered song "Hallelujah." There's an important reason for this. I've often heard people suggest that this song uses spiritual imagery to describe sexuality, with the *hallelujah* serving as a euphemism for orgasm (that was the sentiment of the late Jeff Buckley, who made the song famous and reworked it in a manner that would affect all future renditions). I think this theory has things backward. I think it's a song about spirituality that draws from erotic metaphors and imagery. I believe this even if Cohen himself wouldn't have put it exactly like that. Moreover, I don't believe that it is all that easy to separate sexuality and spirituality; in fact, I'll argue that we disconnect these two aspects of our humanity to our peril.[16] Cohen will be a sort of musical backdrop for our exploration of the ambiguities involved in separating out sin, sexuality, sadness, joy, hope, desire, and—ultimately—Saint Augustine's reflection: "Lord, You have made us for Yourself and our hearts are restless until they rest in You."[17]

---

[16] Check out the insights of my student and young British songwriter Anthony Draper, "Interpreting Hallelujah," *An Englishman in LA* (blog), January 23, 2016, https://anthonydraper.wordpress.com/2016/01/.

[17] Augustine, *Confessions*, book 1, chapter 1.

A Blaze of Light (The Connection between Spirituality and Virtue)

There's a blaze of light in every word,
It doesn't matter which you heard,
The broken or the holy Hallelujah

—Leonard Cohen, "Hallelujah"

Our culture's collective discussion of ethics, especially in the United States, has for too long centered on rules about what we can or can't touch (on the religious and cultural right) and rules of sexual engagement (on the left). We tend to treat only the symptoms of erotic despair but tragically fail to return to the source of virtue itself. We must stop obsessing about the symptoms and get to the root of the problem, which we've identified as inherently spiritual. Now, if I'm right about this diagnosis, what's the prescription? I believe that it is an approach to ethics called *virtue theory* or *personalism*; this business about virtue finds its power in the New Logic of divine love.

There are typically three approaches to these "normative" ethics,[1] each of which seeks ways to resolve ethical dilemmas and help us make moral decisions. The first is called *deontology*; this is a duty-based ethic that focuses on the nature of actions. The second is called *consequentialism*; this approach considers the results of an action, adding up the positive outcomes, especially with respect to pleasure and happiness, and subtracting the weight of negative outcomes. Thus it balances the "pros" against the "cons," especially with

---

[1] Normative ethics isn't primarily about understanding the abstract nature of the good (called meta-ethics), nor does it focus on contemporary practical issues (applied ethics). Rather, it seeks to find a method by which one can make moral decisions in life, whatever the unique circumstances.

respect to pain and sadness. *Virtue ethics* is the third approach, and it emphasizes the character of the person who is acting.

In practice, few individuals, if any, remain rigidly within one normative ethic. We tend to use different approaches to address different sorts of moral quandaries. Often the normative ethic we employ also has to do with our level of maturity. For instance, when we are young, or when we are in unfamiliar circumstances, the guidelines of deontology can be helpful. Children do well not to question their parents when they are told never to cross the street or talk to strangers. As we start to understand the rationale for ethical behavior, we begin to decipher the conventional logic, or consequential reasoning, behind these guidelines. At this stage, for instance, adolescents might learn to when parents require them to come home at a reasonable hour on a school night, because they realize that going to school without sleep makes paying attention in class difficult. When it comes to sexuality, likewise, deontological rules about keeping one's pants on in public are helpful for children who otherwise would roam naked through the park to their own embarrassment, and consequentialism can help teens abstain from sexual intercourse through fear of sexually transmitted diseases or unwanted pregnancy.

Nonetheless, there are several reasons why virtue theory is particularly helpful with respect to sexual ethics in our perplexing times. Deontological principles are often ineffective when circumstances present particularly difficult temptations. Thus many young people who wear purity rings—signifying their commitment to remaining celibate until marriage—desperately attempt to fulfill their promise but fail to do so in practice. Young people who break their own sexual rules don't always reject the rules or fail to anticipate the negative consequences of sexual activity; it's just that they can't seem to keep their hormone-fueled impulses in check.

Virtue goes beyond acknowledging general rules or avoiding negative consequences. It asks important questions such as, Who am I? Who am I in relation to God? Who do I want to be? What is my true goal in this brief time on earth? How can I cultivate the qualities needed to reach my goal? Virtue asks us to consider the sort of moral heroes we want to be when we come to our life's final earthly chapter. Virtue theory treats ethical behavior the way a martial artist thinks about training for a fight. The student of karate, for instance, memorizes a series of moves and practices them repeatedly. In doing this, practitioners prepare to spontaneously respond to any future stressful situation. By habituating proper form prior to a crisis encounter, they don't have to think in the heat of the moment; they just act.

Virtue thinking avoids relying on taboos to guide behavior. *Taboos* are codes of conduct for which the rationale has been lost. The term itself comes from Polynesia. When Captain Cook showed up on various islands, he and his crew discovered a whole new set of sexual and social rules. On the one hand, they encountered a level of promiscuity and modes of dress (or undress) that would offend old European sensibilities. On the other hand, they also encountered a set of seemingly superstitious rules, including some that prohibited certain casual interactions between men and women. When asked *why* they had the rules they did, the islanders often simply explained that it was bad magic or *taboo*. In other words, they no longer knew the reason their ancestors prohibited certain behaviors. Moral codes that might once have had a rather practical basis now became incomprehensible. Virtue thinking, on the other hand, invites a moral agent to internalize the logic behind living justly. This is especially important in our day, when it comes to sexual ethics. I contend that there are good reasons, within the alternative kingdom of Christ, to live lives of erotic integrity. But when we fail to communicate the overall New Logic to believers, Christian teaching about sexuality seems archaic, anti-intellectual, and sometimes cruel. By recovering the New Logic, however, we can rediscover Christian sexual ethics as an invitation to a blessing rather than a set of shackles.[2]

For Aristotle, virtue involves fulfilling one's calling along the lines of excellence.[3] This idea needs to be cultivated in young people through habituation, which helps them eventually internalize those virtues and ultimately summon them when a moral crisis presents itself. In other words, we *fake it till we make it*. This all depends on

---

[2] For an extensive and helpful discussion of taboo and virtue, see the seminal work on virtue ethics: Alisdair MacIntyre, *After Virtue: A Study in Moral Theory*, 3rd ed. (Notre Dame, IN: University of Notre Dame Press, 2007).

[3] He discusses this in *Nicomachean Ethics*.

a good *ethos*, the distinct character of a culture or group. Aristotle believed that if a person followed his or her life's purpose virtuously, this ultimately would lead to happiness and personal fulfillment.

While he seems to employ other approaches at times, virtue thinking is at the center of Jesus' ethical teaching. He was not permissive concerning the rules or duties of the law: he meant it when he said that to be saved, one's righteousness had to exceed that of the Pharisees (Matt. 5:20). Most don't realize that the Pharisees set the moral bar lower than it really was in some aspects of life, such as the issue of divorce, in order to ensure that they might more easily make it over that bar. Granted, they contrived a bunch of extra rules for themselves and their pals in order to create a hedge around many moral pitfalls, but these rules tended to distract people from the essence of righteousness. The following passage is among the clearest virtue teaching from Jesus:

> Woe to you, scribes and Pharisees, hypocrites! For you tithe mint and dill and cummin, and have neglected the weightier matters of the law, justice and mercy and faith; these you ought to have done, without neglecting the others. You blind guides, straining out a gnat and swallowing a camel! Woe to you, scribes and Pharisees, hypocrites! For you cleanse the outside of the cup and of the plate, but inside they are full of extortion and rapacity. You blind Pharisee! First cleanse the inside of the cup and of the plate, that the outside also may be clean. Woe to you, scribes and Pharisees, hypocrites! For you are like whitewashed tombs, which outwardly appear beautiful, but within they are full of dead men's bones and all uncleanness. (Matt. 23:23–27)

Here we see that the legalistic concern for moral bean counting distracted many Pharisees from the better task of seeking a transformation of their fundamental character. For this reason, Jesus accused them of ignoring the virtues of justice, mercy, and faith even as they carried on with their "straining at gnats." This is an all-too-familiar experience within religious circles today, in both the left and right wings. There are several examples of this throughout the New Testament, but an encounter between Jesus and the Pharisees serves to illustrate the point:

> One Sabbath [Jesus] was going through the grainfields; and as
> they made their way his disciples began to pluck heads of grain.
> And the Pharisees said to him, "Look, why are they doing what
> is not lawful on the Sabbath?" And he said to them, "Have you
> never read what David did, when he was in need and was hun-
> gry, he and those who were with him: how he entered the house
> of God, when Abi'athar was high priest, and ate the bread of the
> Presence, which it is not lawful for any but the priests to eat, and
> also gave it to those who were with him?" And he said to them,
> "The Sabbath was made for man, not man for the Sabbath; so
> the Son of man is lord even of the Sabbath." (Mark 2:23–28)

Here, we learn two things: the purpose of laws is to provide a safe
environment in which virtue can take root and also that the rules
are not themselves the ultimate goal. Sabbath creates a space for qui-
etude, contemplation, worship, and spiritual recuperation. It keeps
us from overworking employees and beasts of burden. But it doesn't
ensure that we will love our neighbors or livestock. Granted, observing Sabbath rest helps protect men, women, and beasts from having
the life wrung out of them by greedy and unjust masters. It ensures
that, at least once in a while, humans can stop striving and take time
to live abundantly. The Sabbath, therefore, is a foretaste of an even
more abundant life that the people of God work to create as they
participate in its peace, its rest, its *shalom*, its *shanti*. It is part of the
Jewish rabbinic teaching that God's people are called to *tikkun olam*,
a term that refers to the healing or restoration of the world. Thus
to turn the gift of Sabbath rest into a new burden is diametrically
opposed to its original purpose of repairing brokenness. How tragic
it is that this distortion of justice has become so widespread among
religious types, even among Christians who claim to be "evangelical," which means—by the way—that their focus is supposedly on
the Gospel (εὐαγγέλιον/*euangelion*, literally "good news"). The rules
are meant to limit injustice, but they can also become a mechanism
for injustice when they're in the hands of those who forge idols out
of otherwise helpful rules rather than preserve rules for the purpose of
mitigating human cruelty.

    Addiction to legalism is not unique to the Jewish and Christian
religions. It's endemic to the human race and discernible across ages
and cultures, from ancient Chinese society to secular American

liberalism today. For instance, when progressive mores regarding workplace harassment, inclusive language, and multicultural sensitivity—all, at their core, serious and legitimate concerns—are breached, folks get fired, shamed, and relegated to cultural exile. We expect corporations to swiftly root out such sins, even while the companies from which one is tossed are often complicit in dehumanizing labor practices in impoverished countries and while the networks that fire newscasters for insensitivity are simultaneously benefitting from the exploitation of human bodies to sell light beer during commercial breaks.

Virtue and the Tao

Some of the best reflections on the problem of legalism go back to ancient China, in the teaching of the old Taoist philosophers. Taoist ideas about the connections among spirituality, virtue, and legalism will serve as the underlying framework for understanding the thesis of this book and will point toward how we can regain healthy sexiness today. In short, more rules is not the ideal prescription for the ailment of sexual debasement. The prescription is a return to the center. A return to the *Tao*.

What is the Tao? Anyone who is acquainted with the term probably knows at least one thing: it is undefinable. "The Tao that can be spoken is not the eternal Tao. The name that can be named is not the eternal name." These are the famous opening lines of the *Tao Te Ching* by Lao Tzu. The Tao is the secret chord. Or, perhaps more precisely, the secret chord is inspired by and resonates with the unspoken Tao. Neither ethical rules nor music can contain the Tao, but the secret chord—like all art—is a way humans try to harness it or surf it. The chord is secret not because it is occult or hidden by some secret society. It is secret because it is modest and unassuming. It must be desired before it can be found. Unfortunately, as Cohen reminds us, most don't *really* care for music in the first place. Rules are much easier to manage. Music might seem frivolous to those who lack ears to hear. It is offensive to those who refuse to listen. But such philistinism is no virtue, as Psalm 58 affirms: "The ungodly are forward, even from their mother's womb; as soon as they are born, they go astray, and speak lies. They are as venomous as the poison of a serpent, even like the deaf adder, that stoppeth her ears; which refuseth to hear the voice of the charmer, charm he never so wisely."[4] The psalmist reminds us that some have fallen so deeply into a vortex of vice that divine *eros* has become extinguished. The divine charmer plays a secret chord, but the serpent doesn't hear it. How does such a condition occur? According to Lao Tzu, this is the result of a tragic fall away from the center, away from the source.

You may be wondering, what's with this fortysomething white guy from Southern California appropriating a concept from ancient Chinese philosophy, to which he has no natural claim? Well, maybe you are wondering this because I got ahead of myself and I failed to explain what I mean by the Tao. Tao is at the center of the whole universe, and we all dance around it in one way or another, unless we flee from it altogether in fear of wrath. However we respond to it, it is universal, and it is not the exclusive possession of any particular ethnicity, nation, or race. That makes it useful for broad conversations with people who do not share the same religious tradition. C. S. Lewis is the one who first inspired me to use the term and concept of Tao in this way. He explains:

> The Tao, which others may call Natural Law or Traditional Morality or the First Principles of Practical Reason or the First Platitudes, is not one among a series of possible systems of value. It is the sole source of all value judgments. If it is rejected, all value is rejected. If any value is retained, it is retained. The effort to refute it and raise a new system of value in its place is self-contradictory. There has never been, and never will be, a radically new judgment of value in the history of the world. What purport to be new systems or . . . ideologies . . . all consist of fragments from the Tao itself, arbitrarily wrenched from their context in the whole and then swollen to madness in their isolation, yet still owing to the Tao and to it alone such validity as they possess.[5]

Lewis' approach is quite different from the old platitude that all religions are essentially saying the same thing. This old reductionistic

---

[4] Psalm 58:3–5, from the 1928 Book of Common Prayer.

[5] C. S. Lewis, *The Abolition of Man* (New York: Macmillan, 1961), 103.

assumption that all religions are united in their quest for a mild, tame, liberal, Western ethic is considered obsolete by religion scholars today.[6] Lewis is saying that all the various religious perspectives have a sense that there is something at the core of existence, and there *is* such a something. It's what Paul describes in Romans 1 as the universal recognition of a fundamental truth that we simultaneously grope after and suppress in our unrighteousness and what Acts 17 describes as something related to the reality in which the pagan poets say we "live, move, and have our being."

In theology, we might say that this Tao resembles the *Logos* of Stoicism, the *Dharma* of Hinduism, and even the *Torah* of Judaism. I'm not bothered by the fine distinctions among these concepts, and I recognize that some terms are closer to the concept of "law" and others closer to the concept of "way." I'm not bothered because the sages of these traditions rarely want to equate any of this with cultural *rules*. Rather, the Tao is the fundamental reality behind the structure of the universe, including its rules. It is the good, the divine pattern for the universe, and the wisdom at the core of creation. We're all dancing around this Something when we seek spirituality and ethics. Sometimes we despair whether there really is a Something. But we've heard rumors that it's there, and assuming its existence tends to make better sense of the world than denying it. Mystics try to unite with it, and atheists deny it has a personal existence but nonetheless might seek it with microscopes and telescopes. Alchemists try to tame it for their own gain, drug dealers try to use it to sell substances, and theologians try to tame it in order to get teaching posts. But no one owns it.

As I use the term *Tao*, I should note that I see it as encompassing both the yin and the yang, if you will: it involves the interplay of both Law and Gospel, as Lutheran Christians understand these aspects of biblical revelation. Thus although I appeal to the Christian writer C. S. Lewis in order to appropriate the language of the Tao, I don't think of the Tao in exclusively legal terms. Indeed, there are times when I find myself ironically closer to the graciousness of Lao Tzu. In the following quotation, he describes the Tao in a way that

---

[6] See Stephen Prothero, *God Is Not One: The Eight Rival Religions That Run the World* (New York: HarperOne, 2010).

seems strangely familiar to those who have come to value the distinction and interrelatedness of Law and Gospel:

> TAO is the mysterious center of all things,
> A treasure for those who are good,
> A refuge for those who are not.[7]

I don't believe we can properly approach this Tao apart from divine grace. Nonetheless, we humans seem pretty well convinced that whatever *it* is, it has something to do with ultimate reality and how we should treat each other. If we could reunite with it, soul adventurers believe, we could find significant healing. The fact that this reunion eludes us is precisely where, at least for Christians, the Law points out that we need a New Logic based on the Gospel. In this book, I'll return to the term *Tao* with roughly the same understanding of it that Lewis has. The difference between Lewis' use and mine is that when I speak of the Tao, I include not only natural law but also the whole beautiful logic of the universe, including an awareness of the Gospel center of the cosmic drama. Thus where Lewis connects natural law with the Tao, I include both Law *and* Gospel as fundamental to the Tao, because the Tao is the totality of God's logic. Therefore, while I refer to this logic as the New Logic, I use this language only because it is new to *us*. Ultimately, however, it is actually an ancient logic rooted in the Logos (Christ) that existed before the foundation of the world (John 1). It is only new to us because we humans got off track. It is what Jesus—the Tao incarnate—smuggles into our earthly history in his own body and blood. This is why I believe that Jesus is the only way to recover true virtue.

This takes me to the fulcrum of my thesis: a key passage from Lao Tzu, who offers wisdom even for followers of Jesus to consider. Here is an older translation that captures my point well:

> The Tao is lost, and then virtue
> Virtue is lost, and then benevolence
> Benevolence is lost, and then righteousness
> Righteousness is lost, and then etiquette

---

[7] Lao-Tzu, *Tao Te Ching*, trans. Stanley Lombardo and Stephen Addiss (Indianapolis: Hackett Classics, 2011), 78.

Those who have etiquette
are a thin shell of loyalty and sincerity
And the beginning of chaos[8]

The original word for "virtue," used by the Chinese philosophers was *Te* (pronounced "duh"). In addition to what we normally think of as virtue in the West, this term suggests a kind of power or potency, as when one speaks of the *virtue* of a medicinal plant. Thus *Tao Te Ching* means something like "The Classic Book on The Way and Virtue." The translation can be tricky here, whichever translator you choose. A recent, more precise translation of the text I cited above is therefore the following:

Lose TAO
And TE follows.
Lose TE
And benevolence follows.
Lose benevolence
And righteousness follows.
Lose righteousness
And propriety follows.
Propriety dilutes loyalty and sincerity: Confusion begins.[9]

Here's how I appropriate this as a Christian: when we lose our connection to the Way (the Tao revealed by Jesus), virtue loses a connection to its source and thus eventually decays. When we lose virtue, we rely on personal acts of benevolence, like charitable giving, as if this were the bare minimum for true disciples. Soon, however, because we are starved of internalized virtue, we cease charitable giving and good works; instead, we are content with generic self-righteousness, and we think we are righteous simply by avoiding taboos. Ultimately, when we lose any semblance of self-righteousness, because we live unholy lives, we settle for being polite. We learn the rules of social engagement and mistake etiquette for virtue. In this way, we end up

---

[8] "Tao Te Ching Online Translation," Taoism.net, http://taoism.net/tao/tao-te-ching-online-translation/.

[9] Lao-Tzu, *Tao Te Ching*, 38. Check out a Virtue in the Wasteland podcast (episode 40b) with translator Stanley Lombardo to learn more about his theory of translating ancient texts.

with little more than legalism. We thus lose genuine goodness, and confusion about ethics sets in because we forget why we were trying to be good in the first place.

Isn't this precisely where we find ourselves today? Conservatives champion abstinence and liberals demand consent before intercourse, especially between young adults who've had a few cocktails. Both concerns are legitimate, especially when they have the well-being of vulnerable young people in mind. But even if the sexual rules of both the right and the left became realized and codified in the legal system, this would fail to guarantee erotic virtue. Moreover, if they started with erotic virtue itself, they might have a better shot at helping people avoid exploitative, dangerous, and coercive sexual experiences as well.

This ancient approach to virtue-based ethics is powerful but rarely trusted. Instead, we think that we are safest if we pound our fists and restate rules. We think we need to defend the Tao/way, which leads to Te/virtue. But reality needs no defense. It just is. Therefore, even those of us who think that there is something much more effective and beautiful than legalism must be wary. We must avoid trying to control, to convince with words, or to demand that others see things as we see them. It is much more effective to simply rest in the power of reality. According to Lao Tzu,

> TAO is honored TE is respected
> Because they do not give orders
> But endure in their own nature.
> Therefore, TAO bears them and TE nurses them,
> Rears them,
> Raises them,
> Shelters them,
> Nurtures them,
> Supports them,
> Protects them.
> Bears them without owning them,
> Helps them without coddling them,
> Rears them without ruling them.
> This is called original TE.[10]

---

[10] Ibid., 65–66.

In other words, virtue (*Te*) is not interested in insisting that people recognize its excellence. It uses the power of its excellence to seduce people to itself. Virtue inspires virtue. In an immediate sense, folks scoff at the holy fools, the knights of faith who are following an eternal calling but are misunderstood during their lifetimes. Perhaps, after they've died, they might be recognized as the saints they in fact were. But even if they are not vindicated by the historians, even if they aren't remembered by any of the living at all, even the slightest contribution of virtue and radical love in the human community has a way of producing beautiful fruit to be enjoyed by subsequent generations.

On the other hand, the frantic work of devout legalists can have devastating results. Once again, Lao Tzu recognized this and said it well:

> The more prohibitions and rules,
> The poorer people become.
> The sharper people's weapons,
> The more they riot.
> The more skilled their techniques,
> The more grotesque their works.
> The more elaborate the laws,
> The more they commit crimes.[11]

This is not just some exotic Chinese perspective; it resonates with the connection between the Gospel and a life of sanctification and virtue. Note that Lutheran virtue ethicist Gilbert Meilaender is on the same page. Since society has become unmoored from the spiritual source of the ethical life, it is thoroughly confused about the nature of virtue. "As a consequence," Meilaender writes, "lacking any self-critical powers, the society may degenerate into mere superstition (may be unable to distinguish its moral code from a collection of taboos) and may be unable to deal with external challenge based on critical principle."[12] Don't pass over this quotation too quickly. It gets to the heart of the situation. Especially in evangelical Christian churches,

---

[11] Ibid., 72.

[12] Gilbert Meilaender, *Faith and Faithfulness: Basic Themes in Christian Ethics* (Notre Dame, IN: University of Notre Dame Press, 1992), 5.

the way folks talk about sexual ethics has become ineffective and perplexing to those who listen in from the outside; Christian talk sounds superstitious rather than principled. When this situation occurs, we find ourselves disconnected from the original purpose of all this: to cultivate intimate, loving relationships among partners, parents, and children, as well as society as a whole. Paul thus warns in 1 Timothy 5:8, "If any one does not provide for his relatives, and especially for his own family, he has disowned the faith and is worse than an unbeliever."

The true church must thus engage in continual counterformation if it wants to resist the false formation of the world. It must cultivate a gracious ethos in which older generations are able to train the emerging generations not in a list of strange taboos but in the process of internalizing core values that resonate with the New Logic of the Gospel. As Meilaender explains, "We will need intellectual training in the rules or ideals themselves; training in how to apply and defend them. The aim is that each moral agent should act self-consciously, aware of the grounds upon which he acts and be prepared to defend those grounds."[13]

Part of this formation in the New Logic should involve the idea that embodiment, sexuality, and joy in physical existence are not aspects of life Christians should shun; rather, these are redeemed by the incarnation of the Son of God. As C. S. Lewis explains,

> I know some muddle-headed Christians have talked as if Christianity thought that sex, or the body, or pleasure, were bad in themselves. But they were wrong. Christianity is almost the only one of the great religions which thoroughly approves of the body—which believes that matter is good, that God Himself once took on a human body, that some kind of body is going to be given to us even in Heaven and is going to be an essential part of our happiness, our beauty, and our energy.[14]

Thus the body is not the problem, as the heresy known as Gnosticism presumed. Rather, the problem is the misuse and degradation of the body through vice.

---

[13] Ibid., 5.

[14] C. S. Lewis, *Mere Christianity* (New York: HarperOne, 2001), book 3, chapter 5.

The rest of this book will explore this collapse of virtue, which is a result of our disconnection from the very source of virtue, and offer suggestions about how to regain and apply it to common sexual struggles that occur throughout a human lifespan. I'll argue that religious and secular legalisms are not only unable to reclaim erotic virtue; they are also symptomatic of our deeper spiritual problem. I will contend that reckless promiscuity and cold prudishness are two sides of the same worthless coin. Let the conservatives strive to rid television of naked bodies, and let the liberals strive to ensure that detailed contracts are established between college students preparing to hook up for meaningless coitus. But let us seek something better. Let us set out on a quest for real love.

This quest depends on a renewed encounter and sense of wonder at the profound teaching that is the Gospel. I invite you to embark upon our exploration with a commitment to genuinely trying to encounter and behold this Gospel, not as an abstraction, but as the radical word that it really is. As Kazoh Kitamori rightly states, "Our task is to witness to the gospel. Before we can *talk about* the gospel, we must *hear* it and *see* it. Our words are empty if we talk about the gospel without hearing and seeing it. In witnessing to the gospel, we must first have ears to hear and eyes to see what God would reveal to us."[15] Hearing and seeing the Gospel are thus the first steps on the journey toward erotic virtue.

From Mysticism of the Cross to Ethics

In my theological tribe, it's risky to utter the term *mysticism* unless one is condemning it. Those who know me, or have had me for a class, or have read my essay about false mysticisms in the church.[16] might be surprised to learn that I have come to value sane mysticism. Permit me to explain how I came to appreciate a certain type of mysticism and what I mean by the term.

---

[15] Kazoh Kitamori, *Theology of the Pain of God: The First Original Theology from Japan* (Eugene, OR: Wipf & Stock, 2005), 58.

[16] Jeff Mallinson, "Is Your Church Spiritual Enough?," *Modern Reformation* 24.2 (March/April 2015): 38–43.

I'm the sort of Christian who gets uncomfortable with overly emotional church music. I have considered my life—at least since the sixth grade—a sort of theological quest to learn and exercise the *defense against the dark arts*. I was once in a car chase while helping a gal escape from a cult that's fond of bullying its apostates. I opposed a charismatic missionary in Mexico (who later turned out to be a child abuser) when I was in middle school and she did a bunch of magic tricks she called signs of the Holy Spirit's anointing. I got chewed out for an hour on a conference call because, as a Christian university administrator, I refused to recognize the coursework of the self-appointed prophet and apostle Ted Haggard's Bible college curriculum.[17] I prefer reading philosophical theology to reading Oswald Chambers' devotional book. I don't like long, extemporaneous prayer sessions. I breathe deep during the liturgy. Experiential evangelical culture sometimes makes me uncomfortable. My favorite undergraduate theology professor, Dr. Rod Rosenbladt, beat out any remaining sense that our standing before God depended on some inward, conjured experience; instead, it was dependent wholly outside ourselves. In other words, if Paul was a Pharisee of Pharisees, I'm whatever you'd call a guy with a résumé filled with examples of opposition to sappy, hokey spirituality, whether of the evangelical, culty, Roman Catholic, or new age sort.

Despite all this, mysticism is a real phenomenon.

Perhaps I (and folks like me) have been overly skittish about anything related to religious experience because, too often, people *base* their faith on experience. The danger is that experience can be very unreliable. For instance, on Good Friday, the very guy Christians believe to be the Son of God cried out that God was absent, but God was in fact never more active than on that day in human history. For real theologians, God shows up not in victory or euphoric experiences but with splinters, blood, thorns, and scorn.

As the Formula of Concord rightly explains,

We should not and cannot pass judgment on the Holy Spirit's presence, operations, and gifts merely on the basis of our feeling,

---

[17] This could have gotten me into worse trouble had it not been for Haggard's notorious scandal a year or so later involving a male prostitute and methamphetamine use.

how and when we perceive it in our hearts. On the contrary, because the Holy Spirit's activity often is hidden, and happens under cover of great weakness, we should be certain, because of and on the basis of his promise, that the Word which is heard and preached is an office and work of the Holy Spirit, whereby he assuredly is potent and active in our hearts.[18]

So in a world of power religion, with big shows and no few charlatans in the mix, we are wise to avoid emphasizing religious experience as a basis of our spiritual standing, our theological formulations, and most especially our justification before God. But this doesn't mean we *can't* enjoy the experience. The point is that the experience is the bonus after the realization that Christ did the work of liberating us "outside of us" (*extra nos*). Still, Lutheran Christians have empha-sized that all this can have a positive experiential effect on our lives, as Augsburg Confession article 20 states: "Because the Holy Spirit is received through faith, consequently hearts are renewed and endowed with new affections so as to be able to do good works."

A couple years ago, I was at one of the lowest emotional and spiritual points of my life. I was thinking about quitting life as a pro-fessor, hated living in a boring suburb, and was depressed as hell. My marriage had become a drag. We'd tried so hard to fix it for so long—and sometimes we'd make strides—that divorce started to look like a real possibility, at least during those short days of winter.

About that time, I was doing some research and speaking on biblical antiwisdom. This is the part of the Bible where the dark, perplexing side of existence is recognized. You can find it in one of my favorite books of the Bible, Ecclesiastes, and in Job, which until recently, was my least favorite. We also run into it in the intrigu-ing psalm that the Church of England historically used at funerals. The psalm is worth citing in full because it reflects my state of mind at the time, especially the first part, where the psalmist is pissed at God but has enough decency to keep it to himself:

> I said, "I will watch my ways
> And keep my tongue from sin;

---

[18] "Solid Declaration," art. II, part 56, *The Book of Concord: The Confessions of the Evan-gelical Lutheran Church*, ed. T. G. Tappert (Philadelphia: Mühlenberg Press, 1959), 532.

I will put a muzzle on my mouth
   As long as the wicked are in my presence."
But when I was silent and still,
   Not even saying anything good,
   My anguish increased.
My heart grew hot within me,
   And as I meditated, the fire burned;
   Then I spoke with my tongue:
"Show me, O Lord, my life's end
   And the number of my days
   Let me know how fleeting is my life.
You have made my days a mere
   Handbreadth;
The span of my years is as nothing before you.
Each man's life is but a breath. *Selah.*
Man is a mere phantom as he goes to and fro.
   He bustles bout, but only in vain;
   He heaps up wealth, not knowing who will get it.
"But now, Lord, what do I look for?
   My hope is in you.
Save me from all my transgressions;
Do not make me the scorn of fools.
I was silent; I would not open my mouth,
For you are the one who has done this.
Remove your scourge from me;
   I am overcome by the blow of your hand.
You rebuke and discipline men for their sin;
   You consume their wealth like a moth—
   Each man is but a breath. *Selah.*
Hear my prayer, O Lord,
   Listen to my cry for help;
   Be not deaf to my weeping.
For I dwell with you as an alien,
   A stranger, as all my fathers were.
Look away from me, that I may rejoice again
   Before I depart and am no more." (NIV)

Note that right in the middle of this melancholic poem-prayer, sandwiched between astounding boldness before the almighty, is a kernel of hope: *My hope is in you.* This testifies to the strange power of antiwisdom. It is reflected by Cohen's idea that there is a "blaze of light"—a glimpse of some power beyond this world—that we sometimes notice when we take an honest look at reality, whether in its ostensibly "broken" or "holy" forms. What looks grim from the outside is often the precursor to a breakthrough. Often when a wayfarer gets to his or her wit's end, there's nothing left but a fork in the road between the path to love's joyful rescue and the path to spiritual oblivion. As Cohen sings in "Anthem," "There is a crack in everything, / that's how the light gets in."

The concept of antiwisdom is not about opposing wisdom, or being proud to be ignorant, or opposing God's plan. It is about recognizing the pain and woe experienced by all us wayfaring strangers in this life. The Greek prefix *anti* can mean "against," or—as is the case here—it can mean something like "alternative." This second sense is what's at work with antiwisdom. It is the flip side of standard, wise ideas.

If we think of wisdom as a series of mental progressions, the book of Proverbs offers *conventional wisdom*. It says something like, "Keep your nose clean, marry a nice girl, study hard in school, dress nice for work, and you'll have a good life." This is all true, but we know it's not the whole story. *Antiwisdom* faces the problems of suffering, injustice, and perplexity head on. It lays us low. It smashes our egos. It says something like, "As hard as it is to admit, you could do everything right and yet end up misunderstood, lose a child to cancer, find that your whole line of work is being taken over by robots, and die alone." Such wisdom prepares us to be rebuilt or remain in ashes forever. The third stage, if we are fortunate enough to encounter it, is the *wisdom of the counterorder*. It is found in Jesus. I call it the *wisdom of the New Logic*. Jesus says something like, "Conventional and antiwisdom both rightly capture very real parts of life, but I'll let you in on something wilder than all that: you must die to live, lose to find, suffer to find love, become small; in other words, do the stuff that seems risky, wasteful, foolish, and absurd. Pour out everything you've got as if you had infinitely more in the vessel you're tipping onto the dirt."

As I was wrestling with all this wisdom stuff, I was downcast, reading the darkest parts of the Bible I could find and listening to sad music. Meanwhile, Stacie and I were asking ourselves whether we shouldn't just shuffle our whole life deck, join mixed martial arts fighter Justin Wren in his work liberating the Mbuti pygmies from enslavement in the Congo, or help fight human trafficking in New York with Raleigh Sadler. I was looking for something to give me a deep spiritual kick. I was becoming weary of trying to convince affluent suburban students that theology and philosophy mattered. Maybe I was tired of trying to convince *myself* that what I was teaching mattered.

In any case, after all this, I—a dude who's uncomfortable with overly emotional forms of worship and religious practice—eventually had a realization of the Gospel in a way that can properly be described as mystical. It wasn't that I learned some new secret wisdom. It wasn't that I learned something that wasn't already in the teachings of Paul and Jesus. It was that I internalized and existentially trusted the New Logic *for me* in a way that I had not quite felt before. It was as if God was showing me that I didn't have to do anything to reconcile God and students. God was able to do what he wanted to do. In the meantime, I could devote my life to loving everyone around me without having to go to some foreign land. I realized that God, in Christ, had *agape* for me and that life would be a great joy if I remembered to try to pour out that same inexhaustible love to others in my daily existence.

Some folks, upon hearing about all this, ask me how they might experience something like this themselves. The short answer is that conjuring and formulaic approaches to spirituality are routinely rejected by most sane mystics as well as scrupulous spiritual teachers of other religions. The key to what I experienced is, in one sense, simply treating the claims of the Gospel not as abstractions but as God's promises declared to individuals through preachers, friends, Scripture, and the Eucharistic feast.

The history of religion includes various catalysts for spiritual experiences, including chanting, forms of breathing, yogic stretching, long periods of meditation, sleep deprivation, dancing, and even shamanic use of plants. But to assume that such things can guarantee awareness of God is typically viewed with skepticism, even by folks who advocate the value of such practices. The real deal is, as my dad says, "getting high on oxygen," by which he means taking in the experience of divine beauty in mundane life itself, recognizing God's presence and the beauty hidden within what is right in front of us every day.

Moreover, this question leads me to some important warnings here. First, I must reiterate, don't *base* your faith on religious experience. It's great if you come across positive ones, but if you tie your beliefs to experiences, you'll be miserable before too long, trying to manufacture feelings to prove you are in good with God. Second, though my account might sound like a form of direct, propositional revelation, that's not how I see it. It was more like seeing clearly, or finally consciously recognizing, something I already knew, albeit in a limited way. It came after long stretches of prayer, study, and reflection. It was about connecting the dots that were there all along on my life's road to that point. It was like the apostles at dinner who, after they had been walking with the risen Jesus on the road to Emmaus, suddenly recognized who had been with them all along. It wasn't that they had a new vision at dinner; rather, they had better eyes and perhaps better attentiveness to what was already with them (Luke 24:13–32).

I'd suggest you immediately consult a professional psychiatrist or at least a neurologist if you frequently hear voices or have experiences where some bizarre new facts or instructions occur to you. Abraham heard a voice, and it told him to kill his boy, but if that sort of thing happens to you, *please* see a professional before sharpening any blades! Third, remember that mysticism is the polar opposite of magic. Mysticism is passive and humble. It receives and recognizes the grace of God in joy. Magic is active and conniving and attempts to summon the spiritual realm to do one's bidding. Mysticism instigates a sense of deep compassion and love for the world. Magic seeks hexes to exact revenge on ex-lovers or potions to trick someone into loving you.

Perhaps you still want me to give you a clue as to how you might keep an eye out for the mystical. Fine, I'll entertain such a discussion. But remember, this is not, and I don't believe there can be, a simplistic formula to evoke a genuine spiritual encounter other than a commitment to an honest awareness of reality itself. God isn't a genie to be rubbed out of a lamp. Therefore, trust no would-be guru or spiritual guide who claims to have a simple formula. Anyone who claims he or she has a list of secret steps or an esoteric key to mystical experience is little more than a spiritual snake-oil vendor at best and dangerous to your finances and physical well-being at worst. This does not mean, however, that there aren't common factors at work when most mystical moments occur. As far as I can tell, the following three acts were common to all the folks whose accounts of positive spiritual experience I find trustworthy:

1. They experienced emotional devastation.
2. They carved out space for silence.
3. They paid attention to the connections between and wonder in everything they encountered.

The first part is unpleasant but important. Mysticism is a result not of success and triumph but of blessed failure. To paraphrase Martin Luther, we need to go through hell and damnation if we are to really understand the Gospel. That's where the antiwisdom I mentioned comes into play. This is the Law doing its existential work, laying us low and smashing our egos. Historically, radical spiritual shifts often occur when a person is extremely afraid. For example, Luther decided to become a monk when lightning struck a nearby tree. At other times, such shifts occur when someone is deathly ill, which was the case with Julian of Norwich and Theodore Beza.

The second part involves patience and intentional silence. I'll discuss this in a subsequent chapter. The third part is the goal of genuine mysticism: recognize that this embodied existence, despite its trials, is a beautiful gift, the envy of the angels. It is flooded with divine light, even when that light is veiled. Thus sound mysticism is largely about mindfulness that recognizes the ways in which our lives are enfolded into a divine reality. If there is a logic, a *Logos* in, with, and under this existence, then paying attention to everything around us just might allow us to catch a glimpse of the threads of God's grace, which string together the fragments of our world and pull us up into His infinite joy.

Being affiliated with a brand of Lutheran Christianity that emphasizes the cognitive and orderly side of the faith, as I've said, makes this conversation about mysticism uncomfortable for me. One thing I did, after all this occurred, was to go back and read—or in a few cases, reread—the old mystics themselves. What I found was startling. It was as if some of them had seen precisely what I'd seen.

I also came to realize that two of my favorite theologians, Augustine and Luther, had mystical elements to their own theological outlook. I know that sounds strange to some. It did to me, as an undergrad, when my anthropology of religion professor Garth Ludwig said in passing, "And you know that Augustine and Luther were mystics, right?" I was greatly perturbed by this allegation. Calling these heroes of my faith the dreaded *m* word was almost like insulting my mother at the time. I tossed that claim aside back then. But I remembered it once more after a student gave me a copy of Bengt Hoffman's *Theology of the Heart: The Role of Mysticism in the Theology of Martin Luther*. It turns out Ludwig was right: a form of mysticism is right there in Luther. Hoffman did the proper scholarly legwork, so I'll allow him to make the case if you care to go get a copy and consider it. Note that he is helpful in distinguishing Luther's response to the speculative, Neoplatonic type, which wasn't his style, and the *Germanic* type, reflected by Johann Tauler (1300–1361) and the *Theologia Germanica* (fourteenth century). The latter book, despite being labeled "demonic" by John Calvin, was rediscovered and published by Luther himself. Concerning this anonymous mystical work, Luther said, "Next to the Bible and St. Augustine, no book has ever come into my hands from which I have learnt more of God and Christ, and man and all things that are."

I have come to believe that mysticism has a curious way of relating to epistemology: that is, to our ability to discover truth. Lutheran sociologist Peter Berger suggests this too and suggests that there is a connection between mysticism and understanding the world. He writes,

> Knowledge can be cultivated for its own sake; it can also have very definite existential consequences. It is possible to make the case that existentially (that is, in terms of the individual's existence in the world) true knowledge leads to experiences of ecstasy—of *ek-stasis*, a standing outside of the taken-for-granted routines of everyday life. Bodies and modes of knowledge differ, both in the degree to which they are conducive to such ecstasy and in the character of the ecstasy they provide. There are kinds of knowledge that appear to be quite timeless in this respect.[19]

---

[19] Peter Berger, *A Rumor of Angels: Modern Society and the Rediscovery of the Supernatural* (Garden City, NY: Doubleday, 1970), 28.

Here it's not that mysticism leads to esoteric, secret knowledge. Rather, awareness of reality can lead to a sort of mystical understanding of our world and, most important for our current quest, our relationships.

If philosophy is about goodness, truth, and beauty, and if I am right that these three transcendentals are interrelated, we might expect that there is a connection between mystical experience and ethical action. Hoffman makes precisely this assertion and discusses this at length in his book. To summarize, he shows that Luther's form of mysticism is behind Luther's famous *On Christian Liberty*, where he suggests that our radical freedom, rooted in the Gospel of Christ, can produce moral transformation. On this matter, Hoffman writes, "No one can assume the burden of Christian moral commitment without constant recourse to the incomprehensible power that lies behind and beyond the ordinary logic of things."[20]

Maybe you were expecting this kind of mysticism to appear more fantastical or to be an ideology or system. This was not the case for the Reformer. As Hoffman explains, "To Luther this personal experience was hardly a system labeled mysticism, but rather mystical theology. . . . Mystical theology is thus, according to Luther, the inner, spiritual side of Christian faith."[21] Historically, of course, Luther rejected the "enthusiasts"—those who today might be "barking in the spirit" at a big revival—but didn't exclude experience altogether: "He meant what in English is called 'feeling' in contradistinction to 'emotionalism.'"[22] Recognizing religious feeling is important for making both the teachings and the ethical ideals of Christianity approachable and joyful: "Life on earth [for Luther] always means you can, if you wish, untie your soul, so to speak, down to the disharmony of the demons. The obverse is also true: one can always open up to the music that wells up around Christ and his angels in these spheres."[23] Why didn't I hear about all this before? To answer this question, I asked my friend Dan to explain the role of

---

[20] Bengt Hoffman, *Theology of the Heart: The Role of Mysticism in the Theology of Martin Luther* (Minneapolis: Kirk House, 2003), 15–16.

[21] Ibid., 21.

[22] Ibid., 26.

[23] Ibid., 36.

mysticism in Lutheranism after Luther. He did his doctoral work at the University of St. Andrews on the seventeenth-century relationship between Lutheran Orthodoxy and pietism. Here's what he sent my way.

Guest Contribution: Daniel van Voorhis, "Religious Experience in Arndt"

Within a strain of Early Modern church historiography, the myth of an "age of orthodoxy" among Lutheran Reformers in the sixteenth and seventeenth centuries persists. This is typically dated from the drafting and adoption of the Book of Concord in 1580. Luther had died almost four decades earlier, and the Lutheran confessions, rather than the character and writings of Luther, came to define Lutheran doctrine, especially in the face of a growing Pan-European Calvinism. Effectively, the confessions ruled the church. The success or failure of the Reformation was believed to depend on the acceptance of these documents. Many ecclesiastical leaders and laypeople did indeed confess the faith as interpreted through the Book of Concord, but judging who was or was not faithful to the documents today is hard to gauge when it comes to understanding theologians or parish pastors of the time and almost impossible with respect to the laity. It is unlikely that the laity professed every jot and title of the Book of Concord, despite the best efforts of catechists, especially because the congregation members were illiterate or indifferent.

The "success" of the Lutheran confessions was that they became authoritative to the extent that erring pastors and theologians could be identified and at least partially curbed by the more conservative faculty at institutions such as at the University of Jena and Strasbourg. However, any attempt to interpret this period as a "Golden Age" overestimates the role of dogmatic theology in popular piety among the laity. It even overestimates it within the ranks of many trained theologians and pastors. Nonetheless, this mythic "Golden Age" was useful for establishing the legitimacy of nineteenth-century Lutheran church historians who wanted to enthrone their brand of confessionalism as the only genuine Lutheran expression.

However, one of the keys to understanding the generations that followed the magisterial reformation is the effect of the reformers' thought on the masses. While this is notoriously difficult to do, the increasing availability of books and general education for the middle classes allows us an insight into what they were reading—at least what they were buying—and the general ideas shared.[24] It appears that many Lutherans bought books to include as symbolic components of their libraries, and the choices made tended to depend on either a cursory reading or an interpretation given by someone else that led the person to purchase the work as a piece of self-identification in the first place.

This suggests, therefore, that there is little evidence for a mythic golden age of Lutheran orthodoxy and that the confessions were not initially successful in transmitting the precise theology of the Lutheran Reformation. How did the Lutheran tradition survive? Arguably, it was the image of Luther as a prophet that would resonate with many.[25] The popularity and image of Luther did not come through to the populace via the Book of Concord; rather, it arose from the simplicity and popular piety of Luther. In particular, Luther's popularity was carried forward by pastor and alchemist Johann Arndt. Arndt is often called the "father of pietism" or a "proto pietist," despite living more than fifty years before famed pietist Johann Jakob Spener would write a forward to Arndt's most famous devotional work, which became known as the _Pia Desideria_.

Arndt, whose simple devotional work _True Christianity_ was the best-selling book in the eighteenth century was less of a "pietist" work than it was an attempt to channel the spirit of Luther. After this publication, Arndt would be regularly attacked by theological faculties for not toeing the line and for including mystics in his advocacy of an "interior" Lutheranism. For instance, he consulted

---

[24] See, for instance, the work of Gerald Strauss, starting with his article "Success and Failure in the German Reformation," _Past and Present_ 67 (May 1975): 30–63.

[25] See R. W. Scribner, "The Incombustible Luther: The Image of the Reformer in Early Modern Germany," _Past and Present_ 110 (1986): 38–68.

such mystical writers as Bernard of Clairvaux and Johann Tauler, for whom Luther also had a deep affection. Arndt made it clear that he agreed with the Lutheran Confessions; he signed them and was faithful to them in his teaching and practice. Yet he also felt at liberty to appeal to Luther's works and to the spirit of the early Reformation, a time when theologians were free to borrow from pre-Reformation authors and then appropriate them in the service of the Gospel.

In my graduate research, I uncovered letters of Arndt that previous scholars had not consulted. In the process, I discovered that Arndt was regularly dealing with the question of his fidelity to Luther, the confessions, and his freedom to explore the "mystics" in order to develop a robust theology of the cross and a theology of a broken piety, one that Luther had called "a living and active thing." Among those who defended and vindicated Arndt were Johann Gerhard, Paul Gerhardt, and Johann Heermann.

Arndt rediscovered the inner life of the Christian, despite its secondary and imperfect role. Experiential faith rested on proclamation of propositional assertions about the crucifixion, death, and resurrection of Christ for the sins of the world, but this didn't mean he couldn't draw ideas from monks and laypeople who wrote in a devotional style that diverged from medieval scholasticism. His thought served as a counterbalance to Lutheran scholasticism.

Though Arndt didn't fit the mold of the so-called golden age of Lutheran orthodoxy, he never founded a splinter group, strayed from the confessions doctrinally, or betrayed the church he served until his death in 1621. Rather, he advanced, on a more popular and affective level, the spirit of the early Reformation. Arndt was not the founder of a new movement, nor the synthesizer of Lutheran orthodoxy and personal piety (though that label might go to his parishioner and good friend Johann Gerhard). Yet he represents an example of a Lutheran thinker who tried to be faithful to both his tradition and a genuine inner experience of faith.

Mysticism and Means

Mysticism seeks unity with God. Some (both adherents and detractors included) think of this as an unmediated connection to the divine.

This need not be the case, however. I, for instance, am committed to the importance of the *means* of grace—the spoken word and the tangible sacraments—and remain uninterested in any amorphous, new age sort of disembodied spirituality that avoids the importance of embodiment and incarnation. The theologian who has helped me see the value of a healthy mysticism is Japanese Lutheran theologian Kazoh Kitamori. In one passage, after rejecting the light and easy pseudomysticism of liberal theology, he explains why he still insists on the importance of what he calls a "sound" mysticism:

> Here we face a most difficult problem. Our aim is to secure a sound mysticism. As long as it is mysticism, this immediacy must be retained. But, theologically speaking, this immediacy is unsound. How then can we secure a "sound mysticism"? This is indeed a difficult problem, yet a sound mysticism must overcome it. This is possible because our mysticism is a "mysticism of pain." The pain of God exists by the denial of immediacy. Yet we are dissolved into the pain of God and we are at one with him in this pain. Thus, in the mysticism of pain, *we become immediately at one with God who denies immediacy.* . . . Consequently, in the mysticism of pain, the disobedience of mysticism is completely resolved, yet the characteristic of mysticism is maintained. In theological terms, we may say that mysticism is based on the doctrine of justification. . . . The progression from justification to mysticism is inevitable. A doctrine of justification which does not develop into mysticism lacks power. . . . Our fellowship with Christ's suffering becomes our joy and comfort: . . . Because the pain of God is love rooted in his pain, the mysticism of the cross creates power for sanctification. This love of God produces ethical sanctification in harmony with the order of the Holy Spirit. Mysticism which has justification as its background produces ethical energy—this is our mysticism.[26]

I dig Kitamori's phrase "mysticism of the cross." This should remain distinguished from the late-medieval Roman Catholic approach of contemplating a crucifix or Stations of the Cross in order to gain spiritual merit. Instead, Kitamori is talking about the way in which,

---

[26] Kitamori, *Theology of the Pain of God*, 74–77.

because of the reality of sin and brokenness, the lover and the beloved—in this case, God and His church—find unity. Both parties begin by aching for a restored relationship and ultimately overcome sin by experiencing pain. Christians point to the cross as the archetype of this reality. On the cross, the divine and human became reconciled, but only after we humans executed the one who was the embodiment of goodness, truth, and beauty.

Guest Contribution: Lance Green

One of my favorite students over the years has been Lance Green. I confess, as much as he reflects the best of earnest, theological desire, he had also picked up (sometimes, alas from me) a bit too much *odium theologicum,* or theological anger, mixed with an overemphasis on the abstract and a pinch of youthful arrogance. I mention this not only to my own shame but also to explain my delight when I met up with him again in Los Angeles at a cool little hipster restaurant on Sunset Boulevard. I wanted to confess my sins as a professor and let him in on some new stuff I was exploring. I was thrilled, therefore, to learn he had gone down similar lines without any prodding from me. We are all works in progress, but he found some solid wisdom in his explorations. Indeed, his master's thesis addressed the intersection of erotic desire and Christian spirituality. For this book, I asked him to summarize what he was exploring. The traditions he explored were slightly different from those of Luther's Germanic mysticism, but he is able to provide a helpful introduction to something academic theologians have been exploring lately. I am grateful that he agreed to contribute.

How Christian Mysticism Might Heal Our Sexuality

For Saint Augustine, humans find their ultimate fulfillment in participating in their Creator. This reveals something fundamentally important—and often lost—about the nature of human sexuality: that it is an outworking of our innate desire for fulfillment. In creaturely sexual desire, we see an analogy to our desire for the Absolute. Thus, more than anything in our embodied lives, sex is primarily about how we relate to our God. To speak of God is not to speak covertly about sex; rather, to speak of sex is to implicitly speak of God.[27]

Desire is a relevant theological category today because it opens the door for Christians to see the connection between their sexuality and God. While it might seem out of place to mention desire and sexual passion in the same sentence as God, such an impression only betrays our modern tendency toward compartmentalization. Theology and human sexuality have not always been alien to each other; in fact, there is a rich Christian tradition of seeing the connection between God and erotic love as fruitful for theology. For many ancient and medieval Christian thinkers, *eros* did not denote a merely sexual desire; rather, *eros* encapsulated and completed sexual desire in its pursuit for ultimate fulfillment in God. Understood in this light, human erotic love grounds all desire for God; it is the erotic impulse that sends us out of ourselves to our Creator. This is a fundamental theme in much of Christian mysticism: creaturely *eros* launches the soul's ascent to God. On this spiritual journey, human love is caught up and made holy as one encounters the Divine Lover.

One of the earliest explorations of the place of *eros* in theology comes in the writings of Pseudo-Dionysius. A fourth- or fifth-century Syrian Christian, Pseudo-Dionysius believes *eros* to be an essential descriptor of our relationship to God. Pseudo-Dionysius goes one step further in his use of *eros* when he applauds the citation of 2 Samuel 1:26 as a clear analogy for loving God, defending the use of *eros* against those wary of associating the term with our experience of the divine: "It is clear to us that many lowly men think there is something absurd in the lovely verse: 'Love for you came to me like love for women,' someone says. To those listening properly to the divine things, the name *love* is used by the sacred writers in divine revelation with the exact same meaning as the term *yearning*."[28]

---

[27] Sarah Coakley, *God, Sexuality, and the Self: An Essay "On the Trinity"* (Cambridge: Cambridge University Press, 2013), 10.

[28] Pseudo-Dionysius, *Divine Names*, in *The Complete Works*, trans. Paul Rorem, Karlfried Froehlich, and Jean Leclerch (New York: Paulist Press, 1988), 81.

Pseudo-Dionysius notes that Paul himself was taken by this love: "It is no longer I who live, but Christ who lives in me" (Gal. 2:20). Paul was swept up by God's love in such a way that he was displaced by Christ. Paul is "beside himself for God."[29] Ecstasy (*ekstasis*), which is the notion of being taken up and drawn out of ourselves, is a foundational motif for Pseudo-Dionysius and other mystics. Participating in the rites of the church—the liturgy, sacraments, and prayer—activates this ascent to holiness: "Divine yearning brings ecstasy so that the lover belongs not to self but to God."[30] *Ekstasis* is the result of this yearning for God, the completion of our most fundamental desires.

This journey of ascent is particular to humanity, but the cause of *ekstasis* belongs essentially to God. Our love and ecstasy is grounded in God's "own benign yearning for all," which is "carried outside of himself in the loving care he has for everything."[31] Thus our own yearning for God, our own desire, is grounded in God's own eternal yearning that goes out of itself and infinitely returns. Part of the essence of God, then, is a love for otherness.

Considered the great synthesizer of the mystical and scholastic tradition, Saint Bonaventure (1221–74) asserted it was the cross that brought us into the life of God. Similar to Pseudo-Dionysius, creation is brought into being out of love, but Saint Bonaventure emphasizes the Christological elements—that is, that Christ's crucified love transformed the world.[32] Further, it is Christ crucified that defines the Christian life:

> And then transfixed
> with nails,
> he appeared to you as your beloved
> cut through with wound upon wound
> in order to heal you.
> *Who will grant me*

---

[29] Ibid., 82.

[30] Ibid.

[31] Ibid.

[32] Ilia Delio, OSJ, *Crucified Love: Bonaventure's Mysticism of the Crucified Christ* (Quincy, IL: Franciscan Press, 1998), 126.

> *that my request should come about*
> *and that God will give me*
> *what I long for,*
> that having been totally transpierced
> in both mind and flesh,
> I may be fixed
> with my beloved
> to the yoke of the cross?[33]

In the same way we are yoked to the work of the cross, so is all creation. Christ, as the union of a divine person with human flesh, effectively redeems and restores the whole of the created order.[34] Creaturely *eros*, then, is part of this redeemed reality; but all love is grounded in the sacrificial, self-surrendering love of Christ.

Considering these insights from the Christian tradition, how might mysticism help us redefine our understanding of sexuality? Mysticism shows us that sexual desire is not our defining attribute but rather part of the outflow of our innate desire for the divine. Becoming aware of our fulfillment in God should drastically change our priorities. Properly understood, *eros* is about our relationship to our Creator and the Creator's relationship to us. This implies that our yearning for completion—our ascent toward God—is really about being transformed and sanctified into what humans are meant to be as creatures made in the *imago Dei*. Love defines this ascent because the incarnation is the greatest revelation of love. The power and work of the cross are what make all this possible. Sexual desire should thus be interpreted and transformed through Christ's outpouring of love on the cross. Self-emptying and self-sacrificing are what define Christian sexuality.

One might call this a *kenotic ethic*, an ethic that rests upon Christ's own self-emptying, from Godhead to humanity, as it culminates in the outpouring of his life on the cross. A kenotic ethic refuses the sinful inclination to turn toward the self. Following Christ and the character of the whole triune God, the Christian

---

[33] Bonaventure, *The Tree of Life*, in *Bonaventure*, trans. Ewert Cousins (New York: Paulist Press, 1978), 149.

[34] See Bonaventure's "Sermon of Nativity" and Delio's *Crucified Love*, 120.

should always be oriented toward others. We see this especially in the writing of Hans Urs von Balthasar, twentieth-century theologian of the mystical tradition, whose understanding of a Trinitarian *Ur-kenosis* (self-emptying) grounds and compels all subsequent kenotic acts. Balthasar reads Christ's kenosis—both his becoming flesh and his dying on the cross—into the Trinity itself. The Father gives all of Himself over to beget the Son; the Son is eternally receptive of this gift.[35] Kenosis as an eternal "act" is simply the essence of the divine nature and is something God both does and is.[36] Bearing the image of God, humanity can find the grounding of its own ethic toward others in the primal kenotic act.

This kenotic lens, coupled with a properly attuned desire, pushes back against the dangerous and often damaging turn to the self. Sexual desire without the cruciform transformation of the mystical ascent too easily turns another's body into something to be mastered, dominated, or controlled. The reduction of a body to an object for self-gratification is the ultimate act that separates *eros* from God. In doing this, we bracket our innate desire for God from the ethical implications of the Christian life; Christian mysticism attempts to do the very opposite: interpret our sexuality in light of desire for God.

---

[35] Hans Urs von Balthasar, *Theo-Drama. Theological Dramatic Theory, V: The Last Act*, trans. Graham Harrison (San Francisco: Ignatius Press, 2003), 245.

[36] Ibid., 86.

Spirituality and Physical Beauty

While writing this book, Stacie turned me on to a reality-show couple—Evan and Carly—who illustrate the way in which spirituality can create a sense of physical beauty in a person. The pair was featured in *Bachelor in Paradise*, season 2. I must confess that I didn't want to watch this reality show at all. Especially not this subgenre. I must also confess that I enjoyed the episode she showed me and that she rightly recognized the way it demonstrated the concept I've been exploring in this chapter, though in an even more concrete way.[37] The following is my transcription of the most relevant scene for our purposes, and it occurs as the couple is entering some sort of love shaman's dome hut:

> **Carly.** This is really right up Evan's alley. Like, he loves this weird stuff.
>
> **Carly.** I'm a little nervous about the hut. I don't know what's going to happen in the hut. I just want to be confident that I am falling for Evan, or I'm not falling for Evan.
>
> . . .
>
> The indigenous holy men chant and pour liquid over rocks, which steams.
>
> **Carly.** Because Evan was super into it, it makes me feel like, kind of comfortable in a really weird way. If I went on this date with someone who wasn't on the spiritual plane that I am, that would be bad.
>
> **Evan.** Carly, I . . . one of my greatest fears is that I won't be accepted for all of me. And you have accepted me. All of me so far. My weird and my crazy and my everything. And I'm really excited to see what happens, and I really want to pursue you and what else is in your heart, because it has so far just been beautiful.
>
> **Carly.** When he said, "you accept the crazy," I was like, I don't know that I do, but I should. He accepted me for mine; I might as well accept him for his.
>   You know, you're sitting in there. You're sweating. The body's going all sorts of ways. You have sand everywhere. Your hair is a mess. And he was looking at me like, "You are so beautiful." And it's incredible to be sitting in front of a guy looking

---

[37] Stacie asked me to mention that she is indeed embarrassed that she sometimes tunes in to these reality shows. But she finds they can also reveal interesting aspects of human behavior. In any case, despite the perverse joy of the spectacle known as *The Bachelorette/ The Bachelor*, we have forsworn that as the relationship equivalent of gladiatorial games.

probably your worst and having him just look at you like you radiate. Whoa. That's what we've all been searching for.

Camera cuts to her talking to him.

Carly. I think every day being with you has surprised me. And every single day, I've fallen more and more for you, and it's surprising me every single second. I'm excited about that.

They pour warm, cleansing water over each other.

Evan. This may have been the biggest breakthrough. I just feel like we're connected and we're on the same page, and we're just . . . we're moving as one. It's amazing.

Carly. It blows my mind that I like him so much. And that he's, like, not what I expected. But I think there's so much beauty in that. I'm so attracted to him as a human being and his soul and that's making him, like, look different to me. On the outside as well! Now my lady boner is, like, finally back.

Say what you will about the cultural appropriation at play, the potential for manipulation inherent to spiritual stuff, or the general new age vibe here. But I think the point remains: bodies and faces become beautiful when surfing the Tao. The eyes of a lover can see beauty more accurately, through a nontransactional understanding of love. By becoming a person who is centered on a form of spiritual peace and by ignoring the normal criteria used to judge a partner in our nihilistic world, even otherwise shallow people can have their perspective transformed. Carly was originally uninterested in Evan. She didn't dig his look or his demeanor. But his spirituality made him sexy in her eyes.

This is a good place to pause. It seems I haven't yet arrived at the titillating parts, if that's what you were hoping for. I suppose I haven't been talking *directly* about sex at all. But that is a valuable lesson itself, I think. So wait for it, friends. Slow and low: that is the sexy tempo. Flirtation and foreplay are half the fun, right? Something just might get unveiled in the next chapter.

✓ Best Prrts

✓ CLI oro

Circut late

Shg 6 + webinar

(VDS)

~~Sepill~~

LCEF

new late

stlukes

rev. dan weber
lead pastor
dweber@stlukes-church.com

TEL 253.941.3000
FAX 253.941.8994

515 s 312th street
federal way, wa 98003

stlukes-church.com

A Cold and Lonely Hallelujah
(Masturbation)

> It's not a complaint you hear at night
> It's not some pilgrim who's seen the light
> It's a cold and it's a lonely Hallelujah
> —Leonard Cohen, "Hallelujah"

Cold and lonely. Cold and broken. The word *hallelujah* evokes a religious ecstasy that bears an uncanny resemblance to physical orgasms. That might sound blasphemous, but that is only because, even at our best, we mortals often experience our sexuality as a snare. This tension between what we'd like to be and what we actually are is at the root of our spiritual and emotional distress. Many have cried out, "Wretched man that I am! Who will deliver me from this body of death?" (Rom. 7:24). This realization properly frames the picture of our erotic tragedy. It's not that there's a problem with sexuality per se; it's that we bend the best gifts to our own twisted ends. This is particularly true when it comes to masturbation.

Our tragedy is not exactly one in which self-gratification creates bad karma. Despite Christian adolescent fears, Saint Peter isn't in the business of tallying up negative cosmic demerits in a logbook of masturbatory infractions to be read aloud upon our arrival at the pearly gates. The tragedy is that while the drive for an orgasm is related to our drive for connectedness, masturbation is a solitary act.

After an orgasm is experienced apart from connection to *agape*, it can end in a sense of loneliness and *lament* that there is no connection. Of course, there are hormonal and biochemical reasons for this too. But orgasms in the context of love and safety tend to leave a person with a feeling of bliss. Thus the experience of this almost-grasped but elusive love can occur both within the context of solitary sex and also in the casual, loveless sex. If masturbatory orgasms resemble a hallelujah, they are *cold and broken, cold and lonely* when they are mistaken for the ultimate goal itself or when they reveal the emptiness of our painful lack of real intimacy with God and humanity.

The connection between the Tao and virtue that I described in previous chapters is the necessary backdrop to understand the odd question of whether it is permissible for a virtuous, faithful person to masturbate. In one sense, this is a comically unimportant subject. There are many horrendous injustices in the world that are worthy of the time wasted on this relatively inconsequential matter. Indeed, even if we were to identify masturbation as categorically sinful, it surely remains among the least serious of our ethical failings. Nonetheless, because we take masturbation too seriously in some circles, it can become a pernicious source of inward struggle and self-loathing for many, especially adolescents. During my years as an educator, many frustrated and guilt-ridden young men (young women, for good reason, either seek out female mentors or are more restrained in their habits in the early years) have come to me seeking help in understanding their struggle. Perhaps I come across as a guy who's unfazed by such awkward topics. Still, the prevalence of anxiety regarding masturbation makes me think the subject warrants an extended discussion here.

A Touchy Subject

It's odd that any educator, or any person with a platform to share ideas, would shy away from this topic, despite its private nature. Too much free conversation about masturbation can indeed be a red flag when it is a favorite topic for a teacher, youth worker, or pastor. But I think another reason we have difficulty dealing with masturbation in a mature way has to do with the constraints on otherwise reasonable people: the politics of it all, at least for the last few centuries has been marked by hysteria.

Only a couple decades ago—under *Bill Clinton's* watch, mind you—the first African American Surgeon General of the United States, Jocelyn Elders, was asked during a United Nations panel about the wisdom of teaching about masturbation. The international community was wondering whether there was a safe alternative to dangerous extramarital intercourse, especially in light of the AIDS crisis. She responded, "I think that it is part of human sexuality, and perhaps it should be taught." There are two important but distinct points at work here. The first is that it is *part of human sexuality*. There should be nothing controversial here; it *is* part of human sexuality. You don't need a doctorate in human development to know that it is commonplace, even though we may refrain from discussing it in polite company.

We might go so far as to interpret her words as implying that it is *normal*. I suspect she purposely didn't use this word. The meaning of *normal* can range from a descriptive statement to a value judgment. But technically, normal ought to be understood as value-free and descriptive. Thus farts and toe fungus are normal. There is no guilt or shame in admitting to have a personal acquaintance with such things, even though propriety leads us to hide their existence in public. There are other normal human experiences that are unfortunate, like the fact that puppy love fades as a relationship ages and that hormone shifts can make us irritable. These seem partly benign and partly a matter of the virtues or vices we bring to the table when we handle these realities.

But there's a second, implicit aspect here, which I believe was the primary reason she became a casualty of the American culture wars: she suggested that *it should be taught*. Conservative Americans are uncomfortable with the federal government weighing in on issues they believe are best left for families to discuss with their children. I understand this reason. I, for instance, don't want prayer in public schools, not because I don't like prayer, but because I don't trust the state meddling in the religious training of my children, and I assume that the prayers they would use would be prayers to a generic god of a vague civil religion. I bet Baal worshipers had prayer in schools back in the day.

Similarly, I have no objections to talking frankly about masturbation with my own children. But depending on what it would mean to *teach masturbation*, I might have a concern if it happened at school. Would they assign it as homework? Would they use diagrams to show how to do it right? Is that necessary? Isn't that like giving a teen a jigsaw puzzle and then numbering the pieces so that they can easily be pieced together? I'm against that because it's generally a waste of time and turns our budding sexuality into something far too clinical.

Would they teach students about some things *not to do*, like inserting one's penis into a pool drainage hole? Probably not, though maybe they should, since EMTs I know report responding to emergencies like this on occasion. Would they teach them to chill out about the topic and recognize that it is a behavior that is usually part of normal and natural human development and that they shouldn't become tangled up in shame over the matter? I hope that's what she meant, and keep in mind she only conceded that this *probably* should be taught. In any case, though times have changed culturally since then, I believe this remains an important question for us to consider, though we should give priority to families and other appropriate venues for this sensitive discussion.

What if we set aside the question of the context in which this should be taught and turn to a more fundamental question: should masturbatory health be taught as a normal and healthy and virtuous behavior *in principle* by Christian parents? Before we do consider this question, however, please recognize my own fears when proceeding with this discussion. I didn't yet finish the story concerning Jocelyn Elders. She was fired by Bill Clinton, the notoriously womanizing commander-in-chief, who cited this as the last straw in a list of areas wherein he disagreed with his Surgeon General. Granted, he was losing political capital at the time, but *really*? *This* was the erotic Rubicon that he would not cross? If the topic *was* indeed too taboo for twentieth-century secular America, it seems ill-advised for me to weigh in now, given my affiliations.

Nonetheless, as a Christian father who cares about ethics and the well-being of his children, I must insist that parents should address this topic calmly, without flinching. Moreover, and perhaps more controversially, I think parents who share my faith should assure their children, at the appropriate time in their development, that masturbation in moderation is a normal and usually healthy aspect of sexual development. It should be a relaxed component of parenting conversations, in which parents share wisdom about how to maintain healthy perspectives and habits related to the practice.

What Was the Sin of Onan?

First, some historical reflection is in order.[1] Let's start with the Bible. There's no passage in either the Old or New Testaments that explicitly condemns masturbation as such. Certain practices made someone ceremonially unclean, but the prophets and apostles of the Almighty pay it little mind. That's instructive in itself, since it's not as if our species only discovered self-gratification in the eighteenth century.

The closest thing to a condemnation of masturbation we have is an odd passage in the Old Testament wherein a man named Onan "spilled his seed on the ground" (Gen. 38). God killed him for this. Whenever sensitive consciences encounter God's wrath, we become anxious and try to figure out how to avoid such a doom ourselves. What on earth did this guy do to deserve death?

The answer requires an understanding of something called "levirate marriage," something unique to the ancient Hebrew context. (Incidentally, however, a couple Sudanese students I once had in class told me it remained an element of their cultural mores to this day.) It is described in Deuteronomy 25:5–10. Among many ancient people, lineage was typically more precious than material wealth. It was the only thing that could outlast a person's short span on earth. Moreover, when we are at our best, we are concerned for the well-being of our loved ones and descendants after we die.

In this system, if a man died and left a childless wife behind, the brother was obliged to sleep with the dead man's widow. The express purpose of this was to produce male descendants so that his brother's memory and lineage would not be erased from the earth. There were ways out of it, but even these avenues brought shame on

---

[1] There isn't space to examine all the complex factors leading up to contemporary Christian attitudes regarding masturbation and sex education. The reader can find robust discussions of the topic in several articles, such as the following: Vern Bullough, "Sex Education in Medieval Christianity," *Journal of Sex Research* 13.3 (1977): 185–96; Lee Belford, "Protestantism and Sex Education," *Advances in Sex Research* 1 (1963): 61–66; Sterling Fishman, "The History of Childhood Sexuality," *Journal of Contemporary History* 17.2 (1982): 269–83; Lesley Hall, "Forbidden by God, Despised by Men: Masturbation, Medical Warnings, Moral Panic, and Manhood in Great Britain," *Journal of the History of Sexuality* 2.3 (1992): 365–87; Robert MacDonald, "The Frightful Consequences of Onanism: Notes on the History of a Delusion," *Journal of the History of Ideas* 28.3 (1967): 423–31.

the unfaithful brother. When Onan's brother Er died, Onan didn't refuse levirate marriage, and he slept with his former sister-in-law. But he was unfaithful to his brother and his community because he practiced *coitus interruptus* (the pull-out method). Thus he enjoyed the benefit of physical pleasure but refused the call to self-sacrifice at the root of levirate marriage. It's important to note that though the term *onanism* came to be a synonym for masturbation after the eighteenth century, Onan's offense had to do with birth control, not self-gratification. But that isn't the main point of the story. Note that while the minds of many Christian young people are plagued by shame and guilt related to their self-exploration, the go-to proof text for condemning masturbation turns out to have nothing to do with the topic.

But wrestling with the passage can help guide us all in our endeavor to understand orgasms and human relationships. Leonard Mars offers an interesting anthropological interpretation of the incident, suggesting that the problem isn't even birth control per se but a fundamental offense against Onan's father:

> What Onan did was to exterminate Er, to erase his name from the world of the living. Undoubtedly Er was physically dead but by means of the levirate his name could have been perpetuated; he could have been given life by the magnanimous and altruistic act of a dutiful brother who was prepared to sacrifice his own individual interests for those of his family as a whole. Onan's crime constituted not only an attack on his brother, an attempt to extirpate Er, but also represented an heinous assault on his father, since the murder of Er was the murder of a first-born. It was not simply a case of murder but was an impious act of murdering a first-born brother whose name had been bestowed on him by his father. The first-born was considered to be closer to the father than subsequent children since a greater portion of the father's personality, soul, or strength was embodied in him. Hence by destroying his elder brother, Onan was destroying a major part of his father; in effect, he was committing a form of parricide.[2]

---

[2] Leonard Mars, "What Was Onan's Crime?," *Comparative Studies in Society and History* 26.3 (1984): 436.

Many see God's holy history, as recorded in the Bible, as a continuous story of the fulfillment of the promise to Eve that, though the serpent would bruise her seed's heel, one would come to crush the serpent's head. For those folks, stories about lineage and the importance of genealogies in the Bible have to do with a narrative in which an evil force persistently tries to snuff out God's messianic line. According to this way of thinking then, God's covenant people constantly worked to maintain the purity of that messianic line, while the forces of evil worked to cut the line off. Thus, in that theological context, Onan is attempting to thwart God's ultimate plan. In any case, it is sufficient here to establish that Onan's story has nothing to do with masturbation.

A Most Disgraceful Crime?

Despite what I've just stated, Martin Luther unfortunately perpetuated the older view regarding nonprocreative orgasms. Even those of us who put him among the top theologians within Christian history can't expect him to have rethought every teaching he received from the medieval church. Nonetheless, we should avoid the error of thinking he was infallible. Too often, the weight of his exegetical opinion has led Protestants, and of course most Lutherans especially, to leave his particular biblical interpretations unchallenged. My hunch is that Luther recognized the self-sacrificing aspect of levirate marriage, but he was unable to shed his medieval assumption that orgasms divorced from an intent to procreate are essentially abominable:

> Accordingly, it was a most disgraceful crime to produce semen and excite the woman, and to frustrate her at that very moment. He was inflamed with the basest spite and hatred. Therefore he did not allow himself to be compelled to bear that intolerable slavery. Consequently, he deserved to be killed by God. He committed an evil deed. Therefore God punished him. And this is what I meant when I said that the probity of those who kept this law was outstanding. For it is a great burden to serve another by raising up and preserving descendants and heirs, to beget children for others, to rear and nourish them, and to leave

them a patrimony—and all this in the name of a dead brother. The world knows nothing at all of such love. It is a great annoyance to be only a guardian and tutor of wards, which customarily takes place nowadays according to Roman law. How many complaints and what perfidy are found there throughout the whole world! For it is a difficult task and a mark of outstanding love to be faithful and diligent in protecting the goods of others. Accordingly, this law includes the most ardent love. That worthless fellow refused to exercise it. He preferred polluting himself with a most disgraceful sin to raising up offspring for his brother.[3]

Luther is alluding here to an idea that is based more on an application of natural law thinking than special revelation (Scripture). Natural law, in this context, refers to the idea that we can develop a general understanding of God and morality based on our examination of the natural world. Nature, here, can mean not only the animal and physical worlds but also human psychology.

The chief architect of such thinking in Western Christianity was Thomas Aquinas. Prior to this influential medieval scholastic theologian (who, by the way, reportedly abandoned academic theology for mysticism at the end of his life, by the way), sex was seen as something of a necessary evil. Augustine had already made the unfortunate connection between original sin and sexuality. This was, arguably, due to his Neoplatonism as much as anything else.[4] For Neoplatonists, the body is like a lead weight that keeps us from ascending to higher things and spiritual reflection. This spiritualized adaptation of Plato's thought wasn't identical to Gnosticism—a cluster of mystery traditions that treated the material world and the body as a kind of prison for our souls—but it did have difficulty with the idea that there was something sacred in, with, and under the created world.

Aquinas, receiving his cues from Augustine but also depending heavily on Aristotle, took the practice of drawing moral conclusions

---

[3] Martin Luther, *Luther's Works, Vol. 7: Lectures on Genesis: Chapters 38–44*, ed. J. J. Pelikan, H. C. Oswald, and H. T. Lehmann (Saint Louis: Concordia, 1965), Gen. 38:11.

[4] In his *Confessions*, for instance, he describes a time before his conversion to Christianity in which he and some friends decided to start a sort of philosophical commune, where the guys would remain unmarried in order to avoid earthly distractions. This is evidence that his ideas on sexuality, ideas that greatly influenced subsequent Christian thinkers, were at least as dependent on his prior philosophical convictions as they were on any biblical teaching.

based on evidence from the natural world to new heights. His writings contain curious teachings regarding "emissions." He writes, for instance, "It is evident from this that every emission of semen, in such a way that generation cannot follow, is contrary to the good for man. . . . Sins of this type are called contrary to nature."[5] Accordingly, one finds in Aquinas the idea that oral sex in marriage, anal sex of any kind, homosexuality, birth control, and masturbation are all sins against nature. Thus they are among the most abominable evils because they have nothing to do with procreation.

Incidentally, there is a way in which this business of looking to natural law is now counterproductive, at least in our quest for erotic virtue. Aquinas claimed not to have encountered any beasts who copulated for the fun of it, nor did he know of any that masturbated. Anyone with a male pet dog might chuckle at this claim. I have a psychologist friend whose beagle won't go to sleep without mounting a stuffed animal or pillow each night. Aquinas also never ran into bonobos. These primates greet each other with sexual stimulation throughout the day. They only seem to have one taboo: researchers don't encounter instances of sexual activity between mothers and sons. Unlike chimpanzees, they don't exhibit rape-like behavior. I point to this because they are higher primates who do not fit the natural pattern a Thomist (i.e., a person who adheres to Thomas Aquinas' perspective) would expect to find in the animal kingdom.

Basing sexual ethics on biology is also complicated by human physiology itself. I'm not qualified to evaluate the claims of biologists and anthropological scholars who study such things, but the fact is that nature and grace turn out to be continually at odds, at least as things are in the present reality. For instance, Christopher Ryan and Cacilda Jethá, in *Sex at Dawn: How We Mate, Why We Stray, and What It Means for Modern Relationships* (Harper Perennial, 2012), argue that hunter-gatherer societies were routinely promiscuous, with the ideal of monogamous marriage not really emerging until the agricultural revolution and property ownership. They also note that the human body seems physiologically suited to frequent promiscuity rather than occasional monogamy.

---

[5] *Summa Theologica* 14.5.

Does this imply that nature is pushing us toward behavior that is clearly at odds with traditional Christian teaching regarding sexual ethics? Perhaps. But if so, what would that mean? Would it mean that God *created* us to be promiscuous? Is it merely a result of evolutionary adaptation? Would it mean that we should be sure to produce frequent emissions to avoid cancer? Or if we are committed to traditional values, would it mean that we have to ignore empirical data from scientists? Perhaps we can dispense with such questions by assuming two rather orthodox Christian teachings.

The first Christian doctrine is that nature itself is fallen and disrupted by sin. As Paul writes in Romans 8:22, "We know that the whole creation has been groaning together in the pains of childbirth until now." Here's how this applies to topics like masturbation: the question of whether it is natural or normal is not that helpful if nature is groaning in our present age and people are normally bent inward upon themselves.

The second Christian doctrine is the concept of the *penultimate*, which means "second to last." It's based on Luther's concept that we live in a world characterized by the *already and not yet*. For instance, we are already declared holy, but we are not yet perfectly holy in practice. Luther writes, "Consequently, even if we are not perfectly holy, Christ will wash away our sins with his blood and, when we depart from this life, will make us altogether pure in the life to come. In the meantime we are content with that righteousness which exists in hope through faith in Jesus Christ. Amen."[6] German theologian Dietrich Bonhoeffer made use of this same theme in his *Ethics*, wherein he suggests, to paraphrase one of his more remarkable theses, that it is better to do a naughty thing than to be a bad person. Only a theology steeped in grace can rest easy with odd ideas like this, or with this really unsettling passage Luther wrote to his friend Melanchthon:

> If you are a preacher of grace, then preach a true and not a fictitious grace; if grace is true, you must bear a true and not a fictitious sin. God does not save people who are only fictitious

---

[6] Luther, *Luther's Works*, vol. 54, ed. Theodore Tappert (Philadelphia: Fortress Press, 1967), 375.

sinners. *Be a sinner and sin boldly*, but believe and rejoice in Christ even more boldly, for he is victorious over sin, death, and the world. As long as we are here in this world we have to sin. This life is not the dwelling place of righteousness, but, as Peter says, we look for new heavens and a new earth in which righteousness dwells. It is enough that by the riches of God's glory we have come to know the Lamb that takes away the sin of the world. No sin will separate us from the Lamb, even though we commit fornication and murder a thousand times a day. Do you think that the purchase price that was paid for the redemption of our sins by so great a Lamb is too small? Pray boldly—you too are a mighty sinner.[7]

Some Lutherans get embarrassed by this "sin boldly" passage, which older Roman Catholic anti-Protestant propagandists used to love citing. But here, when it comes to sexuality within our penultimate lives, it's quite helpful. Note that Luther isn't saying we should *sin more*. He's saying that it's best to be honest about the shape of things. We can be honest because, in light of the hope that the Lamb of God was powerful enough to take away the sins of the world, we don't have to hide our misdeeds. Luther's point would make sense to folks in Alcoholics Anonymous: you start by admitting to yourself and others that you have a problem. No one is glad about hearing that someone screwed up and hit rock bottom, yet no one is going to throw the addict out of the room. By denying reality, we ultimately end up in a dark place. Gerhard Forde makes the connection here to addiction in general: "A theologian of glory attempts to cure those addicted to glory by optimistic appeals, that is, by the law. But what happens thereby is only a reinforcement of one's illusions about oneself. The supposed optimism of the theology of glory turns against itself. When the addict discovers the impossibility of quitting, self-esteem plummets. The addict tries to hide the addiction and puts on a false front. Superficial optimism breeds ultimate despair."[8]

---

[7] Luther, *Luther's Works*, vol. 48, ed. J. J. Pelikan and H. T. Lehmann (Saint Louis: Concordia, 1986), 375, 281–83.

[8] Gerhard Forde, *On Being a Theologian of the Cross: Reflections on Luther's Heidelberg Disputation, 1518* (Grand Rapids, MI: Eerdmans, 1997), 15–16.

Here's how all this applies to masturbation: set aside the abstract question of whether or not it is sinful in the abstract. I happen to think there is no reason to think of it—at least essentially—as a sin. But even if it is, the last few centuries of fear concerning the practice have done little to extinguish it from the human experience, but that fear *has* succeeded in creating a lot of anxiety. Let's start by adapting Luther's hyperbole, especially for our young people: *No sin will separate us from the Lamb, even if we masturbated a thousand times a day.* Once we realize that the kingdom in which we dwell is one of grace, we are free to ask the question whether that much masturbation is the best way to spend your span of time in God's garden.

Modern Onanism Hysteria and John Wesley

If we consider the cultural history of masturbation, it turns out that it was rarely a big deal until—surprisingly—the Enlightenment. This is well documented by the exhaustive research of Thomas Laqueur, who contends that it arose as a medical-moral problem in the eighteenth century.[9] First came the anonymous *Onania: or, The Heinous Crime of Self Pollution, And All Its Frightful Consequences, in Both Sexes* (1723). Later, it was addressed by S. A. A. D. Tissot's *A Treatise on the Crime of Onan; Illustrated with a Variety of Cases, Together with the Method of Cure* (1766). The medical "cure" to which Tissot alludes became a booming business, with syrups intended to throttle the libido, bleeding (think leeches), and even cages to prevent boys from playing with themselves during the night.

This business about onanism was quite literally about *business*: it involved a sort of snake oil marketing. Create a problem (in this case, one that affects most people and happens to be titillating), offer free literature about it, and then sell some remedies in the back of the book—remedies guaranteed to tame your sexual urges. We can't ignore here how much quackery and how little research influenced our cultural fears and superstitions about masturbation. This all might have been a quaint aspect of history had religious types not seized upon it. The main culprit, when it comes to presenting pseudoscience

---

[9] Thomas Laqueur, *Solitary Sex: A Cultural History of Masturbation* (New York: Zone Books, 2004).

to young adult Christians, was John Wesley (1703–91). Not only was he a well-known religious personality, but his Methodist Society turned out reams of tracts and books, which were disseminated to homes and libraries throughout England and America.

Before coming across Tissot's work, Wesley did some writing about the medicinal benefits of tea and electricity. But after reading Tissot, he became passionate about getting the antiwanking word out. He edited down *A Treatise on the Crime of Onan*, tinkered with it a bit, added an introduction and some footnotes, and made sure the parts he kept were modest enough to respect Methodist sensitivities. What changed after all this was that masturbation morphed from a relatively minor, relatively unmentioned act to a significant *medical* problem.

Popular consciousness—reinforced by family doctors and pastors—believed and reinforced among young people that several of their ailments were a result of "self-abuse." According to Wesley, "By self-pollution, the young of both sexes frequently contract the infirmities of old age. They become pale, effeminate, dull, inactive; they lose their Appetite, weaken their sight, their memory, their understanding, and contract all the disorders attending weak nerves. Many bring on thereby a general weakness, and paralytic disorders of all kinds: Yea, lethargies, epilepsies, madness, blindness, convulsions, dropsies, and the most painful of all gouts."[10] Hairy palms don't seem to show up here, but we can see that anxiety about masturbation came not merely from superstitions whispered among middle schoolers but from the most respected thought leaders in society. The fusion of religious and medical anxiety about masturbation carried forward all the way to the twentieth century. Even now, though folks no longer tend to believe that masturbation leads to blindness, the shame and fear remains for many. Nonetheless, few seem comfortable publicly allaying young people's shame and fear, at least within Christian circles. That is unfortunate.

---

[10] Cited in James Donat, "The Rev. John Wesley's Extractions from Dr. Tissot: A Methodist *Imprimatur*," *History of Science* 39 (2001): 289.

Graham Crackers and Kellogg's Corn Flakes

Wesley wasn't the only cultural figure to instill fear of masturbation into the American consciousness. Sylvester Graham (1794–1851) invented the "graham cracker," which was originally a bland snack. He originally didn't offer the more modern version caked with cinnamon and sugar. He taught that meat and vibrant flavors led to unrestrained libidos and overly excitable genitals. Since he bought into the idea that masturbation could lead to poor health, he concocted insipid recipes to create his own form of "health food."

The connection among health food, masturbation, and religion became even stronger after Ellen G. White (1827–1915), cofounder of the Seventh-Day Adventists, incorporated Graham's beliefs into her Battle Creek Sanitarium, a Michigan institute dedicated to teaching about holistic health. John Harvey Kellogg (1852–1943) became the director of the sanitarium; in this context, he invented granola and Corn Flakes. None of these had refined sugar at the time. Frosted Flakes would come along much later (1952). Meanwhile, the popularity of a meatless breakfast as a way to tame youthful lust was so popular that C. W. Post (1854–1914) offered his own cereal, called Grape Nuts, and a version of Corn Flakes he called "Elijah's Manna."

In all this, we can see that their strategy for cultivating spiritual and physical health involved suppressing bodily energy and gastronomical stimulation. It is a rather depressing chapter in our history for both erotic and culinary reasons.[11] Opposing such quackery, I contend that we should learn to channel sexiness in a holy direction; in most cases, we should avoid starving sexiness to death, even *if* boring food could accomplish such a thing.

Taming the Big Bad Wolf

When I was a child, my mom didn't want us kids to see scary things on the news. Maybe one reason for this was my bad reaction to a story about the Big Bad Wolf. She once read me a children's picture book of *The Three Little Pigs*, and for many years after that, I had

---

[11] See Brian Wilson, *Dr. John Harvey Kellogg and the Religion of Biologic Living* (Bloomington: Indiana University Press, 2014); also the story is depicted in the movie *The Road to Wellville* (1994).

vivid, frequent, and debilitating nightmares about wolves. She only read the little book once, and after my first nightmare, I think she blamed herself. Unfortunately, her response to my nightmares made them worse.

She didn't want us to see anything that would scare us or induce nightmares. Sometimes her tactics backfired. When the evening news would come on, my mom would let out a little gasp, run to the television set, and slap the off button. This caused my siblings and me to worry that whatever they were going to say on television was bad enough to make even big people terrified. I think the same principle holds true for the way families deal with the question of masturbation. By talking about it in hushed, panicked, or disgusted tones, families intentionally or unintentionally cause unnecessary anxiety. For this reason, when my kids were growing up, we spoke candidly about the subject, starting with the basic advice that they should not play with themselves when other family members were around. It was a matter of propriety and decorum, but nothing to worry too much about.

My wolf nightmares stopped after a dream I had when I was ten years old. I remember it as if it were last night. Here's what happened, with a touch of creative license to fill in the gaps in my memory of the details.

I pushed open the slightly ajar door to my infant brother Scott's bedroom. Inside, I found my old nemesis, Wolf, crouching over Scott's bed. Strangely, though Wolf usually looked like a regular timber wolf—albeit one who could talk—he now was wearing a tweed jacket and green corduroy trousers and was smoking a pipe. Slowly, his menacing stance relaxed and he straightened up, like a man. He moved away from my brother and casually sat down in a rocking chair.

I asked, "Why are you bothering my brother? I'm the one you love to hunt. And why are you wearing people clothes?"

Wolf smiled and rocked back in his chair, laughing quietly and benignly. "You don't have to worry," he replied. "I'm here to say farewell. It was good fun being in your dreams, but they must end—"

"Hey, they weren't fun for me!" I interjected. "They were *bad* dreams! They were nightmares."

"That may be true," he replied with a slow nod. "But you never got hurt, did you? And you weren't doing anything important when we had our fun. Your body was just sleeping. Wasn't it, after all, a nice game of chase? Would you rather have been bored, just lying there motionless? Have you noticed how dogs are always kicking when they sleep? That's because dogs, like wolves, love to play in dreamland. Normal life for dogs, you know, is pretty boring. They just wait for their masters to come home through most of the day. They love walks, of course, but nothing beats the *dreams* they have. Your dog, Bando, for instance, once told me that his two favorite things to do in life were going for walks with you and chasing giant red elk through the Scottish Highlands in his dreams. I think he liked the hunting dream better than walks through the neighborhood, but he's a nice sort of dog who cares about his family, so when he's asked, he says he likes the family walks better than the hunts. But he's just being a loyal dog when he says that. Don't let that hurt your feelings, though. He says it because he loves you and your family."

"Why are you here, Wolf?"

"I just wanted to say good-bye, at least for a while."

"I'll see you again?"

"Yes, you will. And as to why I'm wearing people clothes, I look how I look tonight because you tamed me. You tamed me and will continue to tame other monsters by becoming a scholar. I still have the old rumbly heart, mind you. But I have other interests now as a tame wolf, much more interesting stuff than worrying boys in their dreams. I'm here to say that if you had killed me with a gun or spear in your dreams—like you so often tried (and I don't blame you for that impulse)—if you had killed me, another beast would have returned in my place. You would have had to start the chase game all over again. And it might have been deadlier. But we became friends because you studied hard and learned what makes me howl. I will still howl in the future, but there will come a day when that doesn't make you afraid. Instead, there will be a day when a midnight howl will make you smile and remember your friend Wolf. And let it remind you that you should study hard to tame wolves like me."

At that, the dream ended. Some days, I think maybe Wolf won in the end. Perhaps my academic attempt to tame the terror of the numinous, the erotic, and the theological was merely a way for me to feel safe and comfortable. Maybe Wolf will even now sneak up on me, when I'm off my guard, after all these decades. Maybe Wolf wanted me to *think* that he'd been tamed by science and philosophy so he could pounce on me and devour me for good, as fierce as ever. But then maybe if he did that—say, in a fever dream on my deathbed—he would do it because it would be a good joke. Perhaps it would even be an act of love and grace, reminding me of the sense of wonder I felt as a child and hinting that I was about to enter a new realm, with a new naïveté. Who knows?

I believe this dream has a lot to do with our topic of masturbation. Instead of treating it with extreme fear, we need to see it as a part of life that needs to be tamed, directed, and brought into mature control. This is true of our sexuality in general, and it is a good place to start practicing restraint and virtue. At least on one level, coming to terms with reality—whether in the guise of Wolf or in candid conversation about masturbation—made the nightmares, anxiety, and restlessness give way to tranquility. I want that for young people who are on the path of virtue. I want them to learn to tame the beast our species has always grappled with, not half-pretend it isn't there at all. In doing this, we will learn to recognize the reality of biological forces within our species. We will learn to channel those forces in healthy ways. And we will avoid letting them consume us.

When Masturbation Is a Problem

Now, I realize that there is such a thing as addiction to masturbation. There can be times when folks find that solo sex gets in the way of important, healthy activities. It also can be linked with addiction to increasingly abundant online pornography. It can be an outgrowth of unhealthy lust. It can become an obsession. But the real potential problem with masturbation is when its excessive practice is a symptom of a person having given up on intimacy, embodied relationships, and the quest for holy love. Augustine famously argued that evil has no primary existence. He spoke of the image of God as being a man and woman in unity. For him, evil is a twisting of a good thing to bad ends, or brokenness in a good thing, or a lack of a good thing. Thus just as darkness is the absence of light, cold is the absence of heat, and a hole is a cavity in a thing, evil occurs when a good thing has been bent. I think this is what Julian of Norwich meant when she said that she saw in her visions that "Sin is naught."[12] More germane to the issue of masturbation is Martin Luther's understanding of sin. He famously described sin as humanity curved in on itself (*incurvatus in se*). To the extent that masturbation turns our attention inward and distracts us from our call outward—to be faithful masks of God to our neighbors in the world—we are indeed sinning.

C. S. Lewis understood all this and applied it in a personal letter to Keith Masson, who was wondering about Christian teaching on masturbation. Lewis writes:

> For me the real evil of masturbation would be that it takes an appetite which, in lawful use, leads the individual out of himself to complete (and correct) his own personality in that of another (and finally in children and even grandchildren) and turns it back; sends the man back into the prison of himself, there to keep a harem of imaginary brides. . . . And this harem, once admitted, works against his ever getting out and really uniting with a real woman. . . . For the harem is always accessible, always subservient, calls for no sacrifices or adjustments, and can be endowed with erotic and psychological attractions which no woman can rival. . . . Among those shadowy brides he is always adored, always the perfect lover; no demand is made on his unselfishness, no mortification ever imposed on his vanity. In the end, they become merely the medium through which he increasingly adores himself . . . After all, almost the main work of life is to come out of our selves, out of the little dark prison we are all born in. Masturbation is to be avoided as all things are to be avoided which retard this process. The danger is that of coming to love the prison.[13]

---

[12] This theme occurs frequently in Julian of Norwich, *Revelations of Divine Love* (New York: Penguin, 1998).

[13] C. S. Lewis, *The Collected Letters of C. S. Lewis*, vol. 3, ed. Walter Hooper (London: HarperCollins, 2007), 758–59.

I still think Lewis, in his desire to be faithful to centuries of Christian teaching and because of his association with the Anglo-Catholic approach to Christianity, was more worried about masturbation than he needed to be. But in this passage, he's got a legitimate point. If sexiness is about connecting with others and manifesting the infinite love of God in our reaching out to other human beings, then masturbation *can* pull us in the wrong direction. In this sense, then, we should encourage ourselves and young people to remain mindful of goodness, truth, and beauty in our mental lives. To this extent, if there is in fact a legitimate place for masturbation within erotic development, we should think of it more like a warm-up toss before a game, never as the game itself. I say this because as we see increasing detachment from human connectedness corresponding to online life, I worry that we in the West are coming dangerously close to a phenomenon affecting Japan, where the population is declining, sexual activity is decreasing, and even the government is stepping in to address an epidemic of withdrawal and reluctance to marry.

Indeed, if there is a problem related to masturbation, it's not the act itself that worries me but rather the fact that people are withdrawing, detaching, and failing to experience rich intimate relationships with others. In other words, masturbation as a substitute for erotic love is a symptom of a lack of sexiness. It's not a symptom that there is too much.

There may be a way, however, in which masturbation may have a healthier effect on a person. Sometimes pent up sexual frustration can cause people to obsess on sexual thoughts—even dark, lustful thoughts. There are times when a person's libido causes him or her to spend an inordinate amount of time trying to strategize a way to "hook up" with someone or gratify his or her urges in some other way. In such cases, sexual energy is capable of distracting a person from other wholesome activities, and masturbation can help a person get this distraction *out of the way*. In other words, with moderation, it can help a person put sexual thoughts aside. The key is to avoid turning masturbation itself into an obsession or addiction.

Some will object that the only way to masturbate is to contemplate evil, lustful thoughts. There's no doubt this is common. But I don't believe that is a necessary conclusion. One might, however, focus one's attention on good, virtuous expressions of sexuality. If so, it just aligns a person's sexual energy in a healthy and wholesome direction. After all, the formation of positive mental and moral habits is foundational for Aristotle's approach to ethical development.

Virtue and Habituation

Virtue ethics relies on an approach to moral formation within a community. Whereas Plato spent much of his time pondering the nature of the essence of the good—an abstract endeavor—Aristotle was wisely more interested in learning how to *be* good. He believed that teaching virtue required a virtuous ethos—that is, a community in which the moral development of children was reinforced by the culture of a community or group. This remains essential for our quest. We can apply this within the Christian community by spending less time deliberating on the rules and codes related to touching oneself and more time encouraging, praising, and reinforcing positive romantic behaviors. Aristotle realized that young people wouldn't get it right the first time but needed to practice good behaviors repeatedly until those behaviors became internalized as part of their character.

It's at this point that we find we are in distressing times. We can talk all we want about the abstract rules of Christian sexual ethics, but there is a way in which all the talk in the world crumbles under the weight of secular culture. Here I don't so much mean permissive sexuality within the larger culture; I'm speaking of the subconscious, embedded values in the culture, as reinforced by narratives found on television and in the movies. This is why, while shows like *South Park* are indeed crass, I'm not so worried if my sons watch those shows. I'm more worried about the ways in which some television shows and movies reinforce the deceptive idea that mere physical gratification and sexual conquest are worthwhile ends in themselves. I'm also worried that many narratives assume that we can attain meaning and relationships, or at least seal them, through sexual contact.

The most formidable obstacle today along the path toward erotic virtue is our loss of the very language of true love. This language is indigenous to Christian culture. But even in the church, we often fail to realize that we've lost the Christian logic concerning sexuality that makes the rules intelligible in the first place. Paul writes, "Do not be conformed to this world but be transformed by the renewal of your mind, that you may prove what is the will of God, what is good and acceptable and perfect" (Rom. 12:2). This means we need to constantly check whether our implicit values are part of the New Logic or are instead drawn from secular assumptions. Lutheran virtue ethicist Gilbert Meilaender explains this well: "We can no longer depend on a society at least roughly Christian to socialize its members into anything approaching a Christian way of living, nor can we recapture the kind of serious catechesis by means of which the church once inculcated its way of life even amidst an alien culture."[14] If this is true, then faithful Christians need to let go of their old attempts to reinforce and preserve Christendom. It's too late. And maybe that's not the worst thing. When we Christians hold the reigns of culture, we tend to forget our calling to be an *alternative* culture. Now, if Christianity offers a New Logic and an alternative language for life, it's important to remember that although the core values and assumptions about this language may be ancient and unchanging, that language nevertheless must be *translated*. I am convinced that failure to translate the Christian narrative, especially as it relates to erotic virtue, is at the heart of our current cultural confusion about sex.

Not all religions emphasize the importance or even the legitimacy of translation. The dictated *surahs* of the Quran, for instance, are only considered divine revelation when they are read in Arabic. Many of the ideas and teachings of Hinduism remain untranslated Sanskrit words. Hebrew is essential to training in Judaism. Christianity, on the other hand, has been a religion of translation at least since Pentecost (Acts 2:1–3).[15] The entire Bible has been translated into more than 530 languages, with some portions translated into more than 2,800 languages. Moreover, the Jesus Film Project (for which I once worked as a young man) has translated and dubbed *The Jesus Film* into approximately 1,400 languages.

Surely, therefore, we need to remember to translate well when we are engaged in catechesis and formation of future generations of Christians. Failure to do so would be as problematic as teaching

---

[14] Gilbert Meilaender, *Faith and Faithfulness: Basic Themes in Christian Ethics* (Notre Dame, IN: University of Notre Dame Press, 1992), 8.

[15] On this theme of translation, see Lamin Sanneh, *Translating the Message: The Missionary Impact on Culture* (Maryknoll, NY: Orbis, 2009).

Baptist third-grade Sunday school entirely in King James vocabulary or preaching a sermon to modern Catholics in medieval Latin. In Meilaender's view, we keep repeating our confession until it becomes a reality: "Those who regularly recite the first article of the creed, desiring their world to be shaped by that recital, should expect this. They should anticipate that human beings share a common bond which will enable them to meet—to 'translate' to some extent their ways of life and understand each other."[16]

Perhaps because Western Christians have increasingly seen church as a service that they can take or leave rather than as a radical alternative community dedicated to pushing back against the darkness of this present age, ethical teaching has unfortunately taken the form of legalism rather than a call to a bold witness to a beautiful way of life. As Meilaender writes of Christian virtue, "It was intended to be taught—but taught within the ongoing life of a worshiping community of believers. Abstracted from that way of life, particular rules for Christian living may lack intelligibility and will almost surely lack the power to persuade or the beauty to attract."[17]

To what ought we be attracted? To the Incarnate Christ, who sanctified our embodied selves but points us *outside of ourselves* and, ultimately, to intimate and wholesome relationships with others. Masturbation, then, is indeed a problem if it takes us back to what C. S. Lewis called the dungeons of our own minds. To break free of these prisons, we to keep students chained up not in long examinations of their routinely bent inner fantasy lives but to the cross of Christ. We will stumble along the way, but we must keep our eyes *on the way*. That's what surfing the Tao is all about.

---

[16] Meilaender, *Faith and Faithfulness*, 12.

[17] Ibid., 24.

I Did My Best (Premarital Sex)

I did my best, it wasn't much
I couldn't feel, so I tried to touch
I told the truth, but I didn't come to fool you
                    —Leonard Cohen, "Hallelujah"

Let's be clear up front that, despite a few older theological perspectives to the contrary, sexuality "is a beautiful thing." That's what my father said when he gave me my birds-and-the-bees talk when I was in sixth grade. It made me laugh a little then. But he was right. Embodiment is a gift. An orgasm can be like a dance attuned to the music of the heavens. It's best viewed not as a necessary evil but rather as a glimpse of the holy. According to Miroslav Volf, although sexual intercourse can become a selfish act, "sexual union can be a sacrament of love—not just a sacrament of human love, but also a means of expressing and mediating divine love. Pleasure—pleasure of the soul no less than of the body!—given to the other and for the other's sake *is* then a pleasure received. And a pleasure received by the other is, almost paradoxically, a pleasure returned to the giver."[1] I wish I had heard this more clearly from my own youth group education in Christianity. Because once Stacie and I got married, it was hard to be comfortable in bed together for some time. We had so emphasized the elimination of desire and the naughtiness of sexuality that—despite the many times people insisted explicitly that sex in marriage was of course good—any physical intimacy carried with it the residual sense of guilt.

---

[1] Miroslav Volf, *Free of Charge: Giving and Forgiving in a Culture Stripped of Grace* (Grand Rapids, MI: Zondervan, 2006), 70.

Despite this, the Christian community has rejected the legitimacy of sexual intercourse outside the commitment of marriage since the earliest days of the movement. Meanwhile, though there are indeed many who have "saved themselves" for marriage, even many devout Christian young people have cowered in shame and fear of God's wrath, having "lost their virginity." They have come to realize firsthand that "the spirit is willing but the flesh is weak" (Matt. 26:41). Some who remain committed to Christianity find the old teachings to be obsolete or impossible, and thus they quietly ignore them. The language of "premarital" sex increasingly sounds odd to those who don't plan on getting married in the first place. What's going on here? How should we proceed in these perplexing times?

The Impotence of Doing One's Best

In late medieval theology, a movement known as the *via moderna* embraced a concept called *divine voluntarism*. Participants in this movement held that God is free to choose any number of ways to redeem people. In other words, God is free to treat someone as holy even when a person is in fact not holy; God can choose to do this based on some condition He determines. Some thinkers within this tradition held that God grades on a curve, as it were: if people do the best they can, given the circumstances, God will count *that* as perfect righteousness. A key phrase for this way of thinking was the Latin phrase *facere quod in se est*; that is, "do what is within you," or "do your best, and God will do the rest."

With respect to this approach, Martin Luther responded that, yes, God is free to consider us righteous based on his unbound will, but no, the Bible reveals that God chooses to consider us righteous not because we've made our best effort but rather because of a work outside of us, on the cross of Christ. Thus he said, "When we are lacking the theology of the cross, we misuse the best of things in the worst of ways."[2] In this way, our relationship with God is rooted in His decision to love, not our decision. His love is therefore certain, unconditional, and based on His own gracious love.

---

[2] Heidelberg Disputation, thesis 24; loose translation mine.

In Luther's literary debate with Erasmus, which became known as *The Bondage of the Will* (1525), Luther argued that while we are not predetermined puppets, we naturally act according to our own wills, which happen to be *bound* to sin after the Fall. Thus human free will, in the absolute sense, is an illusion. We must understand this basic point if we want to understand and embody erotic virtue. If Luther was right, any attempt to do the best that is within us is doomed to fail from the outset. We need supernatural help. Accordingly, we need an erotic miracle to break us free from the subtle, often undetectable ways in which sin has affected the very framework of our existence. As Miroslav Volf explains, "Unlike God, we always exercise our will as being constantly shaped by many factors—by language, parental rearing, culture, media, advertising, and peer pressure, and through all these, we are shaped either by God or God's adversary. Often we don't perceive ourselves as shaped at all. If we are not visibly and palpably coerced, we think that we act autonomously, spontaneously, and authentically. Yet we are wrong."[3] Thus simply telling folks to "try harder" to live according to the principles of sexual ethics is unhelpful. This is precisely the problem with evangelical Christianity's regular ability to translate its ethical messages into moral behaviors.

Trying harder is of course a laudable idea; but in our attempt to be faithful to Christian moral imperatives, we can't ignore another core Christian doctrine: our inherited sinfulness. As mentioned in the previous chapter, this sinfulness means we are bent in on ourselves (*curvatus in se est*). We take the good gifts of God and use them for corrupt ends. Within this condition, we turn blessings into curses. Food is good, but we often consume too much as gluttons. Wine can help create a relaxed and festive environment in which we grow closer to friends and family, but it can also devastate a person when it becomes the object of addiction. Likewise, sexual intercourse is a beautiful thing, but it can become one of humanity's most painful subjects when it is twisted into infidelity, degrading behaviors, or rape. You don't have to be a theist, or even a conservative, to recognize that uncommitted sexual intercourse can leave a lot of pain in its wake.

---

[3] Volf, *Free of Charge*, 66.

Now, sin isn't merely something *out there* in the big bad world; we bring sin's infection with us wherever we go, even if we were to enter a strict religious order. Sin also affects our lives culturally and structurally. This is particularly insidious because we routinely fail to recognize the ways in which we subconsciously and uncritically adopt cultural assumptions about the good life and spirituality. This is arguably the most important takeaway from Jonathan Grant's *Divine Sex: A Compelling Vision for Christian Relationships in a Hypersexualized Age.*[4] He explains that one of the biggest problems with discussing sexual ethics today is that Christians often try to overlay traditional rules on top of non-Christian assumptions about life.

> There is a temptation in the context of discipleship to make the same mistake, to start with the question, "What is the Christian vision of sexuality and relationships?" and then move directly to the final question, "How do we live that out within our church communities?" Yet this practice avoids the most important aspect of contemporary formation. The question we must first address is contextual: "What is it about our cultural moment that makes the Christian vision of sexuality seem naive and unrealistic at best and downright repressive at worst, even to many young Christians? Why does the church's view of sexuality, with all its 'rules' and 'restrictions,' fail to resonate with so many contemporary believers?" . . . The Christian story claims that genuine personal wholeness is made possible only through the crisis of the gospel, which required nothing short of God himself taking on flesh to overcome human sin and self-deception. Living faithfully within a Christian sexual ethic requires a radical personal transformation, whereby we walk the same journey into death and new life that Jesus walked.[5]

In other words, simply restating rules or proclaiming warnings more loudly doesn't do much good. It's more helpful to seek and teach *repentance*—that is, we must find enlightenment and radically change our thinking about the basic assumptions regarding the

---

[4] Jonathan Grant, *Divine Sex: A Compelling Vision for Christian Relationships in a Hypersexualized Age* (Grand Rapids, MI: Brazos Press, 2015).

[5] Grant, *Divine Sex*, Kindle Loc. 732–34.

good life. By doing this, we can learn and employ a new "language" about sexiness. I'm convinced that this is far more important for us to reclaim within our communities of faith than are our battles about hot-button sexual issues within the culture wars.

Saint Paul recognized the importance of understanding the core question of one's operating logic when he addressed a case of sexual immorality within the young church. A man was sleeping with his "father's wife," likely a stepmother. Though Paul says the church should not endorse this behavior by associating with the offender, he offers an important clarification regarding the way the church should relate to outsiders: "I wrote to you in my letter not to associate with sexually immoral people—not at all meaning the sexually immoral of this world, or the greedy and swindlers, or idolaters, since then you would need to go out of the world. . . . For what have I to do with judging outsiders? Is it not those inside the church whom you are to judge? God judges those outside. 'Purge the evil person from among you'" (1 Cor. 5:9-10, 12-13). What's up with the difference between the way Paul approaches those within and the way he approaches those outside the church? He recognizes distinct communities working within the context of two different logics. The Old Logic is generally based on transaction, personal gratification, and conquest. The New Logic is about repenting of this system and relating to one another in a manner that flows from grace, has no expectation of rewards, and has no conditions attached. It's a logic of gift giving rather than investment and expectation of a return on that investment. Now, if a person is operating within the Old Logic, Christian sexual ethics is admittedly irrational. After all, why should we not pursue the best avenue to physical gratification if there is nothing beyond the material world? What's wrong with sexual conquest when our logic says it is better to be a winner than a loser?

We must keep all this business about distinct cultural frameworks in mind when we try to impose behaviors that only make sense within the New Logic on those who don't share the logic of the Gospel. For them, Christian ethical teachings look absurd, hateful, intolerant, and dreary. What they need is not an exhortation to *do one's best*; they need to internalize the New Logic that results from the radical claim that God has accomplished the work of reconciling us to Himself (2 Cor. 5:19).

Now, those of us well past adolescence and early adulthood would do well to be empathetic toward the younger generations when it comes to the difficulties of their situation. Anecdotally, no matter how conservative the religious community in which I was immersed, far more emphasis was placed on the sexual abstinence of young people than on those who have been divorced. Meanwhile, just about every year, public scandals in which married pastors have had affairs remind me that no matter how well someone *knows* the nature of Christian teaching, it's hard for folks to *do* what they believe they should do. Paul expresses this well in his epistle to the Romans, chapter 7, verse 18: "I have the desire to do what is good, but I cannot carry it out." This struggle of Paul's is arguably even more difficult for young people, whose very brains are less capable of delaying gratification and controlling impulses. Indeed, the process known as *myelination*, wherein a sheath of fatty lipids and proteins accumulates around the brain's neurons, particularly in the frontal lobe, isn't complete in humans until around the age of twenty-five. Don't get bogged down by the science here; the point is that during the same period in a person's lifespan in which Christians are asking them to control raging hormones, their brains have not yet developed mature planning, decision-making, and self-control abilities.[6] This doesn't mean that young people *can't* delay gratification; it's just that we must keep in mind that this erotic journey through dating and early adulthood is no easy trip, given the physiological realities involved.

I'm the Best Kisser on Consejos

As fun as the early years of dating can be, they also can lead to embarrassment. When I was in the fourth grade, I lived on Consejos Street, which is Spanish for "advice" or "counsel." I wish I had received better advice about making out back then. All in all, though, it was a fun street, with several kids my age living on the block. We would play

---

[6] Elizabeth R. Sowell et al., "Mapping Cortical Change across the Human Life Span," *Nature Neuroscience* 6 (2003): 309–15.

stick ball or touch football in the street. A Mormon gal would come over and play chess sometimes. I'd get in an occasional fight with the blond Argentinian kid down the road.

It was on that street that I had my first kiss. A few of us were on skateboards. It's a weird pastime. Even skillful skaters spend much of their time failing to complete the moves they are trying. Standing with my board in hand one late afternoon, I made the bold proclamation that I was the best kisser on Consejos. I used to make claims like that because my parents' hippy friends in Colorado used to assure me that if I believed anything strongly enough, I could will that reality into existence. They were wrong. Julie, a girl my age, decided to test my claim. I was nervous, but I wasn't afraid of failure. I moved in as romantically as I could. I think up until mouth-to-mouth contact, I was doing all right. But then things went horribly wrong. I just sort of pushed my half-open mouth onto her face. She pulled back with wide eyes and an incredulous smile. "You've never done this before!" Julie exclaimed for all the neighborhood kids to hear. "You aren't the best kisser on the street; you aren't even a decent kisser. You are pathetic." Don't be hard on Julie. I did make a false claim, after all. I don't think she had a lot of experience herself, but I definitely didn't understand the basics back in 1984.

I didn't try again for four years. A friend introduced me to Amy. She was cool. Her family wasn't bad, but neither was it nurturing. I don't think her father was around. But she had the experience I lacked. She invited me over to her house to watch *The Princess Bride*. Though others had seen this classic repeatedly, it was my first time, so I was focused on the movie. Amy was not. She wanted to make out.

This time, I thought I was ready. I had seen a make-out scene in the movie *Top Gun*. In it, I remember Tom Cruise's character did a lot of biting and sucking of Kelly McGillis' lip as Berlin's "Take My Breath Away" played in the background. I didn't have the soundtrack, but I thought I could replicate the technique. I was wrong again. It was a disaster. I was slobbery and annoying. At some point, Amy pulled back, kind but exasperated. "Just stop moving and I will explain how this is done," she said.

After a few moments, I finally had it figured out. It was fun, but I was filled with so much adrenaline, or whatever chemical gets released while you are making out to a classic comedy film, that my stomach ached a little. We made out for at least a half hour. Sex wasn't even on the table, at least in my mind. It was intimate, but no groping took place.

I mention this business about learning to kiss because while many well-meaning parents try to protect their children from early flirtatious or romantic experiences altogether, I believe the romantic dance of my early years was an important part of growing up. I was glad to have learned about kissing the hard way. I didn't lose too much community respect in fourth grade, since we were all in roughly the same boat. More important, I think it is crucial to create a balanced approach to flirtatious engagement. Going too fast ruins the fun, but avoiding the romantic dance altogether causes a young person to miss out on the gift of playful exploration. Different communities and families will work out different ways of exploring this dance. Maybe it happens at an actual dance. Maybe some innocent flirtation takes place at a church youth group ski trip. Maybe it happens on an orchestra trip to Italy with the high school seniors. But so long as people don't get in too deep too fast, I believe we need to help young people safely and respectfully enjoy the art of the sexy flirtation dance. Life is too short to kill all the fun. And it seems the way many conservative Christians have come at romance in adolescence has emphasized the negation of sexiness altogether instead of its appropriate restraint.

The Purity Movement

"You're married?" a twentysomething Irish woman asked Josiah, one of my undergraduate students. She was backpacking through Scotland. He had enrolled in a class I was teaching on religion in the British Isles with a band of religion and psychology students. We were all settling into one of the coolest hostels I've ever experienced. The accommodations were inexpensive but hip and right across from the big castle in Edinburgh. They had, among other cool amenities, a wine lounge, a library, and a room for spinning vinyl records. That's where Josiah found himself in conversation with this perplexed young woman from Dublin. She was obviously strongly interested in Josiah, and for a reason even she didn't quite understand.

"No. Not married. Why do you ask? . . . Ah, the ring," said Josiah. "It's hard to explain. It's something my church group got into: the ring represents a purity pledge. We sign a promise to remain abstinent until we're married. We have a ceremony and then get rings."

"Oh, wow! Like Britney Spears? How novel!" She moved closer, leaning in toward Josiah in order to hear more. Her face flushed.

"Sort of. It's just this thing we did."

"So you're really not going to shag until you're married?"

"That's the idea." Josiah wanted to move on. He casually turned over a Bob Dylan album cover, pretending to read the track list on the back. Nevertheless, the young woman was relentless. It was clear to me that she both respected his well-intentioned pledge and also wanted to be the one to get him to break his word. Perhaps the idea of being attractive enough to get a handsome young evangelical student to commit something like a mortal sin was a turn-on for her. Perhaps the fact that he took his sexual behavior seriously enough to even attempt chastity put Josiah into an economic category like that of Cuban cigars (prior to 2016): *Who knows whether they are really better than others? But I'll be damned if I can't at least get a taste.* Supply and demand seems to work with sex, too, I suppose. So does reverse psychology. (Incidentally, like most young people I know who were involved with the evangelical purity movement, Josiah now sees it as toxic. In a Facebook message posted to his current wife's wall, he describes purity movement guru Josh Harris as "a sack of s***," along with a link to Harris' decision to do a documentary and possible apology related to the now apparent negative ramifications of his 1997 book, *Kissing Dating Goodbye*.)

This anecdote remains intriguing to me. It confirms the idea that if we respect the nobility of sexuality and seek to live with integrity toward each other, this can be incredibly *sexy* to potential romantic partners. It also should serve as a cautionary tale. The purity ring instigated a conversation about sex between two young singles. Because he was wearing a purity ring, sex was what the whole group ended up thinking and talking about for most of the evening. Perhaps this conversation between Josiah and the flirtatious hostel guest helps explain why the purity movement, in its attempt to cultivate abstinence until marriage, has not been as effective as many had hoped. Some alumni of the movement have even found it to have been a terribly disruptive and unhealthy experience.

I leave it to the courageous and wise mom, podcaster, and author Rebecca Lemke to explain why what I say does not stem from some desire for free indiscriminate fornicabula. In her recent book, *The Scarlet Virgins: When Sex Replaces Salvation* (2017), she explains the startling but ultimately understandable connection between the purity movement and sexual dysfunction experienced by many young evangelical adults today. Lemke suggests that the way she was taught about sexuality in her conservative homeschool circles resulted, for many of her peers, in Sexual Aversion Disorder (SAD), rape fantasies, and BDSM, largely because they had for so long dissociated themselves from sexual desire and found it difficult to orgasm without simulated coercion.[7] Check her book out. She is a gem of a courageous lady, not some ideologue, so I think her observations are worth considering seriously.

There's no shortage of studies on the relationship between Christian abstinence education and sexual activity among young Christians. Most suggest that there is only a slight difference, if any, between the sexual practices of nonreligious individuals and those of evangelical Christians. For instance, in one study of Texas Southern Baptists, more than 70 percent of respondents had engaged in premarital sex, though more than 80 percent felt guilty about it, and almost all those who married after twenty-four (women) or twenty-six (men) had engaged in premarital sex.[8] This highlights an important tension for our day. People are waiting longer to get married, but their sex drives remain powerful in late adolescence and early adulthood. My wife's maternal grandparents got married at age sixteen. What would it have been like for their sex lives had they waited another ten years to wed? Would they have even come close to maintaining chastity?

Many of my first-year undergraduate students, when asked casually, surprisingly suggest they aren't even certain they plan to get

---

[7] Rebecca Lemke, *The Scarlet Virgins: When Sex Replaces Salvation* (Norman, OK: Anatole, 2017).

[8] Janet Rosenbaum and Byron Weathersbee, "True Love Waits: Do Southern Baptists? Premarital Sexual Behavior among Newly Married Southern Baptist Sunday School Students," *Journal of Religion and Health* 52.1 (2013): 263–75.

married *ever*. I suspect this will change for many of them over time, but it seems that the expectation that marriage is something to lock in early, perhaps as a way of guaranteeing personal independence, is a thing of the past. My father-in-law once joked with my sons, "Hey, remember, it isn't *pre*marital sex if you don't plan on getting married." He was being silly, but his joke wasn't far from reality when it comes to the young adults I know. They sometimes cock their heads in bewilderment at the phrase "premarital sex," especially when they have not grown up in a church. It's not a phrase they use outside the church much. When I first started teaching at the university level, I got lots of questions from students about sexual ethics, since they were struggling to reconcile their religious beliefs with their sexual lives. These days, I am struck by the number of young people I meet who don't want to get married in the first place. Perhaps they've seen too few successful relationships. Perhaps the economy is too rough to start a family.

In any case, if more and more young adults wait to marry until their midtwenties or beyond, we will find a greater and greater disconnect between the traditional ways of speaking about sex before marriage and the ways sexuality is navigated by younger generations. This doesn't mean the churches should compromise in the way they treat the subject, but we all would do well to recognize the difficulties of our contemporary situation. If nothing else, empathy and awareness of social realities will be important for everyone who is interested in cultivating a virtuous community within God's alternative kingdom.

Not all studies reveal a lack of distinction between believing and unbelieving young people in terms of sexual practices. When Christianity has an effect on sexual behaviors, it seems to correspond to the level of participation in the language and life of the Christian community. For instance, a 2012 study conducted by Grey Matter Research, commissioned by the National Association of Evangelicals, titled "Sex and Unexpected Pregnancies: What Evangelical Millennials Think and Practice" shows that a majority of committed evangelicals had not had, or at least did not frequently have, premarital sex. The study sampled "millennials" who fit their operational definition of "evangelical" and were active in a Protestant congregation. The study found that while a majority (77 percent) indicated that they believed extramarital sex was wrong, 44 percent of eighteen- to twenty-five-year-olds had in fact had sex. Those who did have sex typically felt guilty about their behaviors, expressing regret that they could not seem to live the lifestyle they believed they should live.

Even when abstinence education—whether secular or church based—has had a significant effect, it remains impotent overall. From the perspective of virtue theory, we should expect this. The abstract question "What is the good"? is worthwhile to a degree, but it is far less important than asking how we are able to actually do good and be good. If in fact it turns out we've been doing things wrong when it comes to cultivating erotic virtue, changing our tack is no sign of compromise or licentiousness. Rather, it's a sign of wisdom and true concern for the well-being of individuals and their sexual integrity.

The tension here between faith and practice is nothing new. It was a reality known to a woman known by many today as Saint Monica. She was the mother of the most influential Western theologian, Saint Augustine of Hippo. Monica was overbearing, but she loved her son and wanted the best for him. She was a devout Christian and prayed for him constantly. But she also was realistic. She assumed that her son, despite her moral exhortations, would almost inevitably engage in premarital sex. Her answer to this, while perhaps strange to us today, was not unheard of in her time. Augustine recounts, "My cleansing [baptism] was deferred on the assumption that, if I lived, I would be sure to soil myself; and after that solemn washing the guilt would be greater and more dangerous if I then defiled myself."[9] Monica believed that baptism could clean a person's slate entirely; it could even remove the stain of what might be considered mortal sin. After that, other means would be required to expunge postbaptismal sins. If she could keep the lad alive long enough to get over his "boys-will-be-boys screwing around" phase, she figured she could get him a free pass into heaven. This pass would take the form of a late-adolescent baptism. Though the context and sacramental theology of parents today has changed, many parents indeed seek ways to mitigate the damage done by what they

---

[9] Augustine, *Confessions*, trans. Henry Chadwick (Oxford: Oxford University Press, 1991), 14.

think are likely—if not inevitable—sexual behaviors experienced by young people. Meanwhile, it has been my experience that these same parents—though pragmatic in their own thinking—often refuse to speak frankly and openly with their children about the real difficulties of sexuality in contemporary society.

Augustine reflected a similar realism to that of his mother regarding youthful sexuality. As a young man, he prayed, "Grant me chastity and continence, but not yet." He explains, "I was afraid you might hear my prayer quickly, and that you might too rapidly heal me of the disease of lust which I preferred to satisfy rather than suppress."[10]

I find Augustine's discussion in the *Confessions* of his inner turmoil related to sex to be fascinating and instructive. Unfortunately, however, Augustine was also responsible for con-tributing several unhealthy ideas about sexuality to the Western church in general. He was a complex guy. He's among my favorite theologians. I even named my firstborn after him. But anxiet-ies and fixations in his own life sadly became anxieties and fixa-tions for centuries of Christian thinkers. At one point, Augustine says that proper sex education and some form of external disci-pline might have helped him stay pure before marriage: "If only someone could have imposed restraint on my disorder. That would have transformed to good purpose the fleeting experiences of beauty in these lowest of things, and fixed limits to indulgence in their charms. Then the stormy waves of my youth would have finally broken on the shore of marriage. Even so, I could not have been wholly content to confine sexual union to acts intended to procreate children, as your law prescribes, Lord."[11] Here we see evidence of Augustine's Neoplatonism. Neoplatonists held to a hierarchical view of the world that spiritualized Plato's teaching about the forms. At the top of the hierarchy was the Good, which terminated for Christians like Augustine in God himself. It is as if the individual's quest is to ascend upward, beyond the embodied world. But throughout this quest, physical temptations—especially

---

[10] Ibid., 145.

[11] Ibid., 25.

of the sexual sort—tend to pull a soul down, which is the wrong direction.

Accordingly, Augustine described embodied beauty as among the "lowest of things." He and other Neoplatonic Christians assumed that the spiritual life involved contemplating the higher spiritual realities and untangling oneself from the physical, bodily world. For this reason, Augustine regarded a life of celibacy as nobler than monogamous married life. Moreover, for those who do choose to get married, he believed sex is a necessary evil, permissible only for the purpose of procreation.

Despite the desirability of contemplating transcendental realities and the drawbacks of attention to embodied life, Augustine found himself pulled down to the carnal world through adolescent habituation in a non-Christian set of values: "Among my peer group I was ashamed not to be equally guilty of shameful behavior when I heard them boasting of their sexual exploits. . . . I used to pretend I had done things I had not done at all, so that my innocence should not lead my companions to scorn my lack of courage, and lest my chastity be taken as a mark of inferiority."[12] Note the power of one's community ethos here. He was immersed in a world that did not value committed relationships but rather praised sexual conquest. This is of course prevalent today in locker rooms and television dramas. When young people think that promiscuity is the healthy and laudable norm, they tend to pattern their lives after this perceived norm. Understanding this is essential to cultivating virtue in general and erotic virtue especially. But the patterns set by the secular world do not simply go away when one enters sacred space. Augustine recounts, "During the celebration of your solemn rites within the walls of your Church, I even dared to lust after a girl and to start an affair that would procure the fruit of death."[13]

It always bums me out to reflect on how things went for Augustine and his young relationships. He probably met his "concubine" in a church. I'm persuaded that she was a Christian because they named their son Adeodatus—that is, "a gift of God." Augustine never mentioned her by name in the Confessions. Perhaps he was too

---

[12] Ibid., 28.

[13] Ibid., 37.

guilt-ridden about the way she was treated, or perhaps he wanted to protect her reputation. But I suspect she simply got written out of the story, since that's how things too often go within patriarchal religious communities. The story is about *him*. Her longings, mistreatment, and relational pain were hardly worth mentioning (so it seemed at the time) compared to the ways in which her very existence seems to have derailed—if only for a time—Augustine's search for the true path. Augustine couldn't marry this gal, because even his devout Christian mother knew she was beneath his social stratum. Monica had ambitions for her boy: Christian teaching about equality (Gal. 3:28) be damned.

I mention all this business about Augustine's family situation because, too often, our self-righteous indignation about what the kids are getting away with is a smokescreen for our own personal desires to control our children's relationships. After all, we have a sense that the person our son or daughter ends up with is a reflection on our own quality, legitimacy, and station in life. If we disapprove of a relationship, it might be because we think the potential partner will bring sorrow to our offspring. It might also be that they would be great together, but they don't reflect well on us. Maybe we think we are worthy of a son- or daughter-in-law who might otherwise be a model, or a president, or a ballplayer.

In any case, Augustine recognized that his youthful sexuality was in fact connected to his innate desire for *existence itself*. Ultimately, therefore, his sexual desire was related to his desire for intimacy with God. He writes, "My hunger was internal, deprived of inward food, that is of you yourself, my God. But that was not the kind of hunger I felt. . . . So my soul was in rotten health. In an ulcerous condition it thrust itself to outward things, miserably avid to be scratched by contact with the world of the senses. Yet physical things had no soul. Love lay outside their range."[14] Here Augustine is in line with my overall thesis that spiritual health is required if we are to have sexual and relational health. What is unfortunate, however, is the way in which he concluded that his skewed erotic impulses were evidence that embodiment, the senses, physical things, and the rest are

---

[14] Ibid., 35.

"outside the range" of love. That's where I think he took the Christian intellectual tradition off on an unfortunate and unhelpful track.

Augustine was correct that in seeking intimacy with God, we seek false intimacy within relationships. Likewise, when romantic intimacy is too intimidating, we sometimes turn to substance addiction. All this is true; but what Augustine didn't quite realize is that by discovering intimacy with the divine, touch, taste, and the pleasant echoes of music all become redeemed. They take on new life in light of their relation to God's sublime reality. His failure to see this continued the trajectory of required celibacy for priests and religious orders in Western medieval Christianity.

In any case, please note one important advantage to Augustine's approach to sexuality, despite his mistakes: he recognized that the orientation of our hearts is what really matters in all this business. We can't properly understand the truth of any situation if our hearts falsely drive us back to our own selfish desires. Note also that despite his very serious advocacy of abstinence, Augustine wasn't too bashful about admitting that he didn't come close to living up to the standard for erotic virtue his mother taught him. While his sexual sins caused him regret, they didn't become unmentionable acts for him. This demonstrates spiritual maturity. He boldly admitted his mistakes and hoped folks would learn from them. He didn't get too tangled up in his mind through self-loathing. The alternative is to get so worked up about the issue that we accidentally give the topic of sex and sexual sin the most prominent place in our discussions, at the expense of weightier matters of ethics and theology.

The Sexiest Poem

My favorite Lebanese restaurant is in Long Beach, California. That's where I asked spoken-word, blues, and hip-hop artist Micah Bournes to meet me for lunch. I wanted to catch up on his latest work and chat about his contribution to this book. Almost everything he does creatively blows me away with its guileless but fierce insight into our spiritual, interracial, and global justice situation; he also wrote a poem that encapsulates, in just a few words, everything I've been trying to put into prose. I first heard him recite his poem "What the Back of His T-Shirt Should Have Said" a few years back when we were both speaking at an event near Seattle. In this poem, he embodied the spirit of this book project. Micah is sincere, understands others' struggles, and is faithful to his beliefs. He first performed this poem in an unsavory open-mic bar in Chicago. He wasn't in a Christian venue by any means but was instead offering a prophetic voice in the very place where he noticed a big dude wearing one of those T-shirts intended to be both humorous and also an indication that the wearer is open to a casual sexual encounter.

As Micah and I enjoyed some tabouli and baba ghanoush before our entrée, I was trying to explain why the book would be called *Sexy*. After a pause, he smiled and said, "You know, there was this older woman who came up to me after a performance. I thought she was going to tell me that she thought my poem was offensive. But she said, 'That was the sexiest poem I ever heard.'" She was right, I believe, at least when it comes to the understanding of *sexy* this book is trying to explain. For this very reason, I asked Micah to contribute the following poem, with a short explanation. Keep in mind, dear reader, that the spoken-word genre is best *heard aloud*. Thus if you're close to a computer and want the optimal effect, you might want to download the audio track or watch the video on YouTube[15] before reading the print version below.

Guest Contribution: Micah Bournes

This poem dispels the idea that abstinence until marriage is unnecessary, unrealistic, oppressive, or unhealthy. When it comes to sexual matters, the liberty our culture encourages us to live in often leads to spiritual wounds and circumstances that limit our sense of freedom. The sexual boundaries God calls us to are like stoplights and speed limits. They are intended not to hold us back but rather to keep us alive and well. When it comes to sex, freedom is found within the boundaries of marriage. Intimacy with someone

---

[15] Micah Bournes, "What the Back of His T-Shirt Should Have Said," YouTube video, 2:36, published on March 6, 2013, posted by Nicole Perry, https://youtu.be/NOcooND2Ufc ?list=RDNOcooND2Ufc.

you love, respect, and are in a covenant with is more likely to be enjoyed without a fear of health risk, abandonment, shame, and regret, among other things. In the end, sex is not suppressed by abstinence until marriage; it is celebrated and experienced with the greatest sense of freedom. Also, for the unmarried in a culture that glorifies sexuality, abstinence causes us to see ourselves as far more than mere sexual beings, encouraging deep connections with each other through the many other aspects of our humanity.

What the Back of His T-Shirt Should Have Said

The tiny T-shirt stretched across the pecks and biceps
Of the large, handsome, man, read

"Virginity is Curable."

But the backside should have said:

"However . . .
Genital Herpes
HIV
HPV
Unwanted pregnancy
Or . . .
A plain old broken heart, is not."

Now don't start rolling your eyes,
'Cause I'm not trying to tell you how to live.
I'm just explaining why I choose to live the way I do.
I'm well past puberty and I'm still a virgin.
I have never made love and I will never "make" love.
Love cannot be made and is not a synonym for getting laid.
And just to set the record straight
If I wanted some, I could get some.

But I want some*one*.

Someone who will be in my life past tonight

Past next month
Past next decade
Someone who won't say to five other guys
The same sweet orgasmic lie

"I . . . Love . . . Youh!"

Someone who believes sex is the pinnacle of the relationship
And not the base of the pyramid.
Someone I enjoy being with even when she's not naked and
    in my bed.
Someone I connect with intellectually, emotionally,
    spiritually.
Someone who doesn't insist on protection
'Cause she's not afraid of me or anything I might have
    contracted.
Someone who will be glad to mother my kids.
Someone who won't hate her child because he looks like me.
Someone who will never try her best to eradicate my place
    in her memory.
Someone who knows when her breasts hang low and her
    wrinkles fold
I will not trade her for a porno and my right hand.
Someone who understands that it takes a strong man to con-
    trol his passions.
Someone who looks forward to loosing them.
Someone who will put that song on repeat and ooh wee until
    we faint from fatigue
Then wake the next morning and

Feel
No
Shame.

'Cause we have the same last name
And our nasty is holy
So thanks for the offer, Dr. Lover
But I'll wait for one who also suffers
And we'll cure each other.

Bournes mentions several practical benefits of monogamous marriage. But what strikes me as "sexy" is the fact that he cares enough about his faith and other human beings that he is interested in becoming a virtuous hero in someone's life, not just someone who finds acceptance and pleasure through the use of other bodies. He wants a deep connection with someone. That's who he wants to be. That's virtue thinking, despite the legitimate consequentialist points he mentions. His poem is potent because it calls his audience to a higher understanding of romantic love. It paints a picture of what might be. And it is a beautiful picture—one that is much more helpful than focusing on the negative aspects of erotic vice. In fact, focusing on the negative has a way of drawing us off course.

Object Fixation

When I was dean of theology at an interdenominational evangelical university, some of the freshmen guys started sharing their frustrations with me about a popular phenomenon: young men's study groups centered on a book by Stephen Arterburn titled *Every Man's Battle: Winning the War on Sexual Temptation One Victory at a Time* (2000). Arterburn shared a story that was laudable for its honesty at least. He recounts something that happened while he was driving up the Pacific Coast Highway, along a stretch I enjoy regularly on my motorcycle:

> My eyes locked on to this goddess-like blonde, rivulets of sweat cascading down her tanned body as she ran at a purposeful pace. Her jogging outfit, if it could be called that in those days before sports bras and spandex, was actually a skimpy bikini. As she approached on my left, two tiny triangles of tie-dyed fabric struggled to contain her ample bosom. I can't tell you what her face looked like; nothing above the neckline registered with me that morning. My eyes feasted on this banquet of glistening flesh as she passed on my left, and they continued to follow her lithe figure as she continued jogging southbound. Simply by lustful instinct, as if mesmerized by her gait, I turned my head further and further, craning my neck to capture every possible moment for my mental video camera.[16]

---

[16] Stephen Arterburn and Fred Stoeker, *Every Man's Battle: Winning the War on Sexual Temptation One Victory at a Time*, The Every Man Series (Colorado Springs: WaterBrook, 2009), 11.

Then, it turns out, he slammed into a car that had stopped on the road ahead of him. Here we see a common evangelical morality tale: when women dress immodestly and men don't keep their libidos in check, the men are in danger of physical harm. At least two things frustrated my students concerning this book. First, the emphasis placed on the ways in which women *create* problems by their beauty seemed to contribute to a sexist approach to the subject. They were worried about the problem of "slut shaming" within patriarchal cultures, though they had not yet heard that term. Second, they complained that the constant conversation about sex seemed, paradoxically, to keep their minds focused on sexual lust itself.

This phenomenon reminds me of the problem of motorcycle accidents and *object fixation*. Object fixation occurs when a rider's eyes and head turn toward the very thing he or she is desperate to avoid. Say a biker is cutting a corner fast. He comes upon a tighter bend than expected, only to find a telephone pole precariously close to the road. He might instinctively stare right at the pole. This might cause him to freeze up, orient his body in the undesired direction, and plow straight into the hazard. This can happen when skiing too. But with motorcycles, it involves the strange way in which motorcycles are maneuvered. One steers a motorcycle at speed by leaning; even slight body movements have an effect on one's trajectory. Many don't realize it even while they are doing it, but motorbikes going faster than twenty miles per hour are "countersteered." This means that although bikes moving at five miles per hour steer to the right when the handlebars are turned to the right, when a bike is clipping along, to get out of the way of a hazard on one's left, turning the handle bars to the left, with a good push on the left hand grip, moves the bike to the right. This relies on the curvature of a motorcycle's tires. It's hard to get used to psychologically, but that's indeed how it works.

This analogy is helpful with respect to the question of sex and lust. When we focus intently on what we want to avoid, we often crash right into the moral hazard we are trying to evade. I'm not submitting a new observation. As my outdoor-loving friend Scott Keith says with respect to mountain biking, "Never look at the rock unless you want to hit it!" Others have noted that telling someone *not to think about a pink elephant* tends to create mental images of dancing pachyderms within a person's imagination. I believe, therefore, that it is far more helpful to fix our eyes outside ourselves, on something more profoundly wholesome and transformative. That is, we Christians are usually better off focusing on the cross of Christ, and what that means for human relationships, than focusing on the constant battles of the flesh. In my experience working with young people, focusing on the goal of healthy and virtuous romantic relationships has been far more effective in steering them in rewarding life directions than harping on the dangers of the obstacles. Staying focused on the transformative teaching of Christianity itself—the central message of the New Logic—and then habituation in virtue within the alternative culture of the church are a far more helpful strategy with young people than a barrage of sex talks.

There's a place for discussing and studying the concepts, of course—otherwise I wouldn't be writing this book—but this topic ought not become central for us. In addition to the reality that overemphasis on sexual topics within the church makes people think the church is basically an antisex institution, such overemphasis has undesirable practical results. Moreover, it is arguably one of the main reasons why young people are increasingly leaving the church: it just doesn't seem to understand or help with the complexities of sexuality in our era.

Having already indicated my appreciation for Bournes' poem, which advocates waiting to sexualize a relationship until holy matrimony, I now should note my apprehensiveness about overemphasizing the concept of virginity. Bournes rightly depicts an ideal attitude. But a significant proportion of well-intended young people within Christian communities misunderstand the nature of erotic virtue when it comes to talk about virginity. When hearing the v word, some turn inward in shame or else assume that virginity is something that makes a person more lovable in the eyes of God and others and become self-righteous.

Part of the Western cultural commitment to abstinence and virginity has less to do with spiritual and moral purity and more to do with a dark reality about the way young women have been treated over the millennia. In patriarchal cultures, young women often get treated as commodities. Even today, my friend and former student from South Africa insists that any man who wants to marry her must understand the number of cows she's worth and that any suitor should be prepared to pay her father in said livestock. In such contexts, a bachelorette is the possession of a father, and then, after the father hands her over, she becomes the possession of the husband. As with other types of property, something "unused" tends to be treated as more valuable than something that's been used. Note the lack of balance here: whether consciously or unconsciously, young men are the ones who do the using, while the young women get used. Meanwhile, sexual conquest can raise the perceived stock of the fellows and decrease the assumed value of the gals. Virginity, in such cases, becomes a matter of cultural value, not a matter of virtue. And this business makes me nauseous. Moreover, because of the physical and cultural power imbalance in most adolescent and early adult relationships, a focus on virginity puts an undue burden of shame, especially in conservative Christian circles, on the importance of virginity for women. Especially for those who have been coerced too quickly into sexualizing romantic relationships, I fear that the church does more harm than good with its constant rhetoric about abstinence.

For this reason, I desperately wanted a genuine voice I could trust on this matter. I wanted to hear from a woman who both understood the conservative Christian ethos and was able to provide a circumspect critique of it. Micah pointed me to a spoken-word poet friend of his: Emily Joy. I invited her out to perform at an event in California, and it was there that I realized she has keen insights into the ways in which young women hear the messages preached in evangelical circles these days. I asked her to contribute one of her poems, along with an explanation. One of the coolest things about Emily is that she posts her negative reviews front and center on her website. She knows her voice is not always heard the way it's intended. Some say she's too angry. Maybe. But I believe that, whatever one concludes about her positions on the issues, she has a right to be angry. She grew up in a subculture too often filled with more posturing and declamations than compassion for those in pain. Thus I believe voices like hers deserve thoughtful consideration. As I mentioned before, if you can get to the Internet, it's best to hear her perform her spoken-word poetry aloud rather than simply read it here on the page.[17] Nonetheless, the ideas are important to

---

[17] Emily Joy, "Thank God I'm a Virgin," YouTube video, 2:20, published on March 26, 2015, posted by Emily Joy, https://youtu.be/usfcWXIyXD8.

include in print for your consideration, dear reader. I'm grateful to her for sharing here.

Guest Contribution:
Emily Joy, "The Cult of Virginity"

I grew up in the late 1990s, the heyday of Christian abstinence rallies and "True Love Waits" hysteria. Every adult I knew was wringing his or her hands over the "epidemic" of teens and young people "defrauding" each other by failing to wait for marriage for the onset of sexual activity. I attended special youth group nights, daddy-daughter dances, concerts featuring famous Christian musicians, and more, all dedicated to promoting an ideal of "purity." I had copies of *I Kissed Dating Good-bye* and *Passion and Purity* on my bookshelf, and I pored over them voraciously, hoping that somewhere within those pages was contained the key to making sure that I was able to have holy and righteous marital sex before I died—or before Jesus came back and the rapture happened, whichever came first. I imagined that Jeremiah 29:11—"For I know the plans I have for you, sayeth the Lord: plans to prosper and not to harm you, plans to give you a hope and a future"—was about the future husband God had saved for me. I wrote letters to the aforementioned mythical future husband. I made lists.

At the tender age of thirteen, I promised to save sex, kissing, the words "I love you," and even handholding for the man it was presumed I would marry someday. I was whisked away to a cabin in the woods, presented with scary statistics about divorce and STDs, and given a ring more beautiful and expensive than any piece of jewelry I'd ever owned. I thought it was my only choice. I thought I was doing the right thing by agreeing to the terms and conditions someone else had written for my own sexuality. Like a lot of terms and conditions, I had no idea what I was agreeing to.

"Purity culture," as it is now called, generally has one of two effects. The first, for those who fail to adhere to its precepts (about 90 percent of adults by the age of twenty-five, give or take), is a flood of feelings of shame and guilt and the lingering certainty that you are definitely going to hell and no self-respecting Christian human will ever want you if they find out that you didn't save yourself for them. The second, for those who manage to more or less follow the rules (the other 10 percent), is a sense of smug self-satisfaction and superiority that makes you an absolute terror to be around and a horrible friend to anyone who has made even remotely different choices than you. Being a headstrong firstborn with a deep-seated authority-pleasing complex, I fell into the second category.

I ended up at a conservative Bible college after high school, and as sexually repressed young people in conservative environments do, we talked a lot about sex. And that's when I started hearing variations on the same refrain, particularly from men: "I just don't think I could marry a girl if she wasn't a virgin"; "I've waited, so I'll be offended if my future wife doesn't wait too"; "If a girl's already had sex with someone else. I won't consider dating her." And even though I myself was the statistical 10 percent virgin unicorn—I didn't end up having my first proper kiss until long after I obtained a bachelor's degree—something about these sentiments never sat right with me. And the more that I realized how much traditional evangelical expectations of sexual conduct are predicated on ideas of power and control, especially over women, the less right they sat—and the angrier I got. Every new sexual and relational experience I had, right up until and including getting married, made me angrier, because it struck me every time just how much basically everything I had been taught growing up about sex and dating and relationships and marriage was a heaping pile of possibly well-meaning but definitely destructive lies.

And the virginity cult of modern evangelicalism is not just extraordinarily destructive but entirely extrabiblical if you really start looking at it, unless your definition of "biblical" includes treating women as if they are property, stoning nonvirgins, and requiring victims to marry their rapist—which are, for what it's worth, also "biblical" ideas. I often wonder if we should be more careful about using that word than we presently are. The Bible is certainly authoritative. Our interpretations of it are not. Miguel A. De La Torre, in his work *A Lily among the Thorns: Imagining a New Christian Sexuality*, says, "When the interpretation fosters oppressive structures, then agreeing to disagree can never be an option . . . such interpretations must be condemned for Christ's sake."

So when Jesus said, "You will know a tree by its fruit" (Matt. 7:16), I like to think he meant it. And the fruit of purity culture has been this: broken relationships, sexually dysfunctional adults, shame, abuse, divorce, repression, depression, self-loathing, unhealthy neuroticism, and so much more. You cannot look at a tree producing almost entirely rotten fruit and pretend that it is still good at the core, that some people just misinterpret it. You only get to say that so many times before you have to start examining the tree itself. And when you find that it is corrupt and rancid to the core, you must do the hard work of chopping it down and starting over, no matter how unpopular it may be and how many exclusive Christian "clubs" you get kicked out of for your refusal to turn your head and look the other way.

That is what I was trying to do with the poem "Thank God I'm a Virgin," and it is what I try to do in my writing, my activism, and my interactions with others each and every day. It is a lifelong work, but those who grew up under the oppressive structures of purity culture know that it is very, very necessary.

Thank God I'm a Virgin

Well thank God I'm a virgin,
Or he probably wouldn't want me.
I thought
As I listened silently
While he told me
That he just couldn't be with someone
Who had been with someone else,
Which is like 90% of adults
By the age of 25
So your already limited pool is shrinking very quickly—
But don't let me discourage you.

Carry on.

Tell me how you saved yourself.
How you saved up enough points with God
To buy an unspoiled bride,
And you will not *settle for less*.
Tell me about her white dress,
How it will *mean something*.
Tell me what it means.
Tell me what it's like to have nothing you regret,
To have made it through life
Unscathed by either bliss or pain—
What does that feel like?
Is it very lonely?

Or does it just feel safe?
Like keeping your cocoon heart
All wrapped up and tucked away,
Hoping to God someday it becomes a butterfly
Before it dies from the frost?

I hope whoever she is,
She meets all your expectations.
I hope enough of her heart is intact
For you to feel like the wait was worth it.
I hope she never knows you wouldn't have wanted her
If she wasn't a virgin.

Because everybody knows a girl is only as valuable
As the men who haven't touched her,
Only as desirable
As the experiences she hasn't had.
But baby, when you get to her—
She better know what to do in bed.
She better satisfy your wildest pornographic fantasies,
Know all the right ways to move
Body parts she has never had the chance to use,
Because God would never fail you, right?
You waited on *his timing*,
Now he owes you.

Anything less is not the bill of goods they sold you.

So I hope it works out for you.
I really do.

But if it doesn't,
Just remember what I told you:

That a heart cannot be divided into pieces
And given away until there is nothing left.

That the greatest gift you can give someone
Has nothing to do with your flesh.

That love is really just grace.

That a lifetime of avoidance
Does not prepare one for a lifetime of joy and pain.

That *virgin* is not a sexual preference,
Nor is it your birthright—

Baby.
Your insecurity is showing.
She chose you.
What more do you want?

Evangelical Prom Night

Some evangelical Christians believe they can reach a level of personal holiness called *entire sanctification*.[18] This is said to occur when a person is able, through the power of the Holy Spirit, to conquer sin. Such a person might still make mistakes—occasional, albeit regrettable, actions of the flesh—but will no longer commit premeditated sin. In other words, whereas Luther described Christians as simultaneously saints and sinners (*simul iustus et peccator*), those who

---

[18] This is less common in Reformed or Lutheran circles but stems from an interpretation of John Wesley's approach to personal holiness, as found in his work *A Plain Account of Christian Perfection* (1738).

believe in entire sanctification think that Christians can reach a point where they should not properly be described as "sinners."

So then consider the prom night of some hypothetical thoughtful male high school senior whose church doesn't teach that we mortal Christians are simultaneously saints and sinners. He doesn't plan to have sex with his date. He digs her personality. His convertible is looking sharp and clean. The stars are out. The night is warm. He knows he's probably going to make out a little. For a moment he thinks *maybe* he might have sex at Lookout Point. But that's wrong. So never mind. Sex is out of the question for sure. He's a Christian; he isn't living a carnal life of sin any more. No, sir. He's going to keep his purity intact.

Maybe he should go buy a condom, though. Just in case.

But in what case? No case at all. He's a Christian. No case at all. Sure, he did get pretty close to intercourse over the last couple semesters. All with the same gal. All the same story. He didn't plan on it, but hormones and circumstances got in the way. And they got a bit too hot and heavy. They went too far. But that's not who they really are. So they repented. They prayed for forgiveness. They talked it out. No more sex. Not until marriage.

Anyway, for prom night, he figures, there's a chance that things might go beyond the line of chaste propriety. But not so long as he plans well. So he scraps the idea of going to Lookout Point. Maybe he should try to hang out with other couples and cruise around town with them. Condoms are for sinners who plan to fornicate. He's not that sort of guy.

Later that night, he laments that the idea of hanging with other couples fizzled out. Too bad his girlfriend bought new binoculars, and she wanted to try them out on the city lights. Too bad Lookout Point was the best place to view those lights. Too bad he was feeling so handsome and the night was so romantic.

As the author here, I get to tell you how the story goes. But you won't be surprised. They end up "doing it," and they do it without a condom. A condom would have meant premeditated sin and thus a loss of standing before God. It would, in this particular logic, be an *aggravating* factor in the young couple's spiritual courtroom.

In this story, they also get pregnant, and their parents get angry. Their church looks at them scornfully when they show up on

Sundays. Since this just became a bummer, let's say they also win the lottery, get married, and live happily ever after.

Now, I'd say giving someone a nasty disease—knowingly or not—*is* a sin. And so is carelessly bringing a life into this world that you aren't ready or willing to care for. Don't we want to reduce the frequency of abortions? Nonetheless, because of these other theological considerations I've explained, some young people grow up thinking that the very possession of a condom is one of the most sinful aspects of their behavior. Of course, if you find that any of this describes your personal history too closely, remember that you are loved, forgiven, and welcome to the way of grace. I'm just pointing out here that if you know you are going to do it, there's nothing wrong with being honest with yourself and minimizing the damage that your evening might create. Do this for rather straightforward reasons. There is nothing so ritually taboo about a condom that it will significantly increase or decrease the gravity of your sin.

Likewise, encouraging young people who will likely have sex (this includes the folks in church on Sunday) to be safe or safer is not sinful in principle. It *is* politically complicated, given the culture wars. And there are indeed times when candid recognition of adolescent behavior can appear to be a sign of moral approval. But I contend that, however we navigate our perplexing times, we need to focus more on the people we want to be and how we want to treat others and less on the ritual impurity of condoms and other contraceptives.

Decreasing Sexual Activity among Young People

Despite relaxed and progressive cultural mores, especially with respect to nonheterosexual relationships, young people today seem to be less risky or as promiscuous than previous generations. This holds true for those both within and outside Christian communities. Despite some Christian alarm-sounding about our increasingly debased times, over the past twenty-five years, according to the National Center for Health Statistics, the percentage of adolescents who have had any sexual intercourse whatsoever dropped from 58 percent of females and 69 percent of males (in 1988) to 44 percent of females and 47 percent of males (in 2015).[19] Moreover, the number of sexual partners per person is now declining. For example, the typical baby boomer had an average of eleven different sexual partners during the same age range in which millennials will have an average of eight sexual partners.

What are we to make of this trend? I don't think this decline in adolescent sexual activity is the result of successful church programs, though some individuals may indeed report this to be the case. There seem to be several other factors at work related to changes in society and technology.

There are positive signs in all this, especially with respect to young people's interest in genuine intimacy. For some, like twenty-six-year-old Sam Wei, sex can get in the way of discovering true romantic connections. She explains, "To me, there's more intimacy with having someone there next to you that you can rely on without having to have sex," she said. "I don't want to do anything that would harm the relationship and be something that we can't come back from."[20]

While Christians might be right to applaud the decreasing frequency of extramarital sex, there might be red flags here. Those flags relate to the ways in which individuals are having difficulty experiencing concrete relationships and intimacy. The lack of sexual activity may have less to do with attention to purity and more to do with a lack of sexiness, as I am using the term. Some observers suggest that this decline in sexual activity relates to (1) pressure to succeed in careers and hence little time for romance, (2) increasingly digital and virtual relationships via texting and other digital forms of communication, (3) unrealistic expectations related to body image due to new dating apps, and (4) fear of situations that might lead to date rape.[21]

Pressure to succeed seems to relate to the high pressure under which many young people struggle, given the high engagement of so-called helicopter parents. This pressure increases once young

---

[19] Laila Kearney, "Rate of U.S. Teens Having Sex Has Dropped in Past 25 Years: Federal Data," *Reuters*, July 22, 2015, 131.

[20] Tara Bahrampour "'There Isn't Really Anything Magical about It': Why More Millennials Are Avoiding Sex," *Business Insider*, August 2, 2016.

[21] Ibid.

people realize that the rapidly changing economy requires everyone on the job market to be adaptable and ready to enter emerging industries. This is a reality for many, but it is important for Christian communities to remind young adults that a well-balanced life will typically involve close relationships. There is no need to privilege marriage and sexuality as the only good avenues for such relationships. Indeed, a life of celibacy is a perfectly acceptable vocation for some. A life without *intimacy*, however, isn't worth the career success it may enable.

Life in the digital age might be more problematic still. Instead of the old model of going out on group dates to the movies or hanging out at a beach bonfire, where innocent flirtation can take place, disembodied interaction has a way of creating unhealthy and disconnected relationships. Digital "dating" is not entirely problematic. Indeed, with respect to my younger son, Aidan, I have found that at least some digital communication can help develop maturity when it comes to romantic relationships.

A few years ago, we had to move from Seattle to Southern California for work reasons. Aidan was able to carry on and then conclude an innocent relationship with a girl at his old school. They shared their stresses with school and expressed their sorrow at being apart. It was hard for him to go through this, but his ability to remain connected—albeit in a disembodied manner—at least helped him practice moving through the arc of a relationship in a healthy way.

Later he developed a relationship with a girl at his school in California. He texted her all the time. In this way, he was able to learn more about her life, interests, and struggles than any of my friends ever did before the texting era. In my day, we just fumbled around with our words or performed immature stunts in order to impress the ladies. He was ultimately able to learn a lot from this virtual relationship. She was not allowed to date in the traditional sense, and that was just fine for both of them. They were able to focus on learning about themselves and about the kind of relationship they ultimately wanted. This also ended up allowing him to eventually break off the relationship in a remarkably mature way. Aidan realized that they had different religious beliefs and life goals, so—without negativity or drama—he was able to conclude the relationship on a rather healthy note. They remain friends, and he has a new girlfriend. This has led me to trust that his future relationships will be easier to navigate for him than they were when I was his age.

Consider Facebook and other social media platforms for the moment. Sure, they can be a drag and can distract a person from other healthy pursuits. But they also allow potential romantic partners to get a better sense of what their prospective mate is about. Their online persona may well be misleading. But like with a potential employer, there are things to be learned. Do they party hard? Do they have thoughtful posts about life, culture, and politics? Do they have healthy relationships with their families? Sometimes starting a casual relationship by "friending" someone can be a pleasant way to discover shared interests. We should recognize the good as well as the bad when it comes to new technology.

Nonetheless, the disembodiment involved in our digital age should not be welcomed uncritically. It might set parents' minds at ease that young people aren't in close enough proximity to fornicate, but the distance can also be problematic. Consider the situation in Japan. Culturally, they have even more career pressure than most nations, plus a highly digital way of interacting. And this is leading many to choose careers over marriage. The young men are often too bashful to approach women romantically and turn to other nonrelational outlets for their sexuality. As a result, Japan's birth rate is dropping at an alarming rate—so much so that the Japanese government is stepping in to attempt a reversal of the trend. The key here of course is to foster a healthy balance.

Sex and Self-Worth

When it comes to premarital sex, the real worry for me, as a parent and educator, has little to do with a commitment to upholding taboos or a fear that folks are getting away with rule breaking. There is of course a real concern about the danger of STDs and about bringing children into this world who don't have family stability. But my worry has to do with something deeper. I worry for the spiritual and emotional well-being of the individuals involved. In a world of law and transactionalism, we tend to view too many things as commodities. Sex can be treated like a commodity. So can our own bodies and behaviors. We all want to be valuable and *valued*. The old secular logic tells us that we are only worthwhile if someone will sleep with us. For many, even if only at a subconscious level, this need to be needed spills out into the way we often sexualize relationships.

Consider the selfish bro who gets pissed off if he doesn't "get laid" after he buys a woman a couple drinks. This image—though all too common—is more terrifying to me than the idea of young adults getting too close. In a world of obligation and coercion, sexuality becomes a way to seal deals, prove love, or lock in a relationship. Grace, and the New Logic it brings, recognizes none of this type of thinking. Christian sexual ethics values mutuality, a *celebration* of deals already sealed, an enjoyment of love that already is assured, and a blessing enjoyed when we are able to be vulnerable because our unconditional relationship is already locked in. This isn't because Christians must be prudes; it's because they are called to base their intimacy and affection on a peace that the world cannot bring or even understand.

In *East of Eden*, John Steinbeck insightfully illustrates the connection between emotional issues and sexual activity:

> Violence and shyness—Tom's loins needed women and at the same time he did not think himself worthy of a woman. For long periods he would welter in a howling celibacy, and then he would take a train to San Francisco and roll and wallow in women, and then he would come silently back to the ranch, feeling weak and unfulfilled and unworthy, and he would punish himself with work, would plow and plant unprofitable land, would cut tough oakwood until his back was breaking and his arms were weary rags.[22]

There are of course many possible manifestations of one's off-kilter sexuality, but Steinbeck's example is spot on. It reminds us that when we encounter promiscuous people, our first concern should be about the internal health of those people, not how we can denigrate them and their behaviors. Do they not know that God promises to make all things well? Do they not know that true love is an unlimited resource and yet is—in the fullest sense of the term—*priceless*?

---

[22] John Steinbeck, *East of Eden* (New York: Penguin, 2002), 280.

I told my son once that I'd prefer he didn't get someone pregnant because "that would be cliché." He laughed, but he admitted it was a compelling piece of rhetoric, in context. But then I went on to mention that if I learned he was bouncing around between casual experiences with young women, I'd worry that something was wrong with his sense of belonging in the world. I reminded him that he was already loved unconditionally, at least by God, his mother, and me. I explained that there was no reason to try to extract more meaning or love from the universe. I urged him to treat young women with this in mind: that he should let them know that they are on solid ground and loved and known intimately, regardless of any *carnal* knowledge.

Within the context of the New Logic, in which nothing of cosmic significance can be earned or spent, holy sexuality is never about performance or transaction. It is a joyful expression of abundant love. Thus the pressure of making sure one is not a virgin before graduation—an asinine trope from teen comedies, as funny as they might be—is a symptom of a type of legalism. In this typical cinematic scenario, this legalism is not the uptight Christian type but rather a secular legalism in which one can earn good standing with the secular gods (say, the popular jocks at school) or with a romantic prospect. According to such misguided thinking, one must *do* something, perform well, and "score." How oppressive! Fortunately, as we've seen, an increasing proportion of young people see such transactional business as unprofitable and take their time to find their life direction and sexual partner. Nonetheless, the stakes are high enough, and the emotions fragile enough, for us to spend at least as much time letting our young people know they are loved and valued as we spend telling them not to dance too closely at the winter formal.

Who Are You?

More important than questions like "What am I allowed to get away with sexually?" is the question, "Who am I?" and the related question, "Who do I want to be in relation to others?" If you love someone, you will want to commit to not harming him or her. The question of one's identity is of course, for Christians, bound up in identity with Christ. In the alternative kingdom of Jesus, we are to treat others as brothers and sisters in a sense. Young men should therefore approach relationships by asking, *How should I treat this daughter of heaven that I've taken a liking to?* Young women should ask, *How should I cultivate healthy relational habits that will perpetuate a virtuous community bound by unconditional love?*

In all this business, regardless of our age, we proceed best when we recognize that sexual intercourse is not something that provides a certification of value or worth. In Christ, we have all the cosmic approval we need. Sex cannot be, as Micah Bournes says, the foundation of the relational pyramid. We are all burdened by a desire to feel loved and connected. By cultivating a sense of God's inexhaustible love and approval, and by extending that gracious spirit to everyone we encounter, we have a shot at forming virtuous relational habits. Even when we fail to live up to our own standards, continuing to practice virtue has a way of becoming an unshakable aspect of our identity. This process may be slow and difficult at times, but in all things, the goal should not primarily be a sense of self-righteous purity; rather, it should be the internalized value of love for God and neighbor. There is no simple way to keep one's behavior in line with one's beliefs in this regard. However, focusing on the New Logic and learning to surf the Tao will be of great help in the struggle, especially if we recognize that we proceed under the shadow of God's gracious wings.

Erotic virtue, in this context, involves an interpersonal testimony to committed love. For this reason—not a rejection of embodiment or pleasure—the followers of Jesus strive to refrain from any sexual activity that might treat love as a merely transactional or selfish matter. Thus intercourse apart from the commitment of marriage is vicious if it creates unwanted children, to whom neither love, nor commitment, nor parental protection is assured. Likewise, such an activity is vicious if it treats another person as little more than an instrument for physical gratification. The best sex takes place under the cloak of trust and commitment. It is there we can be vulnerable with another person—spiritually, emotionally, and literally naked.

9.5 Theses on Sex before Marriage

Lest I leave this important matter of premarital sex without being clear about my advice for young people, permit me to suggest some theses. Even if you think I'm wrong about these, I contend they are worth discussing with someone, or at least pondering within one's own mind.

1. *Don't let the impulses of a passionate moment dictate the rest of your future.* Going too far too fast is not in your best interest, nor is it in the best interest of your partner. Regardless of the way you view traditional sexual mores, consider the ways in which any virtuous person will want to be restrained for the well-being of another human being.

2. *Guard yourself and others against manipulation and coercion.* Even the wisest and strongest humans have found sexuality to be a potential Achilles' heel. In our day, there are few legal restraints on your sexual expression besides general rules of engagement, but this does not protect you from the manner in which this seeming liberation can blind you to the ways in which you might be objectified or victimized. This isn't to say that if someone is manipulated or coerced, it is his or her fault—that is a false and odious assumption of so-called rape culture. However, being aware of potential threats in any situation is wise. Accordingly, we should all work to avoid being coercive, perhaps especially when such coercion is subtle, indirect, or unconscious.

3. *It isn't prudish or uptight to take things slowly.* Savor flirting, holding hands, and being coy. Taking things slowly is attractive to most of the love interests you will encounter, whatever their stated religious, ethical, or political values. If they don't dig the art of being sexy, you shouldn't dig them, for they are probably selfish people at best, not yet in possession of spiritual maturity on average, or potential predators at worst.

4. *Be honest with yourself.* If you know you are likely to engage in intercourse in a given situation, plan accordingly. Better yet, if you believe you should take things slow, avoid creating situations in which the sexualization of your relationship will be nearly irresistible.

5. *Despite what some religious folks seem to convey, consensual sexual sin is by no means the worst form of sin.* The root problem is that sex is such a powerful force of life that it can cause you to act against your better judgment and best interests, and thoughtless sex can lead to lifelong heartache and pain. It can lead you to unite with and then sever from more than one person in traumatic ways. Reckless sex doesn't mitigate the offense of premarital sex; it is an aggravating factor.

6. *Understand your relationship with God through the New Logic of Christ before initiating a romantic relationship and also after you fail to live up to your own standards.* Keep striving for and creating habits of erotic integrity, but don't get all tangled up in ethical despair when you don't live like you think you should. If you act in ways you regret, dust yourself off, reconnect to the divine source of all things, and move forward.

7. *Avoid the vicious excess of finding self-worth in numerous sexual hookups.* This can be a sign that you need some spiritual healing before venturing into the world of serious romance. Perhaps consider reading and discussing a book with a romantic interest. Maybe take motorcycle lessons together. Consider getting scuba certified as a couple. Then, as you figure out who you are, you will be in a healthier position to develop embodied intimacy.

8. *Avoid the vicious defect of shunning intimacy altogether.* Intimacy is not a synonym for fornication; it's the bedrock of beautiful intercourse. Some folks try to starve their libidos and train themselves to be unsexy, thinking this will help them avoid the stain of sin altogether. Take a different route, and seek joy in human connectedness. Learn how to have genuine conversations. Master the art of holy flirtation.

9. *Habituate the virtue of restraint and moderation.* Don't allow your libido to pull your heart and mind off course on your quest for faithful and unconditional erotic love. Think of this the way a cowboy thinks about breaking a wild horse. The cowboy doesn't want the horse to be weak

or sullen. He just wants the horse to learn how to channel its energy, responding calmly to the bridle.

9.5. *Know who you truly want to be.* What virtues do you want to cultivate in yourself? Erotic virtue isn't about remaining ritually pure or looking moral in the presence of others; it's about being a good person toward those you love. When you are dating, remember that the other person is a son or daughter of heaven, so treat him or her accordingly.

You Say I Took the Name in Vain (Finding the One)

You say I took the name in vain,
But I don't even know the name,
But if I did, well really, what's it to you?
There's a blaze of light in every word,
It doesn't matter what you heard,
The broken or the holy Hallelujah

—Leonard Cohen, "Hallelujah"

"Sons," I said to my boys one day, during one of my episodes of manic playfulness, "as you start to date seriously, you'll find that folks get hung up on when to say 'I love you' to a sweetheart. Do it too soon, they warn, and you'll look foolish or desperate. Do it too late, and you might look like you're afraid of commitment. But maybe you should tell a gal that you love her on the first date."

The boys laughed, thinking I was once again saying the extreme opposite of what I really meant. I do that sometimes; why else would I dispense such reckless and potentially disastrous advice? But I was serious. They asked why, so I replied, "Because of the Name. The Name is love. God is love. Love God by loving your neighbor. Every gal you meet is your neighbor. Love casts out fear. So don't be afraid to say 'I love you.' Because of the love that is yours, you are free to love all without fear that the love will get used up. So you don't need to search desperately for some predetermined soul mate, as if she is the only one on whom you can spend your limited resource of love."

As we discussed things further, I had to admit that there is something romantic about declaring, at some later point, that a beloved is *the one*, but not because she is able to bring something to the table to complete you or meet all your needs. "She's *the one*," I continued, "when she and you agree to be *the one* for each other and formally become one in marriage. In the meantime, once you've resolved the love question, you can start getting down to the business of figuring out if the two of you can stand to be around each other, whether you have shared life goals, and whether your personalities are complementary or at least compatible."

Granted, this advice I gave my sons might be too radical for some, and it probably will be an unsettling statement for a young woman to hear without the added explanation. My boys also know that I sometimes speak in idealistic terms and that they need to temper my advice in each context. But the principle, I am convinced, remains true. If we remain connected to the goodness of divine love, our natural response will be the realization that we love everyone, even our enemies. We are free to choose one of those people as a partner in love, which will include loving neighbors as well as potential children. Some of those we love are too dangerous, manipulative, or annoying for us to be around. Some have values so different from ours that they threaten to hold us back from loving others freely. Nonetheless, we love all even as we commit to only one.

Ethicist Gilbert Meilaender supports this concept when he explains how our call to love indiscriminately ends up being expressed by particular exclusive relationships:

> Our benevolence can be exercised toward all in the sense that we can pray for all, have good will for all, and be ready to receive the many who cross our path. But since we are finite, this benevolence will in practice have to be expressed most fully toward certain people near and dear to us. Thus, distinctions in love are still permitted: We love some people with special attachment, but we love them as we would love all if we could—with a love of benevolence, not preference.[1]

Meilaender can speak this way because he contends that an encounter with the Gospel empowers virtue. "Grace," he insists, "is fundamental for the life of believers, but that grace must be understood

---

[1] Gilbert Meilaender, *Faith and Faithfulness: Basic Themes in Christian Ethics* (Notre Dame, IN: University of Notre Dame Press, 1992), 52.

both as pardoning word and transforming power."[2] Through this transforming power, to say "I love you" takes on a different meaning. In this context, we don't *fall in love*, responding to some worthiness in the other person. By saying "I love you" on the first date, we learn to recognize that these words are as much an eschatological promise as they are a current reality. They are an invitation to enter into a new reality—the New Logic—and a new way of understanding relationships. In such a relationship, there is no reason to prove our love by sexualizing it.

Despite all I've said thus far, I respect the way in which people avoid throwing "I love you" around too casually. They detect that love is sacred, perhaps even divine. And such matters should of course be handled with care. Language is inherently unable to capture the totality of the reality to which it points. Words that point to transcendent realities, like *goodness*, *truth*, and *beauty*, are not only hard to define; they are also unable to entirely contain the infinite realities they aspire to capture. The word *grace* can be like this. But perhaps the most notoriously difficult word to define and understand is *love*. For this reason, it sometimes feels blasphemous to use *love* or *I love you* in at least three particular contexts:

1. *When we realize that our ability to love falls short of infinite divine love.* We sometimes feel a sense of guilt when we tell someone we love him or her but haven't backed it up with our actions. We feel like frauds when we realize we are failing in our works of love toward others we value.

2. *When we don't really feel love for another person.* In such cases we are of course failing to realize that true love is not about a feeling but about the process of reflecting the infinite love from its ultimate, divine source. We are to be like the moon, reflecting not our own light but the light of the sun. Sometimes the light of divine love gets eclipsed, in which case we feel as if our verbal expressions of love are guilty of taking a holy name in vain.

---

[2] Ibid., 80.

3. *When we are embarrassed to admit that we love someone we don't know well enough to have developed concrete reasons to love.* This is the most misguided of the three, because divine love does not wait for reasons at all. True love has its source in *agape*, which means our love is unconditional. There is nothing to be gained or lost, cosmically. Hence love should not properly be considered a transaction.

There's a long tradition of respecting a sacred name. This was of course important to the people of Israel. Jews today often refer to God as "Hashem," or "the Name." The commandment "Thou shalt not take the name of the Lord thy God in vain" caused such fear among pious Jews that they refused to utter the proper name of God, YHWH. Some English translations likewise added vowels and wrote this out as *Jehovah*, though current scholars write this and pronounce it as *Yahweh*. Nevertheless, most Christian Bible translations remain reluctant to print Yahweh and instead used *Lord* in place of the sacred name, the so-called *tetragrammaton*, or divine four-letter-word. Likewise, I don't expect my boys to break with convention and throw "I love you" around without serious thought.

Today, devout Jews often write out even the generic divine title as "G-d," in order to avoid any accidental blasphemy. Nonetheless, even within Judaism itself, there can be fascinating conversations about what it means to take the Lord's name in vain. Is it precisely about the sounds one makes with the mouth or what one might write on animal skins? Or is it something deeper and perhaps inexpressible? This is the theme of one of my favorite films, *Pi* (1998). In it, a mathematician computer genius named Max thinks he can understand the world, and God himself, through mathematics. He creates a program intended to spit out a number that is God's true name. What follows is a dialogue between Max and a rabbi, Rav, who studies Kabbalah, or Jewish mysticism. Rav and his friends want Max to give them the number that is the name of God. They believe there is extraordinary power in the number.

Rav Cohen. The Romans also murdered all of our priest-hood—the Cohanim—the Cohens, and with their

deaths they destroyed our greatest secret. In the center of
the great temple was the holy of holies which was the heart
of Jewish life. This was the earthly residence for our God.
The one God. It contained the ark of the Tabernacle which
stored the original Ten Commandments that God gave to
Moses. Only one man could enter this space once a year
on the holiest day of the year, Yom Kippur. On the Day of
Atonement, all of Israel would descend upon Jerusalem
to witness the High Cohen's trip into the holy of holies. If
the holy man was pure he would reemerge a few moments
later and Israel was secured a prosperous year. It meant
that we were one year closer to the messianic age. Closer
to the return of the Garden of Eden. But if he was impure,
he would die instantly and it meant that we were doomed.
The High Cohen had a single ritual to perform in the holy
of holies. He had to intone a single word.

Rav Cohen takes a dramatic pause. Max is anxious to hear the
end of the story.

Max. So?

Rav Cohen. That word was the true name of God.

Max. Yeah . . .

Rav Cohen. The true name, which only the Cohanim knew,
was two hundred and sixteen letters long.

A long beat.

Max. (Incredulous) You're telling me that the number in my
head is the name of God!?

Wondrously, Max rubs the scar on his head.

Rav Cohen. (Passion building) Yes . . . it's the key into the
messianic age. As the Romans burned the temple, the Talmud
says, the High Cohen walked into the flames. He took
his secret to the top of the burning building. The heavens
opened up and took the key from the priest's outstretched

hand. We've been searching for the key ever since. And you may have found it. Now let us find out.

Max. That's what happened. I saw God.

Rav Cohen. No, no, Max. You're not pure. You can't see God unless you're pure.

Max. It's more than God . . . It's everything. It's math and science and nature . . . the universe. I saw the Universe's DNA.

Rav Cohen. You saw nothing.

Max. I saw everything.

Rav Cohen. There's much more. We can unlock the door with the key. It will show God that we are pure again. He will return us to The Garden.

Max. Garden? You're not pure. I'm the one who has the Number.

Rav Cohen. Who do you think you are? You are a vessel from our God. You are carrying a delivery that needs to be made to us.

Max. It was given to me. It's part of me. It's changing me.

Rav Cohen. It's killing you. Because you are impure.

Lenny Meyer. It will kill you!

Max. And what will it do to you?

Lenny Meyer. We're pure. Give us the number!

Max. The number is nothing. You know that!

Rav Cohen. We can use it. We can wield it.

Max. It's just a number. I'm sure you've written down every two hundred and sixteen digit number. You've translated all of them. You've intoned them all. Haven't you? But what's it gotten you? It's not the number! It's the meaning. It's the syntax. It's what's between the numbers. If you could understand you would. But it's not for you! I've got it. I understand it. I'm going to see it!

(Whispers to Rav Cohen)

Rabbi . . . I was chosen.

There's a lot to unpack in this scene, philosophically speaking. Max contends that simply knowing a formula, or a word, or a number, is not sufficient. It must be understood and encountered. This relates to using the phrase "I love you." In some contexts, saying it aloud to someone can have no effect. Maybe it isn't sincere. Maybe it's self-deceived. Maybe love itself is hardly understood by the one speaking. However, for the one who has actually encountered the "universe's DNA"—what I see as Jesus, the *Logos* and the eternal Tao—speaking words of love has a direct power. It involves discourse that changes things. It changes reality by bringing a nontransactional relationship to reality. When said in truth, telling someone you love him or her breaks open the prison cell of another human. It creates the reality it names. Again, this is only the case when one is in a position to channel divine love toward a neighbor.

The important principle in all this is not the precise words we use but rather that we should communicate unconditional care and respect for romantic partners, and we should start with the assumption that we are called to love without restraint. This involves recognizing that we are people on the way, who of course will not live up to the ultimate truth that is declared. Martin Luther was right when he observed that we live within a tension between *the already* and *the not yet*. That is, in God's eyes, we are already holy, disciples, righteous, and connected to His inexhaustible well of love. Meanwhile, we don't adequately manifest that love in our words and actions. Moreover, according to Luther, we are simultaneously saints and sinners. Nonetheless, by habituating virtue, by living in hope of a future reality wherein we will be proper conduits of God's love, we begin to transform others as well as ourselves. As Lao Tzu said, "Those on the way become the way."[3] If we follow the way *of the Way himself*—that is, Jesus—we will have a better chance of becoming shaped and patterned after the way of unconditional love in our day-to-day existence.

---

[3] Lao-Tzu, *Tao Te Ching*, trans. Stanley Lombardo and Stephen Addiss (Indianapolis: Hackett Classics, 2011), 30.

Romance of the Cross

Paradoxical language about love's already-but-not-yet character makes sense once one learns to be a "theologian of the cross." Cross-centered theology was one of Luther's most important contributions. It is set against theologies of glory, which seek acceptance through human performance. Glory theology is intolerant of wipeouts while surfing the Tao. One must abandon glory thinking in order to foster healthy erotic lives. A romance of the cross recognizes that just as Jesus' loving desire for humanity led Him to a painful and shameful death, our earthly love typically involves experiences of agony. Nonetheless, the pain encountered becomes endurable in light of an ultimate hope.

A romance of the cross confronts not only our clearly sinful actions but, more important, our self-deceived, self-righteous thinking. "As an attack," Gerhard Forde explains, the cross "reveals that the real seat of sin is not in the flesh but in our *spiritual aspirations,* in our 'theology of glory.'"[4] Those of us who expect a perfect romantic experience in marriage are chasing a *romance of glory*. With a romance of the cross, we enjoy and spill out this love, but we don't get flustered when it is not perfectly realized, nor do we demand it before it becomes a reality in a partner's life. High-minded romance, even of a thoughtful, grace-based sort, can become demanding when it becomes an unattainable expectation. Meilaender is helpful here when he writes,

> This love, so heedless of self, is not a natural possibility by which the world may be governed, nor, even, is it best thought of as something Christians should *require* of one another. Rather it is a love that becomes a new possibility in the lives of those who have experienced grace as a transforming power. All believers are only on the way toward such Christlike love, and a trust strong enough to eschew attempts at self-vindication is better thought of as a new possibility than new law.[5]

---

[4] Gerhard Forde, *On Being a Theologian of the Cross: Reflections on Luther's Heidelberg Disputation, 1518* (Grand Rapids, MI: Eerdmans, 1997), 1.

[5] Meilaender, *Faith and Faithfulness*, 86.

In other words, when we speak about the New Logic of love within relationships, we cannot use our lovers' failure to live up to the standard of infinite love against them as a new legal angle for attack. This is something I find to be a great difficulty personally. When I see people, or my wife, acting in a way I find petty, I tend to become uncharitable. When this happens, I must remember that the invitation to infinite love is not to be confused with a demand for others to fully express it.

I was gladdened when Stacie wrote on my Facebook page, on the morning of one of our anniversaries, "The Tao that can be spoken is not the eternal Tao." I knew immediately what she meant. She didn't begrudge other couples from proclaiming their affection online, but neither did she want to make a public demonstration of it. She realized that trying to communicate something about eternal love might become misunderstood by other couples. Or envied. It wasn't that we perfectly embodied infinite love, nor was she in the mood to try to perform within this post some poetic act that could prove her romantic passion. It was that there aren't words for the joy and connection we've encountered, having spent so many years together. Anything she might attempt would, in a sense, be both too much and too little.

The line Stacie posted to my Facebook wall is the first line of the *Tao Te Ching*, which a recent translation captures in its stark, original form: "TAO called TAO is not TAO. Names can name no lasting name."[6] Now, for Christians, although even the best words, the best theology, cannot entirely comprehend divine reality, this does not mean words are useless. We should say nice, loving things to each other, of course. But the words don't constitute the thing itself. And when both our words and our actions fall short, this doesn't mean they aren't beautiful tokens of a future reality to come, when all things will be made well in God's providence. A romance of the cross is thus comfortable making bold, absolute claims about the infinite resources of gracious divine love. It is also well aware of the difficulties we will face along the way. Thus we muddle through in hope, outside Eden's borders.

---

[6] Lao-Tzu, *Tao Te Ching*, 1.

Love outside Eden's Borders:
Should We Even Be Looking for the One?

Is he *the one*? Is she *the one*? These are age-old questions that many singles still ask today. But this way of thinking is as wrongheaded as it is common. No doubt, some romantic partners are more compatible than others. Shared values, religion, and life goals matter. For instance, if a woman wants to travel the world but the man is a homebody and wants to establish a stable home and career in his hometown, there could be excessive quarreling down the line. If financial security matters to a man, he might wisely decide not to marry a grad student who's getting a PhD in Irish novels. These practical concerns aside, seeking the *perfect* mate can get in the way of a *good* relationship. Most of us intuitively understand this. But romantic passion has a way of tripping up human reason.

Why do we set up false expectations? The answer has to do with something so deeply ingrained in the human consciousness that it often goes unnoticed. We have the whisper, a rumor, of some distant past in which all was well. We were made for Eden, but we are now expatriates, living a good distance from God's fertile soil. One of the best insights into the way in which spirituality relates to psychology and family relationships is found in the work of a World War II hero who once flew a fighter—for fun, mind you—upside down under the Golden Gate Bridge. His name was Paul "Stormy" Fairweather. He was a wingman for the legendary pilot Chuck Yeager, and at the risk of a court-martial, he called off the first attempt at a D-day invasion because of cloudy weather. The man had guts. Partly through things he learned in dogfights with German pilots and partly through time spent with wounded friends, he developed a unique approach to psychology that rejected many of Sigmund Freud's ideas about "regression" to childlike behaviors and impulses. Instead of seeing the desire to return to idyllic childhood as problematic, he viewed this as an attempt to return to the spiritual peace, unity, and well-being of Eden. He called this the human "birthright." As a Christian, he eventually brought his ideas to the psychology program he established at Fuller Theological Seminary in Pasadena.[7]

---

[7] Fairweather's *Symbolic Regression Psychology* (New York: Irvington, 1981) is unfortunately undervalued by the larger psychological and theological community.

I mention Fairweather because his ideas both help us appreciate the longing for perfection deep within each of us and also help us navigate life in this imperfect, penultimate world. He explains that each of us "is born with an implicit sense that life is to be a garden of harmony and delight"[8] and that this sense is what inspires the best human poetry, literature, and music. This often conflicts with our experience of reality. Everything seems to be out of whack. We lack peace. Our relationships are fragmented. We are in disharmony even when we apply all our strength toward creating deep unity. He explains,

> The person especially feels this uneasiness in his family, where it becomes most obvious that intimacy is only partially experienced. His parents teach him that he should feel at peace with life, but in their very way of living there is an implicit demand that he, the child, dispel their own doubts about the promise of life. In this he is asked to perpetuate the very uneasiness which throws doubt on the meaning of his own existence. Thus he learns no longer to recognize the promise as his own. Moreover, he begins to question its reality. At the same time, he has a deep, perhaps unacknowledged sense of its loss. His life has become a contradictory response to this sense of promise: he at once desires it and distrusts it.[9]

It's as if we live between the fading vision of Eden in our rearview mirror and the vision of a future bliss that is still too far down on the horizon for us to see. Our options seem to be either to (1) choose the way of cynicism, despairing of any peaceful union in this life, or (2) become frustrated when those around us fail to live up to the ideal standards of Eden and the coming kingdom. In our irritation with others who fail to relate to us in an Edenic way, we sometimes become intolerable and perpetually angry that something is not quite right. In this way, we spoil potential gardens for romantic partners and ourselves.

But what if something *isn't* quite right? Would that be a pessimistic attitude? Not really. By recognizing the imperfection of our

---

[8] Ibid., 1.

[9] Ibid., 2.

current situation, we can start to heal ourselves and our relationships. Recognizing the depth of sin's infection is freeing and necessary because it is true, and truth sets us free. Honest acceptance of reality does justice to the fact that we were made for something better than we currently experience, and we can work day by day to provide a slight glimpse of the peaceful human connections promised in the world to come.

Accordingly, we must stop expecting our romantic partners to act as if we were living in paradise. Neither of us own real estate in Eden. Thus so long as we expect the other person to be perfect and ignore our shared imperfection, we will never find harmony in our relationships. We will always have a nagging, but obviously unfair, sense that the *other* person is what stands in the way of our bliss.

But once we've realized we won't find a relationship that can perfectly fulfill our deepest needs, there's more to learn. I am not an unfallen Adam, and my wife is not an unfallen Eve. Nonetheless, something within us seeks out such a perfect person, given how we're designed. When we can't find that person, though, we punish each other for failing to be what none of us *can be*. What a tragedy! As Fairweather writes,

> Persons can actually degenerate to the point where they become defensive against the child self's orientation toward its primary needs. Frequently husbands and wives will act toward each other as if they did not really need each other and as if the comforting which any child would instinctively enjoy did not exist for them. Spouses often cannot express their needs for this kind of personal comfort because they are protecting a precariously instilled sense of "adult" dignity and autonomy. They do not understand that dignity and autonomy themselves must be redefined in terms of a more basic reality, which is the nature of the child self.[10]

This means that we must neither expect too much from a romantic partner nor give up on the pursuit of romantic fulfillment. We should seek erotic joy and unity yet avoid expecting the complete experience of such a reality in this mortal life. Practically speaking,

---

[10] Ibid., 48.

we need to give our loved ones a break when they are weak. At the same time, we need to realize that our loved ones were made for the Garden, and some of the frustrating things they do reflect their discomfort with the weeds that inevitably spring up in earthly life.

As a result of our cynicism and fear, we come to think of true romance as a fairy-tale illusion: "As long as a person doubts the validity of the inner child, he cannot risk a loving relationship, for he doubts the reality of his love and of the energies associated with it. This doubt throws one's inner family as well as his inner child into jeopardy."[11] Erotic despair occurs when we give up on the quest for love. Fairweather explains, "When a man senses the discrepancy between his primal sense of promise and his experience of life and then chooses to believe in his experience of deprivation rather than in his birthright, he becomes full of bitterness and despair. He finds he has lost the poignancy of his will to live."[12]

Leonard Cohen describes this in a stanza that has always haunted me from his song "Bird On The Wire (Bird On A Wire)":

I saw a beggar leaning on his wooden crutch,
he said to me, "You must not ask for so much."
And a pretty woman leaning in her darkened door,
she cried to me, "Hey, why not ask for more?"

In other words, because of our fallen situation, we must not expect from others what we cannot hope to get. At the same time, this doesn't mean we should settle for lives of lovelessness. We must not let the embers of love—for God or for connection with others—die out. When we fight against erotic despair, against the idea that we're just animals trying to release some biological tension or that true love is just a fairy tale—that is when marriages are indeed like sacraments.[13] We become a veiled reality of God's ultimate spiritual reality. When we kiss, we celebrate the unity that once was and soon will be, even

---

[11] Ibid., 54.

[12] Ibid., 5.

[13] I'm not making a Roman Catholic theological proposal here. In my tradition, we have only two formal sacraments—baptism and the Lord's Supper—but since the term is not strictly biblical, enumerating the sacraments is not a major issue for us. I believe other things can rightly be called sacramental by way of analogy.

if after we kiss, we end up fighting about who is supposed to take the kids to school in the morning.

So again, remember that *the one* is the one you've decided to make *the one*. Therefore, courageously traverse this wasteland together, despite the obstacles. Decide together that, in patience and hope, you will endure even the agonies of romantic life. You will endure, confident in God's promises that, despite what it looks like today, we will garden together once more, when the cosmic story takes us back to the Beginning once again. In this, I draw on Robert Capon's insights, when he writes,

> Hence none of the passionate accouterments of our relationships—not the extravagant pleasures of our sexual liaisons, not the till-the-stars-fall, death-and-forever promises of our romances, not the lifelong vows of our marriages—are overstatements. They are merely appropriate responses to the passion that calls us Home. But unless we are willing to accept all the breaks into which that passion may carry us—up to and including the Passion itself—we will welsh on the extravagances and so miss the joy. If the love of the Trinity is not without crisis, pain, and death, ours will not be either. Thus, romance, sex, and marriage always lead elsewhere, into the Home that beckons us.[14]

Disembodied Virtual Romance

Part of the difficulty with romance these days is how technology has transformed how we select our romantic partners. Aziz Ansari and Eric Klinenberg, in the delightful read *Modern Romance*,[15] highlight the ways in which our expectations related to dating and marriage have changed drastically. For instance, guys now frequently ask love interests out for a date via text message. Accordingly, there's a whole new set of protocols for how, and how quickly, to respond.

---

[14] Robert Farrar Capon, *Health, Money, and Love: And Why We Don't Enjoy Them* (Grand Rapids, MI: Eerdmans, 1990), 129.

[15] I learned about Ansari's book, which I highly recommend as both an entertaining and enlightening contribution to our subject, when I met his coauthor, Eric Klinenberg, who spoke at David Zahl's Mockingbird Conference IX (2016) in New York. Klinenberg is a witty personality in his own right.

Meanwhile, the growing acceptance and prevalence of finding dates via online dating sites or dating apps have changed the way we view ourselves and others. On the app Tinder, folks swipe right or left on a profile picture as a way of indicating interest or disinterest in a potential mate.

Whereas people used to marry partners from their own towns, if not their own neighborhoods, people now have an essentially inexhaustible number of partners from which to choose. This becomes an almost unbearable challenge for either party because, no matter how attractive, interesting, and kind a date might be, one need only check an app for a few minutes to learn that there are other potential partners who could be even more desirable.

Said another way, older generations were happy to have someone who seemed good enough, after which they could cultivate a rich history together, but younger generations suffer under the tyranny of a world in which we are constantly reminded that we might not have picked the ideal match. According to *Modern Romance,*

> We want something that's very passionate, or boiling, from the get-go. In the past, people weren't looking for something boiling; they just needed some water. Once they found it, and committed to a life together, they did their best to heat things up. Now, if things aren't boiling, committing to marriage seems premature.
>
> But searching for a soul mate takes a long time and requires enormous emotional investment. The problem is that this search for the perfect person can generate a lot of stress. Younger generations face immense pressure to find the "perfect person" that simply didn't exist in the past when "good enough" was good enough.[16]

Ansari goes on to describe a study in which people were offered free samples of gourmet jams. Folks who sampled and then purchased jam from a display in which only a handful of flavors were offered reported a higher degree of satisfaction with their choice. Those who went to a display with a whole array of flavors ended up regretting

---

[16] Aziz Ansari and Eric Klinenberg, *Modern Romance* (New York: Penguin, 2016), 24–25.

their choice. Maybe they got Pineapple Mango-berry but should have gone for Jalapeño Raspberry!

The application of this study to romance should be obvious. The increasing range of romantic options in our technological age creates a world in which younger generations bear a new burden of having to choose from a bewildering excess of possibilities, and this can lead to an increasing sense of erotic remorse. All this choice, this myriad of digital connections and potential connections, puts a great deal of pressure on a person's external appearance and financial success. It is thus increasingly difficult for folks whom society might deem less than ideal to win a partner over through their warm personalities, profound wisdom, or strength of character, for these things require embodied, personal associations and in-person conversations. Even if a person gets selected for a date, these dates are about performance. Fail to perform well during a short date, fail to look hot, fail to say the right thing, and one is in danger of losing a chance at love. This puts such pressure on people that, as we saw in a previous chapter, people are increasingly and tragically removing themselves from the dating scene altogether and retreating to a virtual world, where only their avatars or carefully crafted online profiles become their primary selves. Already Japan is on alert: their birth rate is declining, and people are failing to make meaningful romantic connections. More than 40 percent of Japanese singles aged eighteen to thirty-four report being virgins.[17]

My colleague at Concordia University Joel Oesch wrote his dissertation on the problems of disembodiment in our technical age. He notes not only how online social networks can *unintentionally* produce lives of loneliness and isolation but also how they can fulfill our unhealthy desire to *intentionally* be isolated.[18] Even more threatening is the way in which quasi-erotic online interaction leads to a world that is deceptive at its core. I'm not just talking about the ways in which unhappy spouses can carry out virtual affairs, or even the way in which online platforms like AshleyMadison.com can

---

[17] "More than 40 Percent of Japan's Adult Singles Are Virgins, Says Study," *The Telegraph*, September 18, 2016.

[18] Joel Oesch, "More than a Pretty Face: Using Embodied Lutheran Theology to Evaluate Community-Building in Online Social Networks" (PhD dissertation, Concordia Seminary, St. Louis, 2015), 209.

facilitate real-world "no-strings-attached" affairs. It's worse than all that, because the virtual world introduces profound deception into the formation of relationships, which are best rooted in the soil of honesty and genuine vulnerability. Oesch explains,

> Ultimately, the virtual world forces society to reexamine questions of authenticity and deception, faithfulness and adultery. For more optimistic OSN [online social network] users, self-representation in any world, digital or real, *necessarily requires* a certain amount of shape-shifting. After all, is not every single social interaction, digital or otherwise, marked by a certain amount of withholding and/or experimentation? A young single man, for example, may meet an attractive woman at a bar, and in an attempt to impress her, may stretch the truth about some of his exploits (e.g., where he's traveled, who he knows, how much he earns). Exaggerations, even flat-out mistruths, are not exactly uncommon in embodied attempts at courtship. Yet even in the mistruths of an over-eager suitor, his body cannot be hidden in the embodied exchange; at least one important piece of truth (in this case, what he looks like, his biological sex, and probably his gender) forces its way into the exchange. No such information necessarily makes itself known in the online world.[19]

The New Logic offers a remedy to all this. We can be honest with ourselves and others because we do not judge by or find our worth merely in external appearances or worldly success. As a community formed by the New Logic of grace, the church is thus to be a refuge from the tyranny of perfection and performance. Of course, in practice, churches too often imbibe the Old Logic of the world, with all the accompanying attention to unhealthy standards of judgment. Nonetheless, by remaining close to the way of the cross, to the radical call of Christ for his people to be a new, alternative community, the church *can* offer something that has become far too rare in our times: a safe place to face reality.

Likewise, the incarnation of the Logos in the person of Jesus of Nazareth indicates the value God places on embodiment and

---

[19] Ibid., 218.

physical existence. Unlike the mystery religion called Gnosticism, a competing perspective that the early church fought resolutely, Christians do not hold that the material world is evil, while the spiritual world is good. On the contrary, just as sin has corrupted mind, will, and emotion, it has infected both the physical and spiritual realms. Fortunately, through Christ, God promises a restoration of heaven (spiritual reality) and earth (physical reality). How is this accomplished? Through grace. And grace reminds us that we ought not to base our relationships on legal demands, performance, and transactions. To be sure, we are free to make wise, practical decisions about whom we marry. But our judgment is not a worldly judgment. We are called to look beyond the surface level—something all too easy to fall into within the world of virtual dating—and develop deep connections with fellow embodied travelers through this life.

Despite the perils of virtual romance, discerning singles are admittedly offered new opportunities. Christians are called to be a gracious people, and this means that while Christianity encourages concrete community interactions, it also recognizes that in our perplexing world, people do not always exist within ideal conditions. Thus although it is usually wise to pursue embodied interactions with potential partners, Christian love and empathy invite us to consider circumstances in which virtual romance can offer delightful opportunities.

For instance, some people are so shy, agoraphobic, or embarrassed by physical disfigurement that they are unable to strike up meaningful relationships in traditional ways. Online communication, in such cases, can offer a chance for these people to demonstrate their inner qualities. Though they might run the risk of having their hearts broken after their first physical meeting, I have met several people who have wagered that the potential embarrassment and disappointment in such a scenario are preferable to constant rejection (say, at a singles bar) and a life utterly devoid of interaction.

Likewise, some individuals live, whether by choice or circumstance, in places where potential partners are scarce. In such settings, without online options, they might be forced to choose from one of only two options: (1) marry someone who is unkind or has no real prospects for supporting a family or (2) give up on romantic life altogether. I've known missionaries, rural pastors, and scientists doing extended fieldwork who've been in situations like this.

Thus it is important to remind each other that the Gospel sets us free to pursue ethical relationships in increasingly dynamic and diverse cultural contexts. Although we are right to be wary about the ways in which technology has allowed us to become isolated, deceptive, and relationally impoverished, we must not make our call to community and embodiment a new law or obligation for individuals in unique circumstances. Most importantly, I've known many people in otherwise "typical" circumstances who have found online dating sites to open up possibilities for romance that are clearly preferable to the singles bar scene. They've found connection, started families, and raised happy children. The days when people would be embarrassed about meeting online are, it seems, a thing of the past, but we need not dredge up that sense of scorn in our efforts to remind ourselves and each other that embodiment and community remain healthy ideals.

The Melancholy Dane

Søren Kierkegaard (1813–55) was a complex but profound religious thinker, though we often think of him primarily as a philosopher. Perhaps his best (but underappreciated) book is his *Works of Love* (1847). Its radical message is a strange one, especially since his own romantic love life was tragic.

He was in love with a woman named Regine Olsen (1822–1904). The couple was engaged for a time, but Kierkegaard broke it off. If ever there was a passionate, youthful infatuation, these two had it. During their engagement, Kierkegaard was a seminary student and wrote his graduate thesis. He was the sort who immersed himself in thought and his studies. The time this took, his desire to write, and his apparent chronic melancholy caused him to doubt that he would be a suitable husband. So he broke things off.

Regine pleaded with him not to leave her, and even threatened suicide. In response, he immaturely acted like a jerk so she would move on. Secretly, however, he remained deeply in love with her throughout his life. He never married, perhaps because his heart belonged to Regine. Many of his works cannot be properly understood without recognizing this deep connection, regret, and longing. Ironically, Regine, her (eventual) husband, and Kierkegaard were buried next to each other in a Copenhagen cemetery.

I mention this partly to show that one of the greatest theological and philosophical writers on the topic of divine and romantic love—Kierkegaard—was unable to practice the sexiness he preached. As a neophyte myself, therefore, readers will hopefully forgive *me* for my own failures to live up to the lofty ideals I am trying to set forth. I also mention it to note that you, the reader, should give yourself the grace to recognize the nature of true love when you encounter it, even when you can't imagine a way to live up to its angelic standards.

In any case, I am on the same page with Kierkegaard regarding the nature of love itself, especially when it comes to the strange idea that, despite the beautiful desire to connect deeply with one and only one person, Christian love is *spiritually promiscuous*. That is, Christians are called to love everyone indiscriminately. Preference is not love, he argues throughout *Works of Love*, but rather an example of selfishness. We love preferentially because it is *our love*; it is a love that makes us feel good, feel loved, feel valued. It is our Christian freedom to love an individual. After vows, it is a sacred duty. But we are nonetheless called to love all. He writes of Jesus' invitation to love all neighbors: "The neighbor is every person, since on the basis of dissimilarity he is not your neighbor, nor on the basis of similarity to you in your dissimilarity from other people. He is your neighbor on the basis of equality with you before God, but unconditionally every person has this equality and has it unconditionally."[20] Therefore, if we are to balk at the idea of loving someone on the first date, it is often because we think we should wait to see if the conditions really are right. We ask ourselves various practical questions when we are dating: Is this potential partner sexually compatible with me? Is he rich enough? Is she pretty enough to ensure that people know I'm a quality person? Is he funny? Is she cool enough for my friends? Such questions assume that before we decide to love, we need to be sure that there will be a good chance of a return on our investment of that love. But as Jay Reinke, a lovable ex-pastor who was featured

---

[20] Søren Kierkegaard, *Works of Love* (Princeton, NJ: Princeton University Press, 2013), 60.

in the documentary *The Overnighters* (2014), once told me during a podcast interview, "Love is not an investment; it is a gift."[21]

Beyond this, Kierkegaard's mind was so acute that he further explored the ways in which sin can take us down a selfish path, even when we are loving someone lowly or seemingly "beneath us." Commenting on Ephesians 5:25 ("Husbands, love your wives, as Christ loved the church and gave himself up for her"), he observes, "To love someone because he is more lowly than you can so easily be the condescension of preferential love and to that extent self-love. No, to love the neighbor is equality."[22] For Kierkegaard, we ought not to love the seemingly unlovable or broken in order to feed our egos, make ourselves feel superior, or have a partner who owes us something. Rather, we should love with God's perspective in mind: we are all equally in need of redemption, and we are all equally loved without measure.

With this in mind, Kierkegaard has some good, practical advice on choosing a mate. To get the whole concept, we should keep the overall discussion of the inexhaustible quality of true love in mind but go back a few years to his book *Either/Or* (1843). In it, he writes of the seeming impossibility of choosing in this life. For the *aesthete*—that is, one who seeks pleasure alone—it is in fact impossible to decide. But for the person set free to act, there lies a hope and possibility. The choice is what makes us human. Consider this passage:

> If you marry, you will regret it; if you do not marry, you will also regret it; if you marry or if you do not marry, you will regret both; whether you marry or you do not marry, you will regret both. . . . Believe a girl, you will regret it; if you do not believe her, you will also regret it; if you believe a girl or you do not believe her, you will regret both; whether you believe a girl or you do not believe her, you will regret both. . . . This, gentlemen, is the sum of all practical wisdom.[23]

---

[21] "The Underdog Pastor," episode 133.

[22] Kierkegaard, *Works of Love*, 60.

[23] Søren Kierkegaard, *Either/Or*, ed. Victor Eremita, trans. Alastair Hannay (New York: Penguin, 2004), 1:37.

The virtuous person escapes the trap of the either/or, of the tyranny of choice, by finding a mature joy in recognizing the sexiness of possibility. He writes, "Were I to wish for anything I would not wish for wealth and power, but for the passion of the possible, that eye which everywhere, ever young, ever burning, sees possibility. Pleasure disappoints, not possibility."[24] This brings us to the point where we can take Kierkegaard's ponderous words and apply them to the process of choosing a spouse in a three-point, practical way.

First, the idea that romance is primarily about calculation is not sexy. Adding up *all* the pros and cons can become a burden that is both impossible—since we don't really know all the potential outcomes of a decision—and also not as much fun. For Kierkegaard, life is about the youthful, sexy risk of jumping into an unknown possibility. That's what makes us human. That's what makes life interesting. Of course, we shouldn't jump into dangerous or obviously doomed relationships. But once we have a good sense that we have a good partner, the idea that we need to be scientific about all the potential profits and losses turns out to be misguided. Profits and losses make sense in banking or in a spirituality based on karma. In the New Logic of grace, such things are almost irrelevant.

With the New Logic, we have everything we need. We have infinite divine love. Nothing, in the ultimate sense, is to be gained or lost. Once we recognize this, everything is to be *enjoyed*. The whole journey. The whole thrill of the risk in taking a leap of faith and tying a knot and struggling through the inevitable challenges of marriage with someone who, like you, is interested in the "passion of the possible."

Second, we should not base our romantic relationships on the power of pleasure. The efficacy of opiates, caffeine, and puppy love all end up waning for the one who enjoys them. We build up a tolerance. We need more and more until the returns are so diminished, we become enslaved to such things just to stay *normal*. Kierkegaard insists that pleasure disappoints. This isn't to say that we should be too prudish to enjoy pleasure. It is a warning that immediate pleasure is never going to be a wise basis for any lifestyle, decision, commitment, or purchase.

---

[24] Ibid., 56.

The immediate pleasure will *always* fade, and thus we will *always* be in danger of experiencing buyer's remorse. If we don't recognize this and we get married, we are tragically prone to blame our spouse for something that is beyond his or her control. It would be as if we started yelling at a bottle of Jack Daniels for not being as potent this year as it was when we were in college, when we first started drinking in earnest. In such a case, the problem isn't with the whiskey, of course; it is with our own experience of the whiskey. The problem is on *our* end in such cases.

Third, with the New Logic of grace, we are freed from the tyranny of second-guessing our decisions when inevitable discomfort and conflict come. All this hinges on recognizing the inevitability of regret. It's always odd to me when athletes are interviewed after a major loss for which they are partly responsible and claim, "I have no regrets, man." They probably mean they can't beat themselves up for this, that they prepared well, and that they did their best. Nevertheless, I'd hope an athlete would care half as much as loyal fans, who do in fact regret a loss. Regret is part of life. Kierkegaard's insight here, though, is that we will regret something about *every* path we choose.

At first, this seems to be a pessimistic, depressing idea. But it is liberating and hopeful at its core. We will all regret the roads we didn't travel, not asking someone to the dance, not taking a job offer, not going on a vacation. We regret because there are things we have lost in every decision. Own it. Admit it. There's nothing wrong in that, especially if it is true. The problem isn't with regret; the problem is with obsessing about that regret and with failing to recognize the reality that regrets are inevitable but not the final word on a life well lived. Regret also is an inevitable experience for all of us at some point, since we live all our years pressing on in hope of the future kingdom and with a sense of loss common to all exiles of Eden.

Suppose you are overcome with anxiety about whether or not to propose marriage or whether to say yes or no to a proposal. You should remember that, at some point in the future, you will feel a sense of regret about whatever you decide. Recognizing this will be helpful when that regret comes. For when it does come, you can remember that you would have also experienced regret had you made a different decision. By recognizing this, you can go easy on the partner you decide to marry. After all, usually *he or she* isn't the primary reason for regret. Regret arises because you can't choose an infinite number of paths in the same mortal existence. Face it. Get over it. And give your partner a break.

This doesn't mean we should be cavalier about choosing a spouse. Rather, by dispensing with our fear of making a regrettable decision, we can start thinking soberly about which path we would regret more. I've tried this method on other decisions, and it works like a charm.

Say I want to get some work done at home. I also want to go fishing with my friends. If I stay home, I'll be bummed out when I see the Facebook photos of my friends holding up big fish. If I go fishing, I'll be bummed on Monday when I'm backlogged. Which regret is more existentially painful? If I go out with my friends a lot, then I should get to work. But if I don't see them often, I might miss out on something I'll remember fondly for the rest of my life.

In a romantic context, this is even more applicable. If I don't marry a particular person—recognizing his or her good and bad qualities—how much will this eat me up in the future? That's the question you should ask. To ask whether that same person is *the one* is like asking whether he or she is the sort of person who will provide you with a romantic life in which you will have *no regrets whatsoever*. That is too tall an order for any mortal to satisfy.

In light of this, if you are thinking about getting hitched, here are the three most important questions I think you can ask yourself:

Who am I?
Who should I be for others, given this identity?
Which potential mate can best allow and inspire me to be my
    best self?

Answer those questions and you will have a better chance than most at a happy marriage. You are called to pour out the infinite love God offers you to the world around you. Find someone who will partner with you in that pouring out of love. Pour it out for your children, for your neighbors, and for your enemies. Do this and, along the way, I bet you won't be too stingy when it comes to offering a cup of love to your spouse.

When the Rubber Meets the Road

This book began on the eve of my son Augustine's eighteenth birthday and concluded a few days before his nineteenth birthday. He wrote several contributions and originally planned to respond to most of the chapters. However, in the time between the start and end of the writing process, he grew a lot and eventually ended up in a serious relationship. At first, my wife, Stacie, and I were worried that he had become too serious too quickly in his relationship. We thought, "Sure, we dig his girlfriend a lot. Heck, even if they break up, we hope she'll come around and stay connected to the family. But don't they want to see what else is out there? Don't they need to explore all the options?" But then Auggie reminded me that such thinking, while reasonable in its own way, isn't the way I've been explaining sexual integrity in this book. He explained that while there are some who jump into a relationship too quickly because they are looking for security in a chaotic world, he was after something else: channeling infinite love and committing to someone as a witness to *agape* and the New Logic.

Guest Contribution: Augustine Mallinson, "Applying These Ideas to a Concrete Dating Relationship"

A lot of humanity's collective time and effort has gone into trying to understand God and love. I'd wager that most if not all philosophical dialogues touch on one or the other. I'd wager further that all of these dialogues actually deal with both, even if the connection is only implicit. Yet despite so much ink spilled over the last few millennia on these two intertwined topics, yet we seem no closer to understanding any of it as a society. God and love matter to us, but we can't seem to truly grasp either topic.

More worrying still, it seems that the people who are supposed to be able to offer concrete wisdom on these matters often cannot. I suppose we all get lost somewhere along the way; the experts and gurus are no exception. Those with years behind them often seem to forget what it was like to be young. Those in their youth can't fathom what the tonic called life has done to and for the older folks. We are all just like junior high students talking about sex behind the school before our moms pick us up. We have a lot of wild and bold ideas about making love, but it's not clear that anyone in the conversation has yet experienced the act itself. Similarly, at the risk of offending those in my father's discipline, many theologians appear to have lots of fancy ways of talking about divinity, but it seems that they haven't actually experienced the deep reality of it.

The problem is that many of the professionals, the theologians, and the love doctors have a partial knowledge of the truth, so they feel more confident than the rest of us when making bold statements. They forget how much they don't know, how much mystery remains in the world. They forget that they know little more about real love and the divine than junior high kids know about sexual intercourse. I don't blame any of us in this ignorance, though. I'll admit the romance experts and theologians know much more than I do, but it's easy to forget how unfathomable these subjects are.

All this to say I believe we should take everything we hear anyone say about God or love with a grain of salt. We must evaluate everything we are taught with a critical eye or ear (depending on the medium). My dad is as compelling as most teachers I've heard on the subject tackled in this book, but even he doesn't have comprehensive knowledge about the mysterious movements of God and women. He may even change his mind about some of what he wrote before the book is a year old. And that's OK. For me, what matters is that we maintain both curiosity and humility when we approach the topics of sex, God, and love.

The most I have to offer here is my personal experience. In my own relationship with my girlfriend, Sydnie, I'm bold to say that I'm "in love." That sounds like a big statement for a young man, and it is a serious one, I'll admit. But we've been together for some time now, so it isn't outrageous by conventional standards. Yet I can say I love her without waiting to see if in fact this is true, because while there are indeed deep emotions involved, this love is not about emotional responses to something Sydnie has or hasn't done. It doesn't depend on what she can do for me in my life, how good she'll make me look as an adult, or how much she'll boost my ego.

Whatever he might get right or wrong in this book, I'll always agree with my dad that no matter how miserably I fail in the attempt, I should try to love everyone. I should offer love to the waiter at the restaurant I might go to. I should offer love to the driver who cuts me off. I should offer love to everyone around me and to everyone living far from me. *Everyone.* That doesn't cheapen the love between two people in a relationship. Instead, I can be confident in my love of Sydnie because we have a shared story, we have developed shared interests, and we support each other in our struggles. The only difference between my ability to promise to love her and my ability to love others is that it is easier for me to love her than to love my enemies. Should she do something to irritate me, that would hardly be a good reason to stop loving and move on as you might with that anonymous driver who cut you off.

As much as I agree with my dad's idea of erotic virtue in principle, I thought he was being a bit hypocritical when he worried that I might be committing to someone too soon. There are, of course, bad relationships that become serious too quickly, especially when one or both people in the relationship are insecure about themselves and their place in the world. But I don't think that holding off, perpetually waiting for the "perfect" girl to appear before your eyes, is consistent with the bigger idea that true love is independent of what is gained from a relationship. In a transactional relationship, you give love until you stop receiving it. You are not giving love freely; you are giving it to one person merely because he or she gives it back to you. You are putting energy into the relationship as an investment, and if that relationship's stock starts crashing, you might plan to sell your shares and move your love investment somewhere else.

True love is what comes before and flows from this relationship. This sort of relationship results in the couple saying to each other, "No, I'm not going to be yet another person who runs away from you when times are hard." For this reason, I told my dad that if I only did one good and significant thing in my life, I wanted it to be that I showed someone else love. This also fits my Lutheran approach to Christianity, in which *vocation* in all aspects of life is vitally important. Accordingly, the vocation of husband, wife, boyfriend, or girlfriend is not a post one abandons at the first sign of trouble. Instead, the vocation of love is to be a partner through life and to be someone the other person can count on to be there through all of it, even the troubles. The pair will share experiences, good and bad, and they will be able to laugh about them at the end. Along the way, it is this relationship that will allow one to pick the other up and allow them to move forward together when the need arises. This message of love is so powerful that I hope to be able to pass on the wisdom of erotic virtue to my own children. I have seen it at work in my folks' life, and it is beginning to take shape in mine. One day, maybe I'll get the chance to share this sort of love with my own children.

You Saw Her Bathing on the Roof (Porn and Commodified Bodies)

Your faith was strong, but you needed proof
You saw her bathing on the roof
Her beauty and the moonlight overthrew you
—Leonard Cohen, "Hallelujah"

A little dust devil of a music festival takes place in the desert near me. It isn't a big mad event like Burning Man. It's a bit more family friendly. Not knowing much about the festival prior to our visit, my family went to see an Australian artist perform whom we don't get to see that often. During one evening at the festival, my wife and I sat down on a rough wooden bench to watch something we figured might be important to investigate for this book: a burlesque act. A Southwest desert rock band plays music between and during performances in which the musicians' wives dance, stripping down to old-timey lingerie. Stacie and I were curious to understand the phenomenon of burlesque, especially given the diversity of its enthusiastic audience. We were surprised to find that, instead of an audience filled with lecherous and drunk men, the most ardent fans included ostensibly happy adult couples, a few teen hippy girls, and a lot of smiling adult women.

Once the show started, Stacie was seated on a crowded bench a few rows back from the stage, and I stood behind her, since there wasn't room on the bench. Enthusiastic women started crowding nearer to us, straining to see the show. So I decided to get a bit more space by sitting down closer to the stage. That way, though my view of the stage would be obstructed, I could stretch and ease the tension on my lower back and observe the crowd. This vantage point turned out to be helpful in my attempt to understand the burlesque phenomenon.

First, I focused on faces in the crowd. I had a direct view of the bandleader, who played slide guitar and sang while his wife was dancing. He gave me a knowing look, as if to confirm that we were both in on a joke. But what was the joke? Perhaps it was that the parody of an old-fashioned adult show was not an exercise in lewd titillation, though that's what a casual observer might have assumed, but a celebration of something good. These performers were people who had passed through trials. By "these people," I'm referring to the whole lot of us: the musicians, the dancers, and the audience. These were people whose hearts had been broken, whose bodies had been objectified and perhaps abused. Despite all that, the dancing was a celebration of an emotional resistance to a tragic world. The dancers had a variety of body types. None of them resembled flawless supermodels. And they danced with abandon, fearlessly. There definitely was an inner beauty on display.

Part of burlesque etiquette is that the audience is supposed to hoot and holler when a sexy move is made. For this show, people were invited to throw bottle caps as if they were tipping the dancers. As the commotion continued, I turned my attention to the young women watching the performance. Their eyes weren't lustful. They were filled with celebration. They were reveling in the power of women to dance with minimal clothing, with beautifully imperfect bodies. Thin and wiry, heavy and curvy, or acne scarred: these women were recognized as *sexy* by the whole group.

Burlesque isn't for everyone. Some of you dear readers may be distressed simply by the thought of Stacie and me attending this show. But hear me out when I suggest there was a strength on display that had nothing to do with what one associates with a seedy strip club. Granted, they didn't capture or perfectly reflect what I'm hunting down in this book. But they definitely kept the mystery alive and kept me on the quest for something beneath the surface of modern sexuality. They did point in some odd way to erotic virtue.

There's probably no way to confirm my suspicion, but I'm certain at least some of the dancers were there to take back something that had been taken from them earlier in their lives. I was startled by my own response to this moment. We were there in the cool desert evening, re-creating an old western saloon with melodramatic characters. A comforting darkness surrounded the dimly lit stage.

The women moved to perform a scene on a side stage, just behind the bench where Stacie was sitting. Instead of standing up to see the scene—not out of prudery, mind you, but mainly because I was achy and lazy—I found myself wanting to stretch my lower back out even further. It had been a long day of walking and setting up tents. I closed my eyes and smiled. I prayed a prayer of gratitude for life. My life. I might have residual resentments and childhood regrets, but as a suburban white guy with loving and protecting parents, I was pretty fortunate. I was also grateful that, at least for that moment, I could let down my guard. I'm the oldest of eight children, with the youngest five being girls. As an educator, I've been constantly about protecting students from manipulation and exploitation. Over the years, I've heard too many infuriating stories of manipulation and coercion to recount. In each of those tales, the mistreatment—particularly of young women—took place in the ostensibly holy, safe, and respectable halls of society. *Here* we were at an ostensibly licentious place, at a seemingly bawdy spectacle. And yet I could rest for the moment knowing that, for some reason I still don't fully understand, there was no reason to fear sexual misconduct in that place, that night. Here, in this anarchic desert party, the women were in charge of their own personal space. They had the power. And they were dancing as much for themselves as for the audience. In any case, this wasn't a strip show or a show for "gentlemen," and it certainly wasn't as tragic as the ways in which bodies are displayed throughout our culture in order to sell products.

Exploitation in Upstanding, Corporate Contexts

Lest you think the sin of commodifying female bodies is something one only finds in dodgy strip clubs or in other recognizable dens of iniquity, our erotic illness has infected the very core of Western society. Because our exploitative approach to women's physical allure is a part of everyday culture, it has a way of habituating our society toward a deep and unfortunate vice. To illustrate this, I turn once again to the poetry of spoken-word artist Micah Bournes, who offered the following poem when I first asked him to contribute to the book. It gets right to the heart of the point I'm trying to make in this chapter. *Note*: For those readers in the eastern United States, Carl's Jr. is the same fast-food burger chain you know as Hardee's.

Guest Contribution: Micah Bournes, "Carl's Jr."

If you are a fan of vagina, breasts, and butt
eat this hamburger
If you like seeing women in bikinis and booty shorts
watch this sport
drink this beer
drive this truck
use this cologne
chew this gum
dine at this restaurant
buy this . . . anything
You see, the problem does not begin in the brothel
The problem goes beyond pimps and johns
The problem starts, with little boys like me

This, is how I learned to be a man
I remember being three chin-hairs past puberty
Watching . . . basketball
When a commercial came on
a nameless model in a tiny bathing suit
was throwing soap suds all over herself and a black SUV
All because Carl's Jr. wanted to sell me . . . a sandwich

Everything I saw
the car, the meat, the woman could all be mine
I just had to open my wallet
and buy combo number 3
and buy her dinner
and buy her a drink
and buy her a ring
and buy her
but be a gentleman about it

tip her well at the gentleman's club
take her to a five star restaurant
so she really does owe you

This, is not a holier than thou rant
I also have been in bondage to my desires
Now I'm Harriet Tubman pleading
with slaves who believe their master is kind
Enjoying your vice is not the same as freedom
Understand, we have been brainwashed
My entire life, I was taught that
buying sexual satisfaction was an American right
Love, is a sentimental fantasy, sex is harmless pleasure
and yes my beautiful parents taught me better
but they could not save me from the sexy cheese-burgers
the commercials
the billboards
the little-boy talk in middle-school locker rooms
the problem does not begin in the brothel
the problem starts with little boys like me hearing myths
    about virginity
Like having it makes a girl pure
but makes a boy less of a man
while taking it makes him more of one
but giving it makes a girl a whore
and having it stolen makes her unstable
un-healable, untouchable

The truth is, the purity of your spirit
has nothing to do with your sexual history
There are saints with a dark past
and virgins with lustful hearts
Discipline and self-control makes you more of a man
not less of one
And any woman that endures abuse and survives should
be honored for her strength not despised for her scars

We have all been betrayed
by each other
we all need forgiveness

pointing fingers is pointless
macho men and seductive women
are boys and girls living out the lies we were taught
we did not chose this time and culture
we are both victim and culprit
we have all suffered
but we are more than our suffering
we are able to heal, together
to truth-away the lies
to re-wire our manipulated minds
to remember the beauty of our bodies
will never be an enterprise
we are nature that cannot be owned
we are mountain, ocean, moon
We are creatures reflecting
the divinity who created us
we are loved
we are love that can never be sold
we are beauty that can never be bought

A Rabbi and a Playboy Bunny Walk into a Bar

Rabbi Shmuley Boteach and veteran actress and former Playboy Bunny Pamela Anderson wrote a thoroughly sane opinion piece for the *Wall Street Journal*: "Take the Pledge: No More Indulging Porn."[1] Their admonitions are worthy of consideration:

> From our respective positions of rabbi-counselor and former Playboy model and actress, we have often warned about pornography's corrosive effects on a man's soul and on his ability to function as husband and, by extension, as father. This is a public hazard of unprecedented seriousness given how freely available, anonymously accessible and easily disseminated pornography is nowadays.
>
> Put another way, we are a guinea-pig generation for an experiment in mass debasement that few of us would have

---

[1] Shmuley Boteach and Pamela Anderson, "Take the Pledge: No More Indulging Porn," *Wall Street Journal*, August 31, 2016.

ever consented to, and whose full nefarious impact may not be known for years. How many families will suffer? How many marriages will implode? How many talented men will scrap their most important relationships and careers for a brief onanistic thrill? How many children will propel, warp-speed, into the dark side of adult sexuality by forced exposure to their fathers' profanations?

Notice that this talk of *debasement* isn't coming from the evangelical right here. This is a matter of universally accessible wisdom, what the rabbis call *chochmah* in Hebrew. *Chochmah* can be found among the pagan nations, so the rabbinic perspective goes, and should be embraced, though if these same pagan teachers claim to have *Torah*, or God's revealed Law, it is not to be believed.

Boteach and Anderson recognize that it is not feasible to stamp out pornography through strong legislation or Internet regulation. Rather, they rightly point to what this book is exploring: the cultivation of virtue within a caring community and a return to healthy eroticism. What I'm calling a return to *sexiness*, they describe as a "sensual revolution": "The sensual revolution would replace pornography with eroticism—the alloying of sex with love, of physicality with personality, of the body's mechanics with imagination, of orgasmic release with binding relationships. In an age where public disapproval is no longer an obstacle to personal disgrace, we must turn instead to the appeal of self-interest. Simply put, we must educate ourselves and our children to understand that porn is for losers—a boring, wasteful and dead-end outlet for people too lazy to reap the ample rewards of healthy sexuality."[2] Dialogue like this can help build unlikely coalitions and strengthen virtue formation in our society. And why shouldn't it? Now that the dust has settled on the sexual revolution, and now that explicit Christian concerns are no longer directly dominant in the public square, we can start asking about what matters: the health of our communities. Perhaps we are mature enough as a culture to start talking about porn the way we've learned to talk about mental health and alcoholism. This need not

---

[2] Ibid.

be a matter of private shame and despair. Rather, it is a public health concern that we can address collectively and with love.

Bathsheba Wasn't the Villain

When I mention Pamela Anderson, I fear that some are inclined to turn up their noses, thinking that a "slutty bimbo" has nothing valuable to offer in terms of erotic virtue. Even when "women like her" say something appropriate and wise, we have a way of ignoring them. Worse, we persist in blaming those who have been objectified rather than recognizing the ways in which those who have profited from (or secretly leered at) her body can go about their daily routines as dignified professionals without being scorned. Blaming the desired body for male sin is nothing new. It's as old as postagricultural society. In "Hallelujah," Leonard Cohen sings about the episode in 2 Samuel 11, where David sees Bathsheba undressed:

> It happened, late one afternoon, when David arose from his couch and was walking upon the roof of the king's house, that he saw from the roof a woman bathing; and the woman was very beautiful. And David sent and inquired about the woman. And one said, "Is not this Bathshe'ba, the daughter of Eli'am, the wife of Uri'ah the Hittite?" So David sent messengers, and took her; and she came to him, and he lay with her. (Now she was purifying herself from her uncleanness.) Then she returned to her house. And the woman conceived; and she sent and told David, "I am with child." (vv. 2–5)

The king, a *man after God's own heart*, responded to genuine beauty with a long string of injustices. He committed adultery and impregnated a woman who was in a position of weakness relative to his social power. David then tried to cover his tracks by encouraging Uriah to go home and sleep with his wife. That way, Bathsheba's child could be passed off as Uriah's own. Uriah, however, was too faithful a soldier. He refused to have fun while duty called. So David ended up sending Uriah to the front lines to die.

The root problem in all this wasn't Bathsheba's nakedness. Maybe she should have been more careful about where she drew a bath, for her own sake. But to focus on that—as if modesty were the moral of this tragic tale—would be to heap injustice upon injustice. The problem is that women have been treated like property far too often in human history. But even when they are honored as something more valuable than mundane property, we still tend to blame them for the trouble caused by lusting and coveting. And when that trouble comes, we sometimes objectify further, shifting the blame onto the body that men apparently find too irresistible to leave alone. The problem is with the human heart, therefore, not the exquisiteness of the object of lust.

This should be at the forefront of all our conversations regarding modesty. There's a place for modesty, to be sure. But there is also a way such thinking can have unintended, negative consequences. For instance, I invited a Muslim acquaintance to speak to my world religions class a while back. He spent a lot of time talking about how hard it is to pray if you accidentally glance at a woman's ankle. That, he explained, is why women—even veiled women—have no place in a house of worship alongside men. My point isn't to pick on Islam. Rather, it's to note that, whether we are talking about halter tops and yoga pants or burqas and hijabs, lustful eyes have a way of finding something to ogle, no matter how little skin is revealed. The way to resolve this problem, I believe, is to align the human heart and refocus human eyes, not to put tarps over all the objects of desire.

By way of application, Christian communities are right to challenge secular habits of selling things through overly sexualized ads. It's good to protect young people from the bombardment of sexual images that can distort healthy development. It's even appropriate for parents to offer wisdom regarding attire. But the problem isn't with nudity in museums or even in movies: the problem is the way the human form is presented, treated, and used.

One of the most beautiful, intimate, and—dare I say—erotic passages in the New Testament is in Luke 7:36–50. Jesus goes to a Pharisee's house to have a meal and reclines at the dinner table. In older Hebrew custom, people would usually sit cross-legged on the floor to dine. But this practice reflects the Persian, Greek, and Roman custom of lying sideways. Hearing about this, a "sinner" runs in to be near Jesus. The text offers no guarantee that her sin was sexual, though many through the ages have assumed she was a prostitute. I suspect this was the case, not because sexual sin is the only sin the Bible cares about, but because it's the sort of sin that would cause a community to label her in this way. If this was the case, the image of this woman touching a reclining Jesus is an intimate one indeed.

She must have heard Jesus preach before, from the way she responded to his presence in her town. And whatever he said in his sermon, it must have been packed with the New Logic, because she couldn't be held back from inviting herself over to the Pharisee's house to meet Jesus. This woman came in with an alabaster jar of essential oil, the sort of thing popular in the Middle East (and hippy boutiques), and then had the audacity to go right to the prophet from Nazareth. Then, "standing behind him at his feet, weeping, she began to wet his feet with her tears and wiped them with the hair of her head and kissed his feet and anointed them with the ointment" (v. 38).

That had to have been an unforgettable scene. Note how tenderly, how sensually, this scene played out. I'm sometimes uncomfortable when people want to hold hands in a circle and pray, because touching skin to skin is unmistakably intimate. Feet, bodily fluid, and hair are all involved here. Jesus didn't blush. He didn't pull back. As we might expect, the Pharisee disapproved and remarked, "If this man were a prophet, he would have known who and what sort of woman this is who is touching him, for she is a sinner" (v. 39). Of course, even a nonprophet might withdraw from this woman's act in polite company.

Jesus didn't flinch, however. Instead, he tells a parable about forgiveness, then explains,

> "Do you see this woman? I entered your house; you gave me no water for my feet, but she has wet my feet with her tears and wiped them with her hair. You gave me no kiss, but from the time I came in she has not ceased to kiss my feet. You did not anoint my head with oil, but she has anointed my feet with ointment. Therefore I tell you, her sins, which are many, are forgiven—for she loved much. But he who is forgiven little, loves little." And he said to her, "Your sins are forgiven." (44–48)

From this, we get two important lessons. First, Jesus is on the side of the sinners, including women who—for whatever reason, often because of poverty and abandonment—are in the sex trade. Accordingly, anything we say against pornography, prostitution, or adult performance must keep this reality in mind. Second, Jesus isn't distressed by human touch, beauty, and feminine proximity. Why not? Because His heart was in the right place as he let this woman draw near.[3]

Leaders in the church should take note of this whole episode in Luke 7 and ask, Are the sermons we offer the sort of messages that cause sinners to run *to us* with gratitude and tenderness or the sort that cause sinners to flee in shame and sorrow? Is our teaching something so desperately needed that people will break with normal protocols of polite society to weep with us? If not, this is a good time to reframe our conversation about sexuality and invite a weeping world to come to an alternative community of holy intimacy.[4]

Adultery in My Heart

Former president Jimmy Carter created media waves when he spoke about lust in a manner that was familiar to evangelicals but in a way that sounded odd to secular ears. In a 1976 interview with *Playboy* (which has now, interestingly, shifted to nonpornographic content), he said the following:

> Christ said, "I tell you that anyone who looks on a woman with lust has in his heart already committed adultery." I've looked on a lot of women with lust. I've committed adultery in my heart many times. This is something that God recognizes I will do—and I have done it—and God forgives me for it. But that doesn't mean that I condemn someone who not only looks on a woman with lust but who leaves his wife and shacks up with

---

[3] Note, however, that I don't mean to suggest that men in positions of influence, especially pastors, should allow themselves to be in intimate positions that they might exploit for their own gratification. The number of stories I've heard about such goings-on is nauseating. I'm simply pointing out that there is nothing inherently wrong with loving, nonsexualized touch and that erotic virtue doesn't hinge on keeping women covered and at a distance.

[4] This isn't to say that Christians ought not be clear about sin, injustice, and holiness. On the contrary, I'm convinced that Jesus' clear understanding of the woman's situation was the basis of her respect for whatever it was he taught.

somebody out of wedlock. Christ says, don't consider yourself better than someone else because one guy screws a whole
bunch of women while the other guy is loyal to his wife. The guy
who's loyal to his wife ought not to be condescending or proud
because of the relative degree of sinfulness.

At the time, this interview generated a lot of negative criticism. This fact
alone was unfortunate, since Carter was only stating—under the cloak
of grace—what I assume is a real experience for many faithful church-
goers. In addition to his own confession, he was also trying to communicate a nonjudgmental attitude regarding those who did not live up
to biblical standards in other areas of life. His words should have been
received more charitably, I believe. There's one exception I must take,
however, concerning his interpretation of Jesus. Granted, his interpretation seems to be in line with what most conservative Christians believe
about the nature of lust and the Sermon on the Mount. But we might not
have properly understood his message.

The original statement from Jesus is as follows: "You have heard
that it was said, 'You shall not commit adultery.' But I say to you that
every one who looks at a woman lustfully has already committed
adultery with her in his heart" (Matt. 5:27–28). Most interpret this as
equating an inner experience of sexual arousal or desire with the act
of sleeping with someone else's spouse. This interpretation is only
partly true.

This business about the relative weight of sins is always a tricky
one. When Christians point out that we are all sinners in need of
redemption and that we should not judge others, they are making
an important point about our relationship with an absolutely holy
God. In that vein, Jesus reminds us not to be judgmental in order to
avoid receiving judgment upon ourselves (Matt. 7:1–3). In this, He
is not obliterating the difference between sins but instead is stating
that when we get into the moral bean counting game, we always lose.
Thus we should avoid calculating the weight of sins because we are to
spend more of our time focused on the healing and gracious cover-
ing of sinners rather than on measuring their condemnation.

James 2:10 tells us, "For whoever keeps the whole Law but fails in
one point has become guilty of all of it." This is a statement that takes
us back to the devastating thrust of the commandment(s) against

coveting.[5] Think you've fulfilled the demands of the Decalogue? You didn't kill anyone? You're generally honest? Fine, but is that because you have a pure heart, or is it because you are afraid of human and divine wrath? Do you *want* to break the commandments? Then you too are in need of redemption. The commandment against coveting, in other words, reminds us of humanity's universal need for redemption. This is a very important spiritual reminder.

But none of this entails the idea that all sins are morally equivalent. For example, speeding on a clear freeway in the morning is not as heinous as genocide. To think otherwise is to dissolve moral reasoning entirely. Ethics, as a philosophical discipline, is frequently about finding ways to choose the lesser of two evils within a dilemma that pits two values against each other. But to make every infraction equal is to inadvertently give permission to abandon moral reasoning. The moral evaluation of actions, we must remember, is an invitation not to self-righteousness but rather to self-improvement. By recognizing the gravity of *this* versus *that* course of action, we can take steps toward being better, albeit imperfect, people.

Now recall Jimmy Carter's rhetorical point: He was saying that while he remained committed to the biblical teachings, he wasn't in the business of looking down his nose at others. He understood that this life was a struggle involving a tension between who we'd like to be and who we in fact are. But to go to the extreme position that all deeds are equivalent is wrongheaded. Classically, the idea that sins are all equal was a peculiar Stoic doctrine. Stoic philosophers taught that one either does or does not have virtue. An act either is or is not on the right path. Virtue isn't divisible, and neither is vice. The Stoics were pretty serious about virtue, and I tend to like these writers, especially Seneca, whose writings contain far more wisdom than folly. They did the best one could with the Old Logic. But the New Logic emerges from the ashes of the true Law's fire sermon. It roots out hidden sin, lays sinners low, and accuses. It brings us at last to the holy fear expressed in the Requiem Mass, particularly the part called the "Dies Irae," or Day of Wrath:

---

[5] Note that some church bodies, such as Lutherans and Catholics, number the Ten Commandments in such a way that nine and ten are both about coveting, whereas Reformed and evangelical Christians end up with only the tenth commandment condemning coveting.

What shall I, frail man, be pleading?
Who for me be interceding,
When even the just are mercy needing?

Even the *just* are mercy needing? This raises the moral bar beyond even the Stoics' reach. In his Sermon on the Mount, Jesus intensified the severity of the Law or, more precisely, He revealed its true intensity. Then He invited all this divine fury into His own tortured body. For a moment during his lifetime, He wasn't sure if the Father in heaven was there with Him anymore (Matt. 27:46). This is the centerpiece of a theology of the cross. It is the core of Christian proclamation.

The crucifixion of all our guilt should, in a sense, be the end of it. It should, but I've encountered far too many young adults who grew up in devout evangelical churches who believe that Jesus can cover all sins, but they spend extraordinary proportions of their lives obsessing over their sense that they commit adultery every time they see an attractive person of the opposite sex and experience some form of arousal. Self-loathing and obsessions about obsessions can become an unproductive cycle of frustration for young people. It's similar to substance addiction. I've never met an addict who claimed that self-loathing helped him or her get clean. Rather, I've heard many accounts of lives wherein self-loathing led to increasingly destructive inebriation.

People obsess about perceived or real guilt, unless they are psychopaths. When it comes to the question of lust, it is true that unholy desire reminds us we are spiritual beggars like all the rest. If lust becomes a major part of our thought lives, we do well to take note and assess whether we've gone off course. Perhaps our excessive lust indicates that something else is wrong in our lives, and it can lead us to moral and emotion vortexes whose force is beyond our power to escape. Thus if someone says that he or she constantly feels attracted to a beautiful passerby or that the thought of that person causes a level of physical arousal, that's normal. If, however, someone confides that he or she is scheming to seduce or is obsessing over someone else, this is something worth trying to quell.

I wager that the *lust* Jesus is talking about in Matthew 5:27–28 is not about natural physiological responses to routine visual stimuli.

It isn't about passing mental images. It's about a deep longing for something unlawful, scheming for something wrong we would do if only there were a foolproof plan to get away with it. It's about envy and ravenous hunger.

The same word (γυναῖκα) that most translations render as "woman" indicates that the person is a "wife" in more than half of the instances where it occurs in the New Testament. Perhaps more interestingly, the Greek word that most translations render as "lust" (ἐπιθυμῆσαι) is the word the Septuagint (the Greek translation of the Old Testament in use at the time of Jesus) uses for "covet." The Septuagint's command not to covet a neighbor's wife includes the same Greek words used in Jesus' statement about lust and adultery.

Many people suffer under a burden of shame when hearing Jesus say, "Every time you get aroused, you are despicable and adulterous," but he's actually saying something more like this:

> Didn't you self-righteous religious folks remember what you learned when you were kids, studying the Ten Commandments? You go around feeling pretty good about yourselves, gossiping about colleagues who have had affairs. But don't you remember how the commandments wrap up by reminding us that coveting is a sin? You wish you could get away with what your shamed adulterer did. You yourself keep trying to flirt with your friend's wife, but the only reason you didn't sleep with her is that she rebuffed your uncomfortable advances. That wasn't virtue; that was cowardice. You are still in need of redemption. Your heart is sick.

Too often, instead of hearing the words of Jesus directed at themselves, religious people deflect the sting of this convicting word and direct it toward poor young adults, who are filled with new hormones they didn't ask for, and tell them that the new brainwaves firing should cause them to weep spiritual tears until the day they quench the fire of their libidos. Woe to us all for setting up such a tragically tortured situation for young adults, who have enough trouble as it is in our perplexing times.

Again, I'm not trying to render a Christian *fatwa* on the topic of what we can and can't get away with in our thoughts. I'm questioning why we in the Christian world spend so much time worrying about something that is at best a peccadillo (such as an occasional sexually explicit thought) when even our big sins don't disqualify us from the love of Christ.[6] Martin Luther encourages us to remind each other of the comfort and freedom offered by the Gospel, even with respect to the uncomfortable topic of lust, however we define it. As Luther explained, commenting on Galatians 5:18,

> And with these words: "If you are led by the Spirit you are not under the law," you may greatly comfort yourself, and others that are grievously tempted. For it often happens, that a man is so vehemently assailed with wrath, hatred, impatience, carnal desire, heaviness of spirit, or some other lust of the flesh, that he cannot shake them off, no matter how hard he tries. What should he do in this case? Should he despair? No, [God forbid]; but let him say to himself: your flesh fights and rages against the Spirit. Let it rage as long as it wants: only make sure that, in any case you do not consent to it, to fulfill the desires of that lust, but walk wisely and follow the leading of the Spirit. In so doing you are free from the law. It accuses and terrifies you (I grant) but this is altogether in vain. In this conflict therefore of the flesh against the Spirit, there is nothing better, than to have the Word of God before your eyes, and therein to seek the comfort of the Spirit.[7]

Here Luther admits that earthly life is plagued by internal impulses that conflict with our higher objectives in life. We aren't to become discouraged. Rather, we are to take note of the base desires within us, not in order to fulfill them, but to be alert so that we don't fulfill these urges by committing a bad action. One of the ways to redirect the mind, Luther says, is to dwell on higher things, not to focus on the fleshly desires themselves. Luther illustrates all this in simpler terms by citing an analogy offered by an old hermit: "You cannot

---

[6] I recognize that there is a concept of mortal sin within Lutheran theology. I have always been uncomfortable with this. I recognize that Luther, starting with his Heidelberg Disputation, turns the concept of mortal and venial sins upside down. Nonetheless, in the Lutheran context, a mortal sin is a one committed out of a lack of faith, out of hopelessness, which is despair. There isn't sufficient space to explore this topic within this book.

[7] Martin Luther, *A Commentary on St Paul's Epistle to the Galatians*, trans. Philip. S. Watson (London: James Clarke, 1953), 509. I have modernized the translation for readability.

prevent the birds from flying over your head. But let them only fly and do not let them build a nest in the hair of your head. Let them be thoughts and remain such; but do not let them become conclusions."[8] In these passages, Luther is referring to lustful thoughts about unlawful acts. Sexual desire, however, was not in principle problematic. On the contrary, he saw such desire as a gift of God, since it motivated people to marry and create families. Thus "when nature's sound," Luther explains, the "ongoing of a man for a woman is God's creation," and "the act which attracts sex to sex is a divine ordinance."[9]

This said, there is indeed a way in which we can linger and cultivate unhealthy imaginary landscapes. I agree, therefore, with John Chrysostom (c. 340–407), who wrote concerning Matthew 5:27–28, "Once one has kindled the flame of lust, even when the object of lust is absent, the one who lusts is forming continually images of prohibited actions."[10] That is, the problem with this imaginary lust is that it habituates a person toward vice, forming patterns of desire that draw a person away from life in the New Logic. Nonetheless, Chrysostom rightly recognized that Jesus was primarily concerned with an active lust toward an actual person, "for he did not simply say 'whoever shall desire,' since it is possible for one to desire even when sitting alone in the mountains. Rather, Jesus said, 'whoever looks with lust,' that is, one who thinks about another solely for the purpose of lusting, who, under no compulsion, allows the wild beasts to intrude upon his thought when they are calm. This intrusion no longer comes from nature but from self-indulgence."[11]

---

[8] Cited in Eric W. Gritsch, *The Wit of Martin Luther* (Minneapolis: Augsburg Fortress, 2006), 53.

[9] Luther, *Luther's Works*, vol. 54, ed. Theodore Tappert (Philadelphia: Fortress Press, 1967), no. 1659, no. 4153.

[10] *Ancient Christian Commentary on Scripture: Matthew 1–13*, New Testament Ia, ed. Manila Simonetti (Downers Grove, IL: InterVarsity Press, 2001), 108.

[11] Ibid.

The True Ethical Problems with Porn

We must ponder God's question (and our own possible answer to the question) originally posed to Adam: "Who told you that you were naked?" (Gen. 3:11). Who indeed? And what changed that this should be a problem? In other words, the problem isn't with the nude form, or our own nakedness, but with the sinful ways in which we use nakedness, or the ways in which we might impose nakedness on others who do not desire to behold it. Pornography as an industry, along with those who consume it, is often regarded—both within and outside religious frameworks—as icky, shameful, and degrading. But Christians should remember that it is not problematic because the beauty of the human form is somehow impure or because pleasure is inherently naughty. Our embodiment is a gift. The human form is enchanting. Recognizing and celebrating beauty can be tasteful and responsible. The problem with porn, however, has more to do with the nature of virtue and vice than codes of ritual purity.

First, virtue, as classically understood, is cultivated through habituation. Throughout our lives, we either feed the darkness or nourish the light in our lives. We shape our hearts and minds by what we do day to day. Pornography often creates an unhealthy situation in which a consumer experiences a need to perpetually increase its intensity (similar to the way drug addicts need increasing doses). This tends to twist the mind away from an erotic life that seeks intimacy and mutuality with others. Pornography thus habituates its consumers toward vicious perspectives on romantic love.

Second, pornography habituates vicious tendencies to objectify others.[12] Through porn, we begin to see others as instruments of our own gratification. This is inconsistent with the New Logic, in which we value mutual gift-giving and intimate concern. It trains us to treat other bodies as commodities for our consumption rather than

---

[12] An anonymous friend made the following helpful observation regarding this point: "John Calvin talked about the unique challenges of veterans coming back from war and not being able to see the face of God in their neighbor anymore because of all the killing. Having been exposed to much porn when I was young (sad to say), I think pornography, like the trauma of war where humanity becomes so much strategically used meat, can leave us (at least for a time) with a kind of PTSD, burned over on the subject of sex, and somewhat disconnected. I think the damage is to the imagination and to desire with no real way to assess the extent of the wreckage."

as beacons of love. Moreover, it can shape unrealistic expectations of our embodied partners. After all, our flesh-and-blood partners can never live up to the airbrushed images that porn can offer.

Third, porn is vicious because of the abusiveness involved in much of the industry. Even when porn actors and actresses insist that they are happy to participate in their careers and that they have taken precautions against life-threatening STDs, they may not always recognize the injuries to their self-esteem or the unjust social contexts in which the adult industry became a legitimate option for them. Often porn "talent" first became involved through a tangled web of manipulation and coercion. The worst form of vicious coercion, by the way, is precisely that which causes participants to act against their best interests and think they are acting freely. There are all sorts of situations in which responsible adults refrain from giving money to companies and organizations that act unjustly. Porn should be put into this category. If we refrain from purchasing meat from factory farms, produce controlled by multinational corporations like Monsanto, or purebred dogs from puppy mills, surely it is virtuous to refrain from supporting the exploitation inherent in the adult entertainment industry.

Fourth, porn can easily become a life-derailing addiction. Life in the New Logic is rich when we focus our thoughts and energies outward, in mutual love toward our neighbors. By turning inward, and living in an imagined world of mental orgies, we withdraw more and more from the sometimes frightening but potentially meaningful relationships possible with those around us. We are called to serve others outside us rather than fold in on ourselves.

Fifth, porn can be detrimental to a consumer's ability to enjoy an embodied romantic life. I've heard report after report from young adults who grew up in a world full of easy-access porn, and they overwhelmingly lament the ways in which it ruined their sexuality. Many say that porn has essentially "fried the wiring in their brains," overloading their brains until they stopped functioning properly. I've heard from some psychologists that this may not be true—that there are not long-term negative effects of porn use on sexual performance—but addictions are never good for the well-rounded life.

This isn't just a boogeyman conjured up by traditionalists to scare off young people. Rather, the alarm about the psychological effects of porn and virtual sex has been sounded by none other than Philip Zimbardo. He's the same psychologist responsible for the famous Stanford Prison Experiment, in which he found that given certain unfortunate conditions, we will almost always act in vicious ways. Similarly, pornography is an external factor that can negatively affect our mental health, no matter how virtuous we think we may be at the outset. In a recent book, Zimbardo contends that porn especially inhibits male development in all aspects of life.[13] Pornography and online life create a world in which young men aren't in danger of being rejected. It negatively affects their ability to learn in school, focus on work tasks, and develop social skills necessary to success in the workplace. Note that Zimbardo's research identifies the effects of online existence in general, including nonpornographic gaming. This shows that what's at stake here is primarily about the ways in which people turn inward, into their own private worlds, and fail to make genuine connections as they mature.

Counselors (some practicing therapists and lots of pastors) and counselees (many young adult males with erectile dysfunction) contend that viewing porn is causative in erectile dysfunction. There may be something to this, especially given how many people seem to believe this is true. I wager that as the medical and psychological research continues, there will indeed be conclusive evidence that porn ruins sexual performance, at least under circumstances related to the frequency and type of porn consumed. I'm sure, for some, the evidence is already overwhelming. Nonetheless, people have only recently been willing to self-report sexual dysfunction. Likewise, it hasn't been that long since the Internet unleashed virtually unlimited pornographic content for developing young people to potentially consume.

History is full of too many cases where researchers were overoptimistic about their research results when they supported the preconceptions of either religious or mental health practitioners. There have also been many cases of pseudoscientific research based on religious concepts of sacred sexual energy. Maybe one's mojo, chi, or Tantric energy can become depleted through visually stimulated lust

---

[13] Philip G. Zimbardo and Nikita D. Coulombe, *Man (Dis)Connected: How Technology Has Sabotaged What It Means to Be Male* (London: Rider, 2015).

and masturbation. Maybe this works only at a metaphorical level. But I am not in a position to evaluate such claims empirically.

Therefore, I'll refrain from offering the dogmatic conclusion that porn consumption leads definitively to sexual dysfunction. But that's not the primary ground for a Christian rejection of pornography. Indeed, I wonder whether the ascetic, celibate monks of the church would have welcomed a good overload of Internet porn to cauterize their libidos, if in fact that's how it worked! Actually, that's not too far off from the odd spirituality of the raving "holy man" Rasputin (1869–1916), who tried to relieve his sexual obsession through heavy drinking and sexual exploits.[14]

To the extent that I love all, I ought to be concerned for the sexual satisfaction of married folks who have consumed porn. But I am far more interested in the sorts of people porn might habituate us into becoming. It is much more tragic for our hearts to be numbed by degrading pornography than for our libidos to be numbed by pornographic overstimulation. The goal of virtue, while it is concerned with the character of the individual person, is to create the power and habit of being heroic and loving toward our neighbors.

One's level of porn consumption seems to be a sort of spiritual barometer in a person's life. I can't even conceive of a scientific study that could verify or falsify this, but I'm convinced that when a person is rightly aligned to goodness, truth, and beauty, pornography simply becomes less interesting. Extreme porn becomes nauseating. Likewise, even tame but exploitative sexual advertisements seem tragic instead of alluring. I'm not saying it is always easy to find that proper ethical, intellectual, and aesthetic alignment; I am saying that if you *do* seek that, the other stuff will be much easier. It is also more enjoyable to think on things that are edifying (Phil. 4:8), letting these positive objectives crowd out unedifying thoughts, than to focus all the time on what you don't want to look at online.

---

[14] One can find salacious details in Frances Welch, *Rasputin: A Short Life* (New York: Atria, 2014). I share this not to aid in readers' titillation but largely to remind readers to be vigilant against manipulative, culty religious people. I've known many in my own short existence, though I must admit that none had the swagger and charisma of the infamous mad Russian monk.

Is Viewing Porn the Moral Equivalent of Adultery?

So if lust in one's heart is about longing to unite with a person to whom one is not committed, is not pornography an example of the "self-indulgence" Chrysostom was talking about? Indeed, Jesus' words can point us to this conclusion. Nevertheless, the rhetoric He used needs to be carefully considered, lest we do more harm than good for people on their quest for erotic virtue. Remember, Jesus spoke in true but hyperbolic ways at times, such as when He said we should hate our mothers and fathers (Luke 14:26) or pluck out our eyes (Matt. 18:9). It is said that the early church theologian Origen of Alexandria castrated himself, taking such teachings too literally. Even if this story isn't true, it remains the case that the rhetoric of a cause needs to be tempered when applied to actual people who are struggling to align their beliefs and actions.

Recently, television therapist Dr. Phil McGraw posted several theses about porn on his website; these have been reposted and adapted broadly. Perhaps the most controversial is the following: "It is not OK behavior. It is a perverse and ridiculous intrusion into your relationship. It is an insult, it is disloyal and it is cheating."[15] For Dr. Phil, porn consumption is the *moral equivalent* of adultery in the practical, civil sphere and indicates a fundamental betrayal of one's spouse. It is a sign that the consumer is perverted, is despicable, or no longer desires his or her partner. This sort of talk runs the risk of conflating Jesus' powerful theological point with practical life questions. I concede that porn isn't good in the sense that it feeds vice and involves human degradation. But I believe Dr. Phil's approach can be detrimental to the process of healing relationships. If porn were considered adultery in both the spiritual and civil spheres, would it therefore be grounds for divorce, even if it were an occasional rather than a debilitating habit? I don't think most pastors or counselors would think so, but it could certainly be read this way by offended spouses.

Suppose also that a man, though unsavory in his viewing habits, found himself addicted to porn. This would not mean that he stopped loving his wife. He might be more devoted to her than

---

[15] "Is Internet Pornography Cheating?," DrPhil.com, September 3, 2002, http://www.drphil.com/advice/is-internet-pornography-cheating/.

most husbands are toward their spouses. He might think cheating unthinkable and instead turned to pornography as a way to find release *instead* of seeking a risky affair. As unsavory as this option would be—and as misguided—it would nonetheless be unwise to introduce into his wife's mind that his actions were necessarily a sign of fundamental betrayal. Such thinking could lead to the unnecessary dissolution of an otherwise salvageable relationship; likewise, it could lead to the wife's unfounded sense that her husband found her undesirable.

Indeed, in my experience, a wife's fear that her husband's consumption of porn is a sign that she herself is unloved or undesired is a common emotional response. It's an understandable, but by no means necessary, conclusion. Many men are unregulated in their habits. Some of their habits are unsavory and need to stop. Given this, it's good for these men to know how their behaviors make their wives feel and then make necessary changes for the sake of love.[16]

Nonetheless, I worry about the histrionics and furious indignation of folks who speak like Dr. Phil does about this matter. Dr. Phil says porn is a "ridiculous" intrusion. Maybe he meant "silly" or "unnecessary." But the root of his chosen word is *ridicule*, which literally means to treat someone with contempt or even to mock them. Crushing a dude with an extra load of shame is likely to lead to additional trouble in a relationship. What good is it to cause a man to curl up into a cocoon of his own self-loathing and degradation? Telling a person that a porn-viewing spouse has committed an act of nuptial treason can create a broken relationship that could have remained intact.[17]

From a theological and spiritual perspective, I'm not always sure what's behind the question "Is porn cheating?" when people ask it. Are they wondering whether it is reasonable grounds for divorce? I suspect even the most moralistic pastors would deny that it *is* a

---

[16] Women also consume porn. The reason I'm focused on the man here is primarily because, at least anecdotally, the men I know rarely worry that their partner's viewing of porn reflects negatively on their own physical worth. I'm sure there are indeed cases of this, though it isn't a big issue among the couples I know.

[17] Note that I'm not talking about illegal or violent porn here, which might indeed be a red flag for other reasons. Nor am I talking about sexting—Anthony Weiner style—which can lead directly to actual affairs.

good reason for divorce, at least in most cases. If so, to insist that porn is cheating could encourage the dissolution of many marriages that might otherwise be restored to harmonious, healthy homes for the raising of children. Again, this is not to condone unwholesome behavior, nor is it an excuse to ignore the pain felt by spouses who disapprove of their partners' porn use; it is a simple plea for everyone to try to keep a level head when this common, albeit unsavory, matter turns up in the life of a family.

The point of virtue theory is to spend less time weighing the relative moral value of this or that action in terms of our standing before God. Instead, we seek to shape our lives in such a way, with behaviors that habituate the sort of qualities we want to strengthen in ourselves, and avoid becoming what we believe is contrary to the kingdom of Jesus. For this reason, the early Christian document called the Didache explains that Christians are to avoid lust because it shapes us into fornicators just as anger is to be avoided lest we become hate filled, murderous people (ch. 3).

Prostitution

The oldest profession isn't prostitution. It's hunting. The hunter is the pure manifestation of direct action and result. An archaic man slew a beast. This labor fed his family, however extensive that concept might have been. Gardening, by the way, was not the oldest profession. It was no profession at all. It was reception of abundance and goodness from cosmic powers beyond the power of humanity. The sun radiates its energy to plants. The gardener receives these with the gratitude of the sailor who receives the energy of the wind that fills the sails. Professions are meant for life in the land of transaction, not pure grace. They effect survival in a world of death and scarcity.

The *second* oldest profession is prostitution. A woman with weaker hunting skills noticed the hunter's kill roasting on a spit. To get a portion of seared animal flesh, she offered her own flesh. Sex for food: older than recorded history. Perhaps it was not as pure a profession as that of the hunter, but at least it was close to the raw reality of life in the wasteland, exiled from the garden. Hunter-gatherer societies tend to place communal sharing at the top of the hierarchy of virtues. Therefore, the act of exchanging sex for food in any explicit way would be to sin against the ideal of sharing with the community and not hoarding. By way of extension, therefore, prostitution in a deeper sense is any career that depends on a transaction, one that exchanges an act or object of beauty for something else of mundane value. In this sense, all laborers are prostitutes of a sort. No one who has worked for a corporation can completely deny this.

The third oldest profession is that of priestcraft. A man who had no hunting skills came upon a feast with only two feasters: one was a hunter, and the other was a prostitute. Either the foodless man was unwilling to exchange sex for food—such behavior being culturally unacceptable, perhaps—or the hunter found him undesirable as a sexual partner. So he promised that if he could get a portion of the kill, he would offer supernatural blessings for the next hunt. In this way, the one who claimed a connection to divine power could exchange a tangible commodity for a supernatural blessing. In a sense, however, this profession was one step removed from the primary societal value of hunter.

Lest you think I—a layperson who teaches theology—intend to denigrate the office of the holy ministry, let me place myself into a category even further removed from the primal authenticity of hunter. The old adage goes, "Those who can, do; those who can't, teach." I'm not ordained to bless a hunt. I guess I'm merely in the business of teaching others how to bless a hunt. I train young adults who may go on one day to be ordained to offer blessings. Guys like me are too untamed or undisciplined to instill in others the confidence that the heavens would listen to my entreaties, I suppose. In other words, there's a way in which, in the human hierarchy, I'm a few levels beneath the harlot.

Of course, I'm messing around a bit here. I'm not saying that a life of prostitution is wholesome or that clergy are all swindlers. Or that educators are inept. But Jesus did say prostitutes would be at the front of the line into the kingdom of heaven (Matt. 21:31). More important, my pseudoanthropological excursus here is meant to tease out the ways in which prostitutes are, in most cases, put into their positions because of societal structures beyond their control. Hunter-gatherer societies—societies where there is not a sense of an individual having a *profession* as such—require no exchange but tend to be communities in which there is a system of cooperation and mutual gift-giving. They are not communities of transaction.

Prostitution is, therefore, best associated with structural sin, societal injustice, and the cruelty of patriarchal societies in which women are property. Valued virgins, in such a society, get the "privilege" of being handed off to a respectable husband. Those who are somehow less valuable only get rented. This cultural tragedy, therefore, must never be addressed primarily by criminalizing the prostitute-victim. After all, much of what sophisticated men and women do within the world's Old Logic of transaction is only a thinly veiled form of prostitution. Go back to my hypothetical archaic prostitute. She offered her body for food. Transactions like this take place today, unfortunately, whenever a man thinks a woman "owes him" for buying her a nice dinner and ordering a couple cocktails. They take place when a woman in a poverty-stricken land sells her body to feed her children.

If we want to oppose and reduce prostitution in our land, we need to address the big picture and all its complex factors. Poverty, addiction, hopelessness, abuse, and organized crime ought to be the primary targets in any righteous campaign in this regard. Meanwhile, it's entirely consistent with a Christian ethic to support the decriminalization of prostitution when it comes to the sex workers themselves. To throw a victimized or at least unfortunate prostitute into jail merely to release her back to their manipulators after a day or two of further humiliation behind bars is hardly an act of superior justice. Pimps and johns are probably legitimate targets for law enforcement. But even then, the best approach to the sex trade, and all forms of human trafficking, needs to be as nuanced as the problem itself is complex.

I had the chance to meet pastor and abolitionist Raleigh Sadler, director of Let My People Go.[18] With his organization, he works to end human trafficking in New York City. My friend Dan and I had a chance to interview him on the Virtue in the Wasteland podcast. Through our conversation, he opened my eyes to subtle ways in which vulnerable young people are lured into prostitution and locked into a sad cycle of exploitation.

---

[18] Check out the organization's website at http://www.lmpgnetwork.org. He's slated to publish a book on the subject with the Virtue in the Wasteland Books imprint, by the way.

Often, he said, people who are being trafficked don't realize it. A woman is sometimes told, for instance, that she needs to trade her body for sex in order to get a "boyfriend" out of a debt. Her will is broken; her self-esteem is snuffed out. Often these trafficked women attend our churches, but without getting to know their stories, their congregations are unaware of their plight. In a *Huffington Post* article, for instance, Sadler told the story of Anna:

> While still in her late teens, she met and fell in love with an older man who gave her what she craved. "Could he be the one to love and accept me for who I am?" she wondered. This longing for love made her vulnerable to her "boyfriend," who had different plans for their "relationship." Over the ensuing months, she would be subtly manipulated into becoming part of his special "art project." Unknowingly, she was trafficked into the world of pornography.
>
> . . . As Anna shared her story with me, I couldn't shake a nagging question. "How did the local church serve you during your exploitation?" Hearing my question, she laughed out loud. "For years," she replied, "I went to church regularly. No one noticed anything. Everyone thought I was happy, so nothing wrong could be going on."
>
> Anna's story is not uncommon.[19]

In this case, the victim of human trafficking wasn't exchanging intercourse for money, but the pattern often leads there if folks like Sadler don't intervene.

On the podcast, we asked Sadler why he decided to drop what he was doing and lead Let My People Go. He responded quickly: "the Gospel." For him, his fight for freedom isn't about earning merit points for heaven, or looking like a good guy, or "virtue signaling." It's about getting to know real humans and listening closely to their stories with the sort of mercy born of the New Logic. He thus travels around the country, speaking to any audience who will listen, to bring attention to the "least of these" (Matt. 25:40). He urges people

---

[19] Raleigh Sadler, "When Human Trafficking Victims Are among Your Congregation," *Huffington Post*, January 12, 2016, http://www.huffingtonpost.com/raleigh-sadler/when-human-trafficking-happens-in-church_b_8958050.html.

of the cross to invest in the lives of those who are the most vulnerable, such as immigrants, the homeless, orphaned young people, and those who struggle with addiction.

Meanwhile, futile acts of heroism aren't the answer. Sadler told us about a well-meaning man who learned that there was a brothel in his city. So he leaned a ladder against the second-story window where the women were staying and whisked them away from their pimp. He says that, in addition to risking a pimp's possible retaliation against the women themselves, that fails to address the reason the women were in their situations in the first place, so they often just find themselves back in their old miserable situations. Some are not citizens. Some have no support network to transition to a new life. They need comprehensive restoration.

We—all of us—must treat the sin of the sex trade as if it were *our* problem, as if the sins committed were *our sins*. We don't hear people talking this way much these days. Nonetheless, Christians are uniquely called to be people of confession. We are to take on corporate guilt even when we are technically without blame or when we are only implicated in structural evil beyond our control.

I used to get angry when I sensed that people were trying to lay the guilt of my ancestors on my shoulders. After all, *I* wasn't responsible for the federal government's treatment of Native Americans or the European colonization of Africa. Moreover, my maternal great-grandfather came from Germany to America to fight against slavery as a Civil War captain, which meant he left long before his offspring might have sullied themselves by involvement with the Nazis. Racism, exploitation, and injustice, I used to insist, were not my problems at all. But two theologians have changed my mind: Isaac the Syrian (613–700) and Martin Luther. While we might not bear the guilt of our parents in a legal sense, Christians are invited to take on those past sins as if they were their own. Isaac was a thinker saturated in grace. He writes,

> Spread your cloak over those who fall into sin, each and every one, and shield them. And if you cannot take the fault on yourself and accept punishment in their place, do not destroy their character. What is a merciful heart? It is a heart on fire for the whole of creation, for humanity, for the birds, for the animals,

for demons, and for all that exists. By the recollection of them
the eyes of a merciful person pour forth tears in abundance.
By the strong and vehement mercy that grips such a person's
heart, and by such great compassion, the heart is humbled and
one cannot bear to hear or to see any injury or slight sorrow in
any in creation.[20]

People of the New Logic don't take the sins of the world onto ourselves because of liberal guilt or direct legal obligation. Rather, dispensing with the demands of the law, we become free to take up our
neighbors' guilt because we don't need to fear divine punishment for
this guilt. Thus Luther writes,

> We give this rule: the good things which we have from God
> ought to flow from one to another and become common to all, so
> that every one of us may, as it were, put on his neighbor, and
> so behave towards him as if he were himself in his place. They
> flowed and do flow from Christ to us; He put us on, and acted
> for us as if He Himself were what we are. From us they flow to
> those who have need of them; so that my faith and righteousness
> ought to be laid down before God as a covering and intercession
> for the sins of my neighbor, which I am to take on myself, and
> so labor and endure servitude in them, as if they were my own;
> for thus has Christ done for us. This is true love and the genu-
> ine truth of Christian life. But only there is it true and genuine
> where there is true and genuine faith. Hence the Apostle attri-
> butes to charity this quality: that it seeks not its own.[21]

Therefore, in a sober, concrete sense, we should indeed recognize the
ways in which injustices to which we have contributed as a society
have led to the reality of prostitution. But like Raleigh Sadler, we
should seek our motivation for transformation not under the burden
of guilt but in the delight of the Gospel's freedom. We are free to care
for the seemingly unlovable. We take their sins onto our shoulders

---

[20] Hilarion Alfeyev, *The Spiritual World of Isaac the Syrian*, Cistercian Studies 175
(Kalamazoo: Cistercian Publications, 2000), 372.

[21] Martin Luther, *Concerning Christian Liberty*, in *Machiavelli, More, and Luther* (Harvard Classics, vol. 36), trans. R. S. Grignon (New York: P. F. Collier & Son, 1910), 41–42.

because our shoulders have been unburdened by the work of Christ, who took *our* sins with Him to the cross.

Prostitution Isn't Sexy

I doubt anyone would be surprised to learn that sex workers themselves typically do not find their work sexy. It's work. It's a business. But based on a few conversations I've had with folks who've confessed to hiring prostitutes, even they don't find it sexy.

One day, after I spoke to a church group, a guy came up to me to thank me and share a bit about his experiences. He said that despite being a seemingly normal family man and churchgoer, he had descended—almost out of the blue—into a couple weeks of risky encounters. He said the strangest part of his experience was that he realized he had really wanted intimacy, not physical gratification. In these encounters, he would often be unable to perform sexually, even if he had wanted to. Usually, he ended up paying a lot of money to talk with escorts, hear their stories, and share some of his own frustrations.

Eventually, he cleaned up his act. Recounting the final days of his descent into sexual despair, he recalled, "I went to a clinic to get tested for STDs, and luckily I was clear. I showered until layers of skin were being removed out of shame. I had been trying to enlarge my experience of the sexual only to realize that when two bodies with a cash agreement meet and immediately begin feigned sexual encounters, they find themselves in a sink hole of shame and debt." He continued: "Many of the women are sexy on the surface, I suppose. But there was nothing sexy about our arrangements and transactions. The chase, the money, the adrenaline from reckless behavior: that is what high-end prostitution is about. Sex is an almost incidental by-product. The utter lack of sexiness in the sex business has left me ashamed and uninterested. I'm searching to return to something noble and fulfilling."

Compassion

The New Logic goes deeper and deeper the more we let it sink into our ways of living and thinking. At first, realizing divine grace may cause us to repent erotically. At this initial stage, we might wish to redirect our attention from viewing commodified bodies in porn or at a strip club to serving our neighbors in love. Later, we start to realize that grace isn't just about avoiding lust; it's about loving the seemingly unlovable. It's about understanding the complexities of various life circumstances. I've had to wrestle with this reality a few times after talking about these themes on the podcast. I was shocked to find so many folks writing in—people who often were conservative Christians—angry that I didn't understand the difficulty of their particular situations. One gentleman suggested, for instance, that porn was important for him because his wife hadn't touched him in years. He wanted to stay married, but he said he needed sexual release that didn't involve risky behavior. Another listener wrote that she was severely disabled and never expected to have a chance at physical intimacy; thus she occasionally turned to escorts for physical touch that she could never hope to experience otherwise. A dreadfully lonely man in the Midwest wrote to explain that the idea of sex robots kept him pressing on with life, which had otherwise become too unfulfilling to continue. These ideas are foreign to my own experience. And I believe that there is a type of sexual fulfillment *above and beyond* what we usually include in our typical list of options: I believe there is a possible sexual energy or connectedness that is spiritual, meditative, and almost otherworldly. I believe that there is also a possible sexual energy from recognizing the beauty and trace of the divine in an ocean swim or a barefoot walk through cool spring grass. Nonetheless, I believe the New Logic invites us to avoid treating folks in their various circumstances as disgusting or icky. It inspires us to offer an extra helping of compassion, human camaraderie, and sincere love to all those around us who wrestle with issues of erotic virtue.

Love Is Not a Victory March
(Surviving Marriage)

Well baby I've been here before
I've seen this room and I've walked this floor
I used to live alone before I knew you
I've seen your flag on the marble arch
Love is not a victory march
It's a cold and it's a broken Hallelujah
                            —Leonard Cohen, "Hallelujah"

Even when we attune ourselves to the melody of eternal love, we must constantly *retune* throughout our lives. If you've played guitar or violin, you know that even a virtuoso sounds terrible with strings that are *out* of tune. Likewise, we occasionally become spiritually and emotionally untuned, and this causes friction in marriage. While I was writing this book, I found this reality frustrating. It slowed me down for at least six months. I had hoped that simply understanding what true sexiness was could be a once-and-for-all cure to all that ailed my own marriage. Alas, it was never that easy. We remain in the penultimate world: we know the ultimate love of God is ours to reflect toward our loved ones, but we remain sinner-saints in need of perpetual repentance and forgiveness.

Despite the difficulties that occurred—or perhaps *because* of this book project—Stacie and I encountered a fortunate reality too: once we discovered the joy of gracious nontransactional ways of thinking about our relationship, the nature and expressions of our frustrations changed character. With each experience of interpersonal friction, we now take comfort in a deeper sense that we cannot be shaken from eternal love, and that means our little arguments don't threaten us with a fear that we are in danger of ultimately losing love itself. This idea at least de-escalates things.

What we ought *not* to do is exist too long in a frantic state of trying to shake free of our discomfort. We need peace—the peace that surpasses understanding. Perpetual bliss is not in the cards for us in this life's sojourn. The best we can hope for is an occasional taste of that ultimate bliss and a resolute hope for the bliss to come, when time itself will be transcended. In the meantime, we need to remember that married relationships are not about winning and losing. Everything's already been won. The task at present is to learn to rest in that reality and be kind to each other even through difficult times.

Grace isn't just a theological concept. It's something that reorients our relationships. Instead of counting on merits and demerits to earn affection and respect, we realize that love is a complete gift. With the New Logic, we don't just try to treat people as they deserve to be treated; we don't even treat people the way we want to be treated. We seek to treat people as God has treated us, with unmerited favor, remembering this is the key to surviving.

Why Marriage in the First Place?

Christian sexuality finds its expression within marriage because the commitment of marriage fits beautifully within the New Logic of love. In this, we seek commitment to someone in a way that appears irrational from a secular standpoint. In this way, Christian marriage is a manifestation of an earthly, unconditional love that draws upon a promise of unconditional heavenly love. But what if we find that we are sexually incompatible with a partner? What if we turn out to have different tastes in music? What if my partner fails to complete me the way he or she promised? Such questions only become vexing when we assume that there is, at bottom, a transactional aspect to marriage.

What if, however, we were to view marriage in light of an unconditional call to love *all*? And then what if we decided to love one particular individual to hell and back, if necessary? In this way, to the extent that we choose to love in marriage unconditionally and without concern for a return on investment, we have something much stronger than uptight traditionalism about the insoluble nature of marriage. In a later chapter, I'll address times when divorce might be an option. For now, however, recognize the beauty represented by the ideal situation: two people promise to stick together through thick and thin, sickness and health, wealth and poverty. What isn't nifty about that? We all want this from others. That's not the problem, then. What irks us is that we just don't want to be *forced* to offer this unconditional love to others, and sometimes to one particular other whose annoying habits we've discovered. But if we consider that a committed, monogamous marriage embodies the New Logic of a nontransactional relationship, then we offer this to each other as an act of worship. Indeed, when freely offered, we might think of marital monogamy as the new kink! Refraining from random encounters can be more than a sign that someone knows how to follow the rules. It can be a sign that someone is willing to perform a herculean feat because that's what true lovers do for each other, even when they don't feel like doing it.

Perhaps this will make more sense with respect to nonsexualized friendships. How rare but beautiful it is when we find a person on whom we can count, even when we ourselves don't seem worth the effort. When times get difficult—when *we* get difficult—a faithful companion is a godsend. Conversely, how common but ugly it is to learn that many of our friends are really only after something we have to offer. Everyone needs a *true* friend. Likewise, there's supreme value in a faithful lover, who will be with us even when we get lost for a little while. If we don't have faithful human connections, then when we get lost, we are in danger of remaining lost forever, at least humanly speaking. Marriage offers a lifeline in this mortal life, and when a marriage is healthy, the extra intimacy of sexual touch can bind a couple closer than what the bonds of friendship offer.

Aside from the Christian idea that there is a cosmic significance to marital union, there have always been several practical reasons to refrain from extramarital activity. Especially prior to technological advances in contraception, such as the birth control pill and latex condom, sex outside of marriage could be starkly unjust. Bastards—that is, those children born without a claim to inheritance—were often tragically treated like nonpersons. In addition to the emotional damage this would inflict on a person labeled "illegitimate," this often meant a life without financial security. It might mean a fatherless child would be doomed to begging, tinkering, or prostitution. Moreover, a woman who became pregnant in a patriarchal society without the protection of marriage might have her life ruined because she would be treated as used goods. Even today, it's not hard to connect the dots between fatherlessness and societal problems.[1] Thus one need not appeal to special revelation like the Bible to condemn careless sexual behavior. It is a social matter of great civic importance. Even biblical erotic virtue has the well-being of the community as a core objective.

Thus ancient Christian prohibitions against premarital sex served to protect the most vulnerable members of society: women and children. Sexual restraint, accordingly, is related to the early Christian emphasis on caring for orphans and widows (James 1:27). The concern to avoid unwanted pregnancy and ruining the future prospects of young women remains the strongest consequential argument against promiscuity. Moreover, such thinking is far nobler than standard modern consequential arguments and their emphasis on avoiding STDs—that is, a person who contracts a disease receives the consequences of promiscuity in his or her own body. A person who creates an uncared-for life causes the consequences of a sin to fall on another human being.

As contraception and prophylactic measures to avoid disease increase in their effectiveness, some of these older arguments seem weaker to many today than they did in generations past. (Note, however, that infidelity is an ancient and common phenomenon even in times and places where infidelity has been punishable by law.) Thus instead of simply restating the old rules, we need to return to a consideration of virtue theory. From such a perspective, premarital sex is problematic to the extent that it assumes that romantic love can be given a "test-drive." Casually using our neighbors' bodies for gratification is problematic even when we are technically "safe" with respect to our sexual activity, because it habituates us into a life of transaction and selfishness. Fidelity within marriage, at its core, reflects a deep respect for the kind of

---

[1] On the theology of fatherhood, see Scott Keith, *Being Dad: Father as a Picture of God's Grace* (Irvine, CA: NRP Books, 2015).

virtuous person a follower of Jesus is called to be. It also can be a testimony to infinite cosmic love.

Sexy Ink

It was probably inevitable that I'd someday get a tattoo, though I didn't get one until I was forty. I used to joke that my first body art would read "R.I.P., Rick Mallinson." Rick is my father. He was a non-cliché hippy who had almost no rules for the family. There was only one rule: no tattoos.

He would say things like, "I love you kids no matter what, but if you get a tattoo, I'll cut a ten-inch piece of hose and beat you with it to within one inch of your life." That's a quote. We kids would laugh, since he never beat us, but we knew he was serious about his anti-tattoo policy nevertheless. Even after tattoos became more accepted and widespread within American culture, my pop would not budge on his perspective.

My best guess as to why he had such disdain for body art has to do with his younger days back in Boulder, Colorado. The hippy types would go into mountain towns like Morrison and Nederland to get their drugs. Usually, the dudes selling the drugs were tattooed bikers with big bowie knives strapped to their legs. These bikers were often fans of "hippy-killer" culture. The nature loving counterculture, on the other hand, usually refrained from permanent body markings. In such a context, to have a tattoo was to cast one's lot with the violent end of the countercultural spectrum rather than the peace-and-love crowd.

When I was thirty-nine, I invited my father onto the podcast to discuss this subject of tattoos. At the time, he wasn't aware that my cohost Dan had quality ink all over his arms. Ironically, he would often encourage me to look more like Dan. You see, as a professor, Dan would dress like a *GQ* dandy. My dad used to say things like, "Why don't you dress like your buddy Dan? He's got a real 'Mr. Chips' vibe." In saying this, he was referring to a James Hilton novel and its subsequent movie adaption, *Goodbye, Mr. Chips*. In it, a teacher dresses sharply, in a respectable and professional manner that I had failed to channel properly.

What my dad didn't know during that podcast was that beneath Dan's long-sleeve fitted dress shirt were many hours of tattoo work. We were originally going to do a big reveal at the end of the show, but I think both Dan and I got spooked when Dan asked if my dad could ever come to terms with his son getting a tattoo. His response startled me: "I guess I see your perspective," my father finally conceded. "You can get a tattoo, son." I never thought the day would come. Right there, on record, for thousands of witnesses to verify, he gave up on the one and only line he'd drawn in the sand. "But first," he added, "you must get down on the ground, kiss the dirt, and worship Satan, because that's what a tattoo means." He got me again! At least he's entertaining when being stubborn.

In the end, my first tattoo wasn't "R.I.P., Rick Mallinson" after all. Neither did I worship Beelzebub before getting my ink. My dad wasn't showing any signs of relaxing on the matter, so I thought I'd honor him somewhat by representing something he and my mother had witnessed, something that provided an important insight for this chapter on surviving marriage: it was a vision about letting go of resentment.

My dad has been a real estate appraiser for decades. Over the years, he created jobs in the industry for my brothers and a friend or two. They've made their living inspecting homes of celebrities in LA and affluent beach towns of Orange County, California. The Mallinsons never lived in mansions themselves, but we can tell you what they're worth.

Amid the financial and real estate crises of 2008, my dad's business was devastated. Sometimes companies that owed him money would not pay their invoices on time. Sometimes they'd even go out of business before paying the family business what was owed. One company was connected to one of America's largest banks. This company owed my father $70,000 when they went out of business. The big bank, my dad believed, still owed him for his work, but they refused to pay my father for the many appraisals he'd done for them. Unfortunately, my dad had been working almost exclusively with this one account. Thus not only was he deprived of his big check; he was having a hard time paying the bills. One evening, demoralized by the situation, my folks walked down from their home in Dana Point to the harbor. There, they saw my dad's favorite bird, arguably the Mallinson totemic animal: the osprey. This is the only species of raptor that grabs fish where beak and talons make contact with its prey simultaneously. This particular harbor osprey my folks saw had latched onto a massive fish. They watched in wonderment as the bird flapped its wings, hoping to take its prize home to hungry chicks back in the nest.

Unfortunately for the osprey, the hefty fish was tangled in kelp. The osprey frantically tried doing everything it could to extract its prize from the harbor. But it began to fatigue. It soon became clear that if it didn't let go of the fish, it would surely drown. Fortunately, it relaxed its talons and flew up to a tree under which my folks had found shade. It then scanned the horizon for another fish.

This scene was meaningful to my father, who interpreted this as a reminder that holding on to resentments is dangerous. So my dad decided to release his emotional grip on the outstanding $70,000 payment. He realized he would go bankrupt if he focused on a lawsuit to get that lost money instead of working to drum up new business. To survive the injustice, he needed to let it go. I tell this story because this act of letting go of resentments is an essential factor for surviving any marriage. It's far easier said than done, but it is essential. Releasing resentment often feels like giving up useful relationship capital, but such capital is valuable only according to the Old Logic. The way of love, the New Logic, jettisons such things.

My first tattoo, completed in three phases, was an attempt to interpret what my dad saw along the lines of this concept of sexy spirituality. Indeed, the completed tattoo on my upper arm is now sort of like a map of this book's thesis. On my upper arm is a blood-orange setting sun, representing the hope of the Gospel and contentment in the reality that grace will restore all manner of things. Sunsets are beautiful in my part of the world, and they remind me that even when darkness comes, I can count on a hope rooted in God, whose light cannot be overcome. Flying toward the sun is the self, which is represented by the osprey. Wings outstretched, the osprey pursues hope and, in doing this, has relaxed its talons. I use this tattoo to remind me that by letting go of karmic, transactional approaches to relationships, we are free to love *and enjoy love* unconditionally. By releasing petty resentments, we lose nothing and gain abundance.

When my pop finally saw this part of the design on my arm, he was surprisingly cool-headed. Perhaps it was the nature of the image.

Perhaps he had never really learned how to get properly enraged at his kids. He's a generous guy, after all. I think he also realized that for some people, tattoos serve as reminders of an important spiritual lesson they don't want to forget when life becomes challenging. They are an *anamnesis*, a remembrance of some past epiphany.[2]

On the inside of my arm is a personification of the theological virtue of *hope*. A woman pours out two cisterns: one onto the land and one into the sea. She basks in the light of a star. She is reminiscent of the Virgin Mary, a 1940s pinup girl, and the Chinese goddess of mercy, Guanyin. (I realized this only after visiting a temple to Guanyin in China that depicted her doing what the woman on my arm is doing: pouring out unending cisterns of grace.) The motivation for this part of the upper sleeve was the idea that we can experience moments of spiritual joy by pouring out the love of God into the entire world. I think it's a cool design. Eric Jones, a superb philosopher-artist who studied under the Bay Area legend Juan Puente, created the image as it is now.

The final part of my tattoo represents the release of resentment. At first, I thought of making the fish my folks saw into a sea serpent. But I eventually decided to make it a mermaid. Thus what the osprey thought was dinner turned out to be a siren, who might lead a man to death by drowning. This was the perfect finishing touch because, for Stacie and me, a key to healing our relationship has been letting go of painful, deadly resentments. I asked Eric Jones to give the mermaid a distinctly fish-scaled tail; otherwise, why would the osprey have been mistaken about its prey? I asked him to make the torso and face skeletal, to represent the deadliness of resentment. But Eric knows a thing or two about religion and art, so he added something important. The mermaid indeed has a body of death, and it's good for the bird that it has released her, but her human face is almost smiling. Her hand reaches out to the woman who represents hope. Thus the mermaid is swimming through waters cleansed by the outpouring of mercy and crawling up onto the island of grace, which is watered by hope's cistern. The image thus came full circle, literally.

---

[2] This is why the Greek term *anamnesis* is applied by some social scientists to religious practices that are not themselves spiritual encounters so much as ways to remind people that spiritual encounters had occurred. The line in the Eucharistic liturgy "do this in remembrance of me" is called the Anamnesis.

Agape is so powerful that it can even heal our past pain and trauma, giving mercy even to our enemies. Even the past traumas and people we must release, from God's perspective, can be redeemed.

This last point is perhaps the main point. Anyone who's been married for more than a month knows that couples constantly need to extend forgiveness to each other. Yet we too often forget to forget—that is, we forget to give up on score keeping. We love to cling to our traumas and injustices as treasures, like Gollum's *precious* ring in Tolkien's books. In our addiction to remembering our traumas, we fail to remember Paul's words that love "keeps no record of wrongs" (1 Cor. 13:5). This doesn't mean we can't cognitively recall the history of our past. It means that we refrain from recalling it for the purpose of beating a spouse up emotionally when it suits our purpose. Letting resentments be redeemed means at least two things: (1) we should love and hope the best for those people whom we have had to release from our daily existence, even if they were true enemies, and (2) the events and circumstances from which we need emotional release may someday turn out to become part of a beautiful story of healing and redemption, even if this isn't apparent until the end of time.

A Thought Experiment: Alien Abduction

Now, if even decent marriages involve no victory marches, why try marriage in the first place? That's a question students have been asking me lately. They wonder why any of this attention to cultivating a healthy marriage is worth the trouble, given the fact that some of them can't point to a single marriage that they would describe as enviable. On the contrary, they too often see brokenness, arguments, defensiveness, divorce, and anger.

Despite their understandable concerns, I insist the struggle is worth it. It's not just worth it; it's the prize itself. The trials of married and family life are *part* of the gift of living. I came to realize this one night, having fallen asleep to an *X-Files* episode. The theme on the show had been alien abductions. Nodding off, I dreamed that I had been beamed up to an alien craft that was on a research mission. My dreaming self was pleased to find that the intergalactic anthropologists were benevolent. They were collecting two members of each species from the various planets they visited; it was a sort of interstellar Noah's Ark. After showing the abducted guests their groovy spacecraft, they offered each of us a choice. We could either return to earth and live out our lives as if nothing had happened, with a small gift of technology that could earn us riches, or else travel to the ends of the galaxy, living for about a thousand years, aided by their advanced medical technology. If we left, we would never see our families again, but we would learn the mysteries of the universe.

Pause here for a moment and *make this a thought experiment for your own relationship situation.* Which would you choose: longevity and astounding knowledge or the daily joys and aches of an earthly relationship? Avoid answering too quickly. Avoid trying to convince yourself to say you'd go with whatever the *right* choice is. Once you're done pondering, keep reading, and I'll share the insights this thought experiment provided me.

My dream forced me to confront something a bit tamer than the typical Faustian dilemma. In Christopher Marlowe's *Dr. Faustus* (1604), the protagonist faces the temptation of selling his soul to the devil in exchange for secret knowledge. This thought experiment involves neither eternal damnation nor rejection of any deeply held religious beliefs. But it does force us to evaluate how much we treasure (or don't) physical existence on earth in embodied relationships with other humans. Is knowledge—specifically cognitive, intellectual, and maybe spiritual knowledge—worth the cost of abandoning concrete existence? Is perfected knowledge the highest achievable good in this life? Is longevity without rich human connection worth much at all? For all the things we wish we had, is there anything to be discovered in the universe that could be compared to the things for which we are currently thankful?

As I dreamt and deliberated, my first thought was that I should immediately sign on to travel to the ends the universe. I would gain certainties about philosophical and religious mysteries that have confounded me since my youth. Liberation would come by being able to gain a grand perspective. I would shed my earthbound biases. I could tap into the eternal truths that lurked in the blind spots of *Homo sapiens'* science and theology. Indeed, why *shouldn't* I go? Sure, I'd miss my family. But then, I assured myself, I would want my family members to go on the journey if they were in this sort of position. After all, how cool would it be to know that someone connected to me was out there, somewhere, enjoying an incredible adventure? That person would somehow carry on our family's wisdom and legacy for millennia to come and into the far reaches of the galaxy. Suppose my son Augustine were to be selected: there would be a perverse, narcissistic thrill in knowing that every lesson, every life story, and every creative idea I had passed on to him might be carried beyond our nearest stars. Go, go, go!

Or so I thought at first. But then I started to think through the logistics and process the poignancy of saying farewell to all I would have to leave behind. I could get past the tears, I assured myself. Nonetheless, I had to think about the long-range implications. What would it be like to know everything, from my study in a cold space ship, floating through the void? It would be angelic, hardly lacking anything. But there is one thing I *would* lack: the ability to cuddle with my family on a couch, falling asleep to a classic movie. I'd lack the ability to share a coffee with close friends after a season of grief. I'd miss seeing the grandkids' visit to Disneyland for the first time. I would miss the sexiness of embodiment that gives life meaning and delight. I would miss my wife, even her annoying idiosyncrasies. I suspect I would often wish she were around to hassle me about my tattoos. I wouldn't be happy in space because I'd be living like a disembodied specter—full of knowledge but devoid of passion. I'd become an abstraction. I'd lose existence. I'd lose love.

"No," I finally concluded, before waking abruptly, "I want to stay grounded on this dusty earth. The angels envy each of our time-bound moments, even when we are traversing the wastelands." When I awoke, I went over to my sleeping sons and kissed their heads. I went back and snuggled closer to Stacie. I turned on CNN to watch the collapse of civilization in high definition and dozed back to sleep. I snored, content that real life was more precious than anything even the dream world could offer.

Patient Silence

When a wall of sound floods our consciousness, when visual images bombard our eyes from flickering screens, when endless online chatter creates a virtual din in our minds, something is lost: silence.

When relationship friction produces discomfort in our daily lives, we need to reset, get into a good mental space, and cast out the demons of pettiness. This silence can be something we do alongside a partner, but we also need some moments of solitary silence to reflect and reset.

T. S. Eliot, a poet who converted to Christianity between the composition of his famous "Hollow Men" and his postconversion "Ash Wednesday," emphasizes the importance of silence, especially as it relates to the quest for divine love. Permit me to highlight a few places in "Ash Wednesday" that illustrate the ways in which we can use silence profitably. Eliot wrestles with themes from Dante's *Divine Comedy* and describes an ascent up a spiral staircase, toward greater connection to a mystical reality beyond daily life. Each turn of the staircase relates to his turning away—his repentance—from petty things of life to the New Logic. He writes of turning not from fun, joyful stuff but from the hollow things. In this, he encourages readers to

> pray to God to have mercy upon us
> And pray that I may forget
> These matters that with myself I too much discuss.

Most of us realize we should avoid gossip. Yet that's not our only wasted effort. Incessant but insignificant battles distract us from our true purpose in life and love. Sometimes these battles involve important relationships, political movements, and even religion. But when we approach them in a shallow way, we clutter our days with endless chatter in order to keep out silence. This is because we are too frightened to take an honest look at our spiritual and emotional lives. Moreover, this problem of "too much discussion" relates to a deeper spiritual problem. Often we become like ghosts, clinging to the resentments of the past and caught in a vortex of our own bitterness.

An unhealthy obsession with our own righteousness and the failures of our romantic partner is toxic. In such situations, we congratulate ourselves that we're on an important crusade but fail to cultivate compassion toward our partner. Sometimes these battles are worthwhile. But more often, they are meaningless hills on which to let our relationship die. Frequently, our ostensible commitment to righteousness and idealism is really just our own sense of self-importance. When lovers let us down, we become frustrated, not so much because the principles of goodness, truth, and beauty have been violated, but because *we* surely deserve to have been treated better. How dare others not curtsy before our own majesty? When we start thinking like this, we do well to turn to Eliot's prayer, embedded in the poem, which is both helpful and healing:

> Teach us to care and not to care
> Teach us to sit still.

Of all the compelling lines about the tension between silence and speaking in the poem, my favorite selection is this:

> Still is the unspoken word, the Word unheard,
> The Word without a word, the Word within
> The world and for the world;
> And the light shone in darkness and
> Against the Word the unstilled world still whirled
> About the centre of the silent Word.

The center of the cosmos is the silent Word. Swirling around the Word, the world is a cacophony of chatter created by vexed and frantic men and women. Amid this little hurricane of human life, we must cling closely to the Logos. We must learn to surf the Tao.

Thus we need to get *centripetal* even as our madly spinning world creates *centrifugal* force, drawing us away from God. The unholy energy that tries to spin us out of the Tao's orbit doesn't always appear sinister. In religious circles, it might take the form of theological bickering, church conflicts about building plans, or incessant nagging. Of course, there's nothing wrong with intellectual discussion, architectural planning, or moral service; but we must never become disconnected ("Suffer me not to be separated"[3]) from the source of life itself if our activities are going to have any healing effect on those around us.

---

[3] T. S. Eliot, "Ash Wednesday."

In your own relationship, if you seem to have lost your bearings, pause and seek silence. Amid that silence, listen for whispers of hope that can sustain your internal and relational health. Eliot writes,

> Where shall the word be found, where will the word
> Resound? Not here, there is not enough silence
> Not on the sea or on the islands, not
> On the mainland, in the desert or the rain land,
> For those who walk in darkness
> Both in the daytime and in the nighttime
> The right time and the right place are not here
> No place of grace for those who avoid the face
> No time to rejoice for those who walk among noise and deny
>   the voice

Even though Eliot probably didn't have marriage in mind when he wrote these words, they point us in the right direction. If we avoid confrontation with the divine face and content ourselves with frivolous noise, we will miss the power of this one-way love for us.

When we are missing it, it's impossible to pour it out to others without reserve, because we treat love like a transaction in that bean-counting relationship economy. Once we fall into a cycle of romantic score keeping, it's hard to extract ourselves. In such cases when we think the ledger is tilted one way or the other, we make *noise*: we get pregnant, or go on a vacation to Fiji, or build an extra wing on the house. Such shared activities can of course contribute to the richness and vibrancy of a relationship, but without contentment and peace, none of that clutter can do much more than distract us from our essential despair.

So if you are in a relationship, encourage your partner to seek times of solitude, reflection, prayer, and stillness. If a spouse needs to step out, take a walk, and think, don't interpret this as a threat or an act of aggression. Rather, commit together to embrace moments of calm, after which you can be renewed for loving engagement once more. This would fit with Paul's recommendation: "Do not refuse one another except perhaps by agreement for a season, that you may devote yourselves to prayer; but then come together again, lest Satan tempt you through lack of self-control" (1 Cor. 7:5).

The Tyranny of Completion

I once heard David Zahl make the following astute observation: "There is no more crushing law than the imagined marital command: *thou shalt complete me.*" He's right. Romantic love should be received as a joyous gift, not as a new legalistic burden to perform. Unfortunately, however, in our efforts to complement each other's strengths, we sometimes treat this *complementing* as a burdensome obligation to fulfill.

I wager that one of the most common sources of argument and marital frustration has been the false demand for us to complete each other. Consider the following common sentiments, each of which spells trouble:

- I'm unfulfilled with conversation during the day, so I need you to be my sounding board, even when you're too stressed and tired to absorb what I want to tell you about.
- I'm treated like I'm insignificant every day at work, so you need to let me boss you around in order for me to feel important in at least one setting.
- I'm starved for fun, so you need to be my only outlet for going out on the town.
- I don't have any interests or hobbies, so our romance needs to serve as my only outlet for diversion.
- I have low self-worth, so I need you to be beautiful and interesting so people will think I'm a winner.

Of course, we ought to help provide the gift of ourselves, whenever we are able to provide healing and value to a partner, through our unique qualities. We should be a sounding board for stressed partners, kind lovers who remind disrespected spouses that they are valued, friends who go out together, and people who provide relationships that make life worth living. But things get ugly when one or both partners become the *only* resource for such things.

Therefore, as a practical matter, it's important for both partners to cultivate their own interests and opportunities for connection so they don't emotionally suffocate the one they love. There are times when our own stresses and needs prevent us from being able to fill in the gaps of our partner's life. This reality becomes problematic when we fail to cultivate a sense of our own purpose and meaning. We forget to ask what we truly want.

What do *you* want? What do you want when you are yelling at your spouse about something you want from him or her? This is no simple question. Too often we act as if we are fighting about who's going to do the shopping, or who will finish the dishes, or how to spend money. But these usually are only symptoms of a more basic desire. Do you want adventure? Do you want security? Do you want to be generous to the needy? Do you want to have companionship? These questions sound simple, but we ask them too infrequently. Instead of asking them and answering them properly, we tend to get angry about tangential issues. This confuses our spouse and leads to deep frustration.

For many, asking what one really wants is a frightening prospect. Perhaps we are afraid of what we want. Perhaps the answer might mean we need to venture into new territory, explore new skills, or meet new people who are different. Despite this fear, the rewards gained after honestly asking such questions can be profound. For if we are at spiritual and emotional peace *and* are enlivened by life interests, we will be less likely to become emotionally disrupted when a spouse threatens that peace. Likewise, when we have friends outside of the home, these people can provide camaraderie when a spouse is in a foul mood. This should be interpreted not as a threat to either spouse but as a relief. Finding meaning in people outside the relationship is healthy and can take the pressure off each member of the team.

Despite what I've just said—which is a firm conviction, mind you—I still find myself spending most of my spare time with my wife. I dig her company, and we love to travel, take walks, and check out local music. Occasionally, I sense the need to get some space, but this need not be constant. My friend Dan and his wife, Beth Anne, however, sometimes like to get hotel rooms by themselves; this gives them a break from the kids and time for silence. As an extrovert, I don't find that sort of vacation appealing, though Stacie and I have tried it a few times with some success. But the grace for space Dan and Beth Anne give each other is valuable and worth considering. The point here is not to replicate the exact strategies couples use to find enjoyment outside marriage but rather that we should remember to give each other permission to cultivate interests beyond the relationship. There's a bonus in such a perspective: when our spouses have interests, they come back, cuddle, and enrich the marriage with tales of beautiful adventures.

Treating the Disease Rather than the Symptoms

In the Cleveland National Forest, which blankets the mountains towering above Southern California, mountain pine beetles (*dendroctonus ponderosae*) have laid waste to the idyllic landscape that has inspired suburbanites to build vacation homes in mountain resort areas. Worse, during the dry season, the weakened or dying trees often create conditions that lead to devastating wildfires. In the last couple decades, this has caused the near desolation of some areas. Mud and decaying branches litter the region. The damage has not been limited to these Southern California mountains but extends from northern Arizona to the wilds of British Columbia.

Pine beetles have killed off trees here and there over the centuries. But recently, it has become an epidemic. In situations like this, we tend to focus on the organism that is directly responsible. In this case, the culprit in question is an insect that likes to live beneath bark. We might be tempted to assume that by simply eradicating this pest, all will be made right. But this sort of thinking ignores the root of the problem. Literally. Pine beetles only become a severe threat after drought, pollution, overseeding, and underpruning and other environmental stressors have weakened the overall health of the trees.

The pine beetles illustrate an important aspect of surviving marriage. We are constantly tempted to assume that the main threats to our relationships are the pernicious events and people that add stress and frustration to a marriage. Nonetheless, like the pine beetle, these potential stressors are always around us. They only start to disrupt our daily well-being when we are weakened by a fundamental lack of emotional and spiritual health. If we get healthy, we are better able to fend off negative intrusions. And if we get healthy, we can begin to let go of our frantic desire to control others, get them to do our bidding, make them say sorry, or make them recognize that we've won an argument. We can start helping them heal.

Practically speaking, before seeking relationship counseling, I believe it's usually best to get individual counseling. In this way, we can address the negative mind-sets and behaviors we bring to a marriage. Marriage counseling can of course be helpful to improve aspects of a relationship like communication styles. But we should be careful not to ignore the root problems that led to communication missteps in the first place.

For instance, I know that instead of flipping out when my wife gets frustrated with me, I should go over and give her a hug, not let her moods dictate mine, and shrug off perceived injustices. I know this, and yet I still lose my cool. Often I lose my cool because I'm being defensive, resentful, or petty. This happens more frequently when I'm stressed, overworked, or tired. There is little that a practical communication strategy can do to overcome these basic problems. Instead, I need to address the core disease within me.

Here's where things get practical. Quarrels don't kill a marriage. In fact, they can be a healthy sort of "controlled burn" in a marriage. Such healthy quarrels can only occur when there's a backdrop of love, grace, and spiritual peace. When issues go unresolved through a relational drought, wildfires can end up destroying what we value most.

Perhaps another illustration will help clarify things. This time, it's drawn from popular culture. Now, I've never seen the show *My 600-lb Life*, but Stacie has, and she tells me that there is a common phenomenon for most participants who come onto the reality program to lose weight: they can't succeed in losing weight by diet and exercise alone. They need to address deeper issues in order to reach their goals. As I'm writing this, I'm in the cockpit of my sailboat. Let me go down the ladder, give my laptop to Stacie, and have her explain . . .

Guest Contribution: Stacie Mallinson, "Concerning *My 600-lb Life*"

The TLC series *My 600-lb Life* features stories of people who are severely obese and in need of gastric bypass surgery. A typical episode traces the story of a person trying to get well, usually beginning with an initial physician's consultation. After assessing the patient's health, the doctor provides a weight-loss goal that must be met prior to performing the surgery. If the patient is successful, surgery ensues.

In the few shows I've watched, I've noticed a pattern. After the surgery, the patient loses significant weight rather quickly, yet at some point he or she hits a barrier that cannot be crossed through medical means alone. Patients often realize that to lose additional weight, they need counseling. Inevitably, it turns out that there are deeper psychological issues at the root of their weight gain that must be dealt with in order for them to continue to lose weight and reach their ultimate goal. Interestingly, few seem to admit or confront the underlying psychological issues, and the folks on the show don't force them to address these at first. Instead, they wait for them to recognize that they need to get healthy in more ways than one. In the episodes I've seen, the root problem was often some type of abuse. For these people at least, it turned out that their obesity was a symptom of a deeper trauma.

As with frustrating approaches to weight loss, one problem with couples' counseling is that couples often approach the process as if the problem is primarily with the other partner or, at minimum, a failure of communication style. No, the problem exists most often within our own egos. Sometimes the problem might be even more basic. Do you (or your partner) need to work through childhood traumas or unhelpful ways of relating to others you picked up from your own family? Do either of you need a doctor to get your psychiatric prescriptions dialed in or your hormonal fluctuations under control? (Hormones are an issue for both men and women, by the way.) If so, failure to address those first will likely undermine any good advice a marriage and family therapist can offer. This doesn't mean that couples' counseling is unnecessary or unhelpful. It only means that we do well to see it as a secondary process to fine-tune a relationship between otherwise healthy individuals. There may of course be times when communication has broken down so far that one or both spouses fail to listen to reason and fail to seek personal healing. In such cases, go ahead and drag your stubborn spouse to a couples' therapist. But if you are both committed to healing yourselves and your relationship, take care of your own issues first, then move on to the marriage.

In my experience, if I am surfing the Tao, there's little my wife can do to affect my disposition negatively. If she's in a bad mood, I recognize that I don't need to be in a bad mood. Likewise, if my wife is marinating in the New Logic, it will be easier for her to shrug off times when I'm ungracious or melancholy. If either of us fails to do or say things that might complete or support the other, we can behave much more maturely and generously if we recognize that we have infinite completion and support by the Source of Life Himself.

Understand that I lose sight of this more than most. In ordinary life, it's probably one of my greatest shortcomings. As the son of an alcoholic, I'm neurotic about making sure everyone, and every relationship, around me is in a reasonably good state. This is because, growing up, if members of the family were in conflict, I knew that my world could become chaotic and painful that day. I've unfortunately taken this into my marriage: when Stacie is upset, I have a hard time being at inner peace; I think the world is about to come undone. Nevertheless, I'm convinced that the principle remains true, for when I *am* surfing the Tao, I realize that I don't need everyone else to be surfing a wave. I only need to learn to glide around them as they wade among the breakers—and offer a generous "hang loose" sign as I pass by—should they happen to obstruct my ride. I'm not really going anywhere, after all. I'm just frolicking in the waves and will paddle back where I started soon enough.

It's no easy task to find spiritual balance, or even an approximation of such a peace. Nonetheless, it *is* the proper goal. Any attempt to treat the symptoms rather than the disease is doomed from the outset.[4] According to Christianity, we can't "order ourselves" without a supernatural rescue by the God who loved us while we were yet sinners (Rom. 5:8). Nonetheless, we must recognize that this

---

[4] Chuang Tzu, *Chuang Tzu* (Chicago: Cloud Hands Press, 2015), Kindle Loc. 2366–68: "The Sage does not order the world first. The Sage creates order inside himself before attempting to order the world."

spiritual renovation is a priority—something to address prior to trying to fix others and our relationships.

Buddhism, Christianity, and Suffering Together

I don't like the story about the founder of Buddhism, Siddhartha Gautama, and his first step on the road to enlightenment. Even Buddhists will agree that the historical record of Siddhartha's life is unreliable, and they would add that it doesn't really affect the substance of their religion one way or the other. That's because, unlike Judaism, Christianity, and Islam, Buddhism doesn't depend on supernatural revelation. It is rather an invitation to a method for finding enlightenment, a way to live in tranquility rather than a set of propositions to be believed. Try it, and if it works, go with it. If not, there's no harm having tried it out. I mention all this because I intend no disrespect to actual Buddhists, whose ancient tradition of compassion, mindfulness, and personal tranquility is commendable, when I suggest a criticism of an element of his story. He may or may not have actually done what he's said to have done.

The part of the Buddha's story that troubles me is the moment when Siddhartha decided to set out alone in order to figure things out. Unable to face the tears of his wife and young son, he kissed them good-bye as they slept one night. Then he left them. Now, I admittedly just said a person needs to get his or her own spiritual and emotional self in order before trying to help loved ones. What's problematic in this case, however, is the assumption that a person should abandon his or her family in order to do this work of exploration. Admittedly, to question the path of a man who changed human history is audacious. Most accounts state that Siddhartha eventually returned home once he found enlightenment. That's a good ending, and the story ends well in this case. But I'm a fan of seeking spiritual understanding in community, in human embrace, and with family.[5] I believe that, especially for parents, our vocations as protectors

---

[5] Jesus did say that one must "hate" one's family in order to be his disciple (Luke 14:26). This is a difficult teaching indeed. It made more sense after I met a couple of students from various non-Christian families who converted to Christianity. The greatest obstacle for them was what getting baptized would mean for their relationships: in one case, the student couldn't return home to her country; in another, the student's father sacrificed a goat and

and providers must always trump our desire for spiritual insight or "finding ourselves." My sons are now older, and my youngest will graduate high school in a few years. There'll be more than enough time to go off and meditate in the woods, should I think that's needed. But in the meantime, parenting is too important a post to abandon.

Granted, Siddhartha was interested in a profound spiritual quest. To achieve his goals, he would have to devote all his mental and emotional energy to seeking Buddhahood. He was a prince, born to a king who had tried to protect him from the pain of life. The king didn't let his boy out of the palace. But one day, Siddhartha's caretaker took him on an excursion during which they witnessed sickness, old age, disease, poverty, and death. This devastated Siddhartha. How could all this suffering exist? How might one escape it? These became the questions that affected the rest of his life. After trying out the various intense religious strategies gurus of his time had employed to find peace and understanding, Siddhartha became a bodhisattva, one who attains enlightenment but, instead of departing this world, goes back to it with compassion and a mission to point others toward the true path. His core message was that suffering is caused by desire. Consequently, by letting go of desire, one could break free from the cycle of suffering and death.

Perhaps the reason I always found this story unsettling was that I'd seen this sort of behavior among people of my parents' generation. My folks had lived in a tent near Boulder, Colorado, before I was born, after which they decided to get a proper house. But many of their friends refused to conform to the strictures of life established by the so-called Greatest Generation that had preceded them. At my experimental, quasi-anarchist school, I had become friends with kids whose families lived in hippy communes. Despite my own romantic fascination with Christian anarchy and the bohemian impulse to detach from the system, I knew that many of the kids my age eventually realized their experience was a net failure. Their parents would prance about, talking about peace and love and community. But they

---

called on the gods to curse this young woman who was no longer to be treated as a daughter. This is what religious rejection of family carried with it in Jesus' time. Jesus is not, however, saying that it is virtuous for a Christian to abandon family vocations.

were often spiritual narcissists. Their own kids didn't seem to have been included in their sense of community. While they were off trying to find themselves, and sleeping with each other's spouses (as they had transcended conventional morality), they also emotionally abandoned their children. While trying to find earthly fulfillment, they let go of the parental relationships that are at the root of human fulfillment.

Being sexy is about remembering the importance of embodiment and connection. It rejects any new age strategy to live exclusively in a state of spiritual ecstasy. Granted, sexiness involves regular reconnection to a sense of the transcendent through various spiritual practices, but its ultimate focus is incarnate. For Christians, this is no incidental aspect of the faith but is rather the essence of what it means to be a theologian of the cross. While we Christians may meditate and seek serenity just as Buddhists do, we do these things in order to recharge and focus our attention on serving our neighbors through our various vocations. Among the most important of those vocations are the vocations of being a parent and spouse.[6]

I doubt anyone understood the core difference between Buddhism and Christianity better than Kazoh Kitamori, who explains that while Buddhism seeks to cultivate compassion, it's a compassion made possible by a sort of distance between the Buddhist seeker and other human beings. By eliminating desire, engagement with those who are in pain can be experienced as painless. The Christian call, on

---

[6] There isn't time or space to explore one interesting phenomenon within Japanese Buddhism: the Pure Land Buddhist sects known as Jodoshu and Jodo Shinshu. To one extent or another, these groups recognized the importance of grace. By "taking refuge" in the graciousness of the divine, or the Amidha Buddha (not identical to the Buddha formerly known as Siddhartha Gautama), a person can achieve enlightenment, peace, and a sort of salvation. The implication of this is often that Pure Land Buddhists recognize something like the Lutheran doctrine of vocation, as a primary context for serving others. These sects bore such a strong resemblance to Lutheran theology that (although I've not been able to track down any reliable historical record of this) the Catholic Jesuit Francis Xavier, after going to Japan as a missionary, purportedly exclaimed, "Oh, no, the Lutherans already got here!" Even if this story is apocryphal, there is a reason for its frequent retelling. Nonetheless, as I will explain, there remains a fundamental difference between the Buddhist and Christian approaches to suffering. What Christianity clings to, and that which Jodo and Jodo Shinshu traditions lack, is the element of pain involved in love. They typically seek, in a manner similar to liberal Christianity, a pleasant, pain-free grace without hearing the deep groans of suffering beneath our current veil of tears.

the contrary, involves sincere desire, not its eradication. Christian desire, by causing us to run toward the unlovable, the dangerous, and the hostile, often causes followers of Jesus to impale themselves on the barbs with which broken people seek to protect themselves. Loving the unlovable is thus a painful endeavor. This is true both for God and for God's people. "Thus," Kitamori explains, "the pain of God is *real* pain, the Lord's wounds are *real* wounds. Buddhism cannot comprehend this real pain."[7]

The theological importance of Kitamori's work is far reaching in its original context. But I believe that the great value of his ideas lies in his disregard for abstraction and his emphasis on the way in which Jesus' message applies the New Logic to concrete relationships. The foremost application here to romantic relationships is the core Christian teaching about forgiveness. We will return to this topic in a later chapter, but it is the centerpiece to our present question: *How can we survive marriage?* The answer is as simple as it is humanly impossible: desire will cause suffering; suffering is addressed through forgiveness. I say that forgiveness is humanly impossible in terms of the Old Logic: in the Old Logic of karma, of reaping what you sow, of brutal cause and effect, forgiveness is absurd. But it's also essential to the New Logic. This is no idle claim. Jesus puts it right in the middle of the Lord's Prayer: "forgive us our sins as we forgive those who sin against us." The idea of forgiveness in marriage brings to mind my friends Debi and Kurt, who've been married for more than four decades. They told Stacie and me that the key to their connubial bliss has been their practice of mutually forgiving each other each morning.

Now, Debi and Kurt are one of those rare couples we've met whose relationship seems enviable. I'm not saying successful and happy marriages aren't out there, just that they seem rare to me. Consider this matter for yourself: maybe create a list of married friends and family you know well. How many of those couples seem to have relationships that you would describe as truly happy? I suspect your estimate falls beneath the 50 percent mark. What's more, I suspect that among those "good" relationships, a decent proportion

---

[7] Kazoh Kitamori, *Theology of the Pain of God: The First Original Theology from Japan* (Eugene, OR: Wipf & Stock, 2005), 27.

of those couples are good at faking it in public and are actually frustrated with the state of things at home. Social media platforms skew our perceptions even further: we tend to post our best moments, our spouse's finest culinary creations, and our children's academic awards, not our setbacks. Only the downers in our circles publicly lament the ugly stuff in their lives, at least until they let us all know they broke up or got divorced.

The potential good news, according to a University of Chicago report, is that my perception of things differs from what married folks self-report. According to a 2014 study, 59.9 percent said they were "very happy" and 36.6 percent said they were "pretty happy," while only 3.5 percent admitted they were "not too happy." Even though the "very happy" group dropped a few percentage points since the same survey two years earlier, these statistics suggest that the overwhelming majority insist they are doing just fine.[8] Dang, I must be too pessimistic, but I just don't sense that those numbers tell the whole story. Look, sociology is not my primary field. It's not even a secondary field, though I respect it very much and value the insights it offers religious studies. What do I know about the methodology and reliability of this particular study?

What interests me, however, is not the precise data points but why my perception of others' relationships differs so drastically from couples' self-reports. After all, even when things are going pretty well for us, we tend to grumble. It might be that these positive self-reports are the product of rampant self-deception. We tend to be masters of this art, and we practice it regularly within the context of marriage. Come to think of it, when I reflect on those couples I don't think have happy marriages, I can recall multiple times when they have made grand claims to having a successful relationship on Facebook. What gives?

I think I have a plausible explanation: for those whose identity and success depend on achieving a successful marriage, to admit to any severe difficulties is terrifying. Even when filling out a questionnaire, such people would create too much inner turmoil if they were

---

[8] Tom Smith, Jaesok Son, and Benjamin Shapiro, *General Social Survey Final Report: Trends in Psychological Well-Being, 1972–2014*, NORC at the University of Chicago, April 2015.

to admit how difficult things are. Most of us unfortunately know at least one person who, though verbally or even physically abused by his or her spouse, oddly insists that he or she is in love and has a great partner. Far fewer of us recognize how often we make a similar move in our own relationships: we deny reality because we don't want to confront the truth.

All this nonsense is like substance addiction. The moment I'm forced to admit I have a drinking problem, for instance, I also realize that I need to make a dramatic change in my daily routine. Simultaneously, if I'm ready to be honest, I'll recognize my own failings and weakness. That process hurts, and for some people, it hurts worse than harsh words or slaps to the face. I wish this weren't the case, but I fear it is. Now, if my own self-worth is tied up in being wanted by someone else, being successfully married, and having a model family, the minute I admit things are amiss, my whole world threatens to fall apart. If I admit to myself and others that I'm not entirely happy, I assume that the next step (perhaps after giving marriage counseling a try) will inevitably be divorce, public failure, and the loss of that which gives me legitimacy in the world as I imagine it.

Notice how this is a sort of theology of glory. Refusing to recognize we are still messy works in progress, we seek to assure ourselves of our proper standing before God and earthlings and that we are worthy of love by pointing to our victories. Take away the victory, and you threaten to take away assurance.

That is an Old Logic way of thinking, though. In contrast, I agree with the New Logic of Luther's Heidelberg Disputation (1518), thesis 21, when he states, "A theology of glory calls evil good and good evil. A theology of the cross calls the thing what it actually is." We might protest and insist that looking on the bright side, counting the glass half full, and putting the best spin on things are virtues. In some contexts, this might be true. However, it can prevent us from growing, healing, and finding mutual forgiveness.

But now imagine what it would be like if this couple were to refuse to admit to each other when they were angry, hurt, or confused by the other member of the team. In such a case, they might fail to encounter the joy of forgiving and being forgiven. Moreover, they would start to store up unacknowledged resentments. Then, at a moment of severe stress—even external stress unrelated to the relationship itself—these resentments might threaten to burst forth. When this happens, such couples make an abrupt change. Whereas they once loudly extolled their superior marriage, they start lamenting the evil character of the person with whom they are now fighting tooth and nail in divorce court. I've seen this firsthand, and all too often.

I'm not pointing out this tragic phenomenon to gloat or to gainsay those who claim they are happy. Thank God for even a mustard seed's worth of happiness, for it can be enough to keep a person from losing hope. I'm mulling over this phenomenon here because it reflects a fundamental wrongheadedness about the nature of grace, love, forgiveness, and marriage itself. It reflects an orientation toward the Old Logic.

The New Logic of grace considers the level of personal happiness in a marriage as important but irrelevant to the question of whether infinite love is present. If married love rests on the promise of divine *agape* rather than an experience of happiness, a lack of happiness becomes an urgent ailment to heal, but not an immediate reason to end the marriage. If married love flourishes when we recognize that our standing before heaven and earth depends on the prior love of God, not our own success, then we can start to be honest with ourselves and others. Most important, we cannot find or give forgiveness if we refuse to recognize—whether in our own actions or those of our partner—what it is that needs forgiveness in the first place.

According to Miroslav Volf, forgiveness has a power beyond merely bringing emotional serenity to the forgiver. It ignites a gracious relationship and can lead to the transformation of both the one forgiven and the relationship between the forgiver and the forgiven individuals. This is because Christian forgiveness refuses to wait for a transformation of life or even an inward state of repentance. "Instead of being a *condition* of forgiveness, however," Volf writes, "repentance is its necessary consequence."[9] The gracious ethos

---

[9] Miroslav Volf, *Free of Charge: Giving and Forgiving in a Culture Stripped of Grace* (Grand Rapids, MI: Zondervan, 2006), 183.

created by an act of gratuitous forgiveness allows the forgiven one to realize that there is nothing to lose by taking a sincere look at his or her own offenses. "In other words," Volf explains, "we are able to genuinely repent only when forgiveness has first been extended to us."[10] Luther agrees. In thesis 28 of his Heidelberg Disputation, he proposes the following: "The love of God does not find, but creates, that which is pleasing to it." Only by connecting to this divine *agape* love can we hope to create love, which may have become only a dying ember.

Make no mistake; forgiveness can be painful before it heals. Forgiveness implies a preexisting sense of judgment. Even admitting to the need for forgiveness is painful, because it confronts a personal failure. It also causes pain in the one who forgives, since it asks the forgiver to absorb something negative without spitting it back in the face of the offender who, according to the Old Logic, is the one who rightly deserves it. True forgiveness does not need to have a precise *record* or enumeration of wrongs, but it does assume that there has been some sort of wrong.

Looping back to where we started, Kitamori's insights on this matter are particularly insightful: "When one truly forgives, he must forget the fact of his forgiveness. This certainly does not imply that forgiveness is easy tolerance. One must bear responsibility for the sinner and suffer pain. However, the pain, if real, penetrates the one who forgives, and issues forth in intentional love. One is not really forgiving others as long as he complains about his own pain in forgiveness. Forgiveness exhibits its true nature, and pain proves to be real, only when intentional love enfolds others, forgetting its pain."[11] Here, instead of the Buddhist strategy of eliminating desire in order to eliminate pain, the Christian strategy audaciously holds that by unchaining desire for another (*eros*), we run headlong into the pain, excise it from our beloved, absorb it, and ultimately overcome it by choosing to forget it.

Of course, when reconciliation occurs after forgiveness, we reflect back on it and recall it as a positive, sometimes

---

[10] Ibid., 185.

[11] Kitamori, *Theology of the Pain of God*, 40. I'm not sure what "intent love" is, so I changed it to "intentional love."

even euphoric, experience. True, but perhaps this is what it's like when a mother gives birth to her child, pushing through intense pain but forgetting that pain once the infant is finally at her breast. In the moment, however, it is typically only false forgiveness that produces pain-free euphoria on its own. False forgiveness occurs when we enjoy watching offending parties squirm, cry, and admit their fault and we imply our superiority in the situation and believe they perpetually owe us a debt of gratitude for our magnanimity. Sometimes a romantic partner forgives with sinful motives. For instance, a husband might forgive a wife (1) to show that he is the nobler half of the couple; (2) to have something over his wife, something she would perpetually "owe"; and (3) to be able to recall this act of forgiveness when the he needs a pardon himself.

The way past this sort of nonsense involves dispensing with moral bean counting altogether. Instead, it rests in the promise that all is well and infinite love is already on offer—freely transferrable to friends, family, and neighbors, by the way—by returning to the fountainhead of *agape*. The tragic alternative is to live in the Old Logic, which depends on Law not Gospel. Relationships that depend on law for their security are all dead ends. The New Logic, however, insists that everything is already and will be OK. As Luther said, "The Law says 'do this' and it is never done. Grace says, 'believe this,' and everything is already done."[12]

True forgiveness releases real screw-ups from the weight of their sins, including screw-ups who don't deserve forgiveness. It is only conceivable if we embrace the New Logic and remember that forgiveness can't depend on the lovableness of the offending party in question. Indeed, as Kitamori writes, "We must love the unlovable. . . . When our fellow becomes an 'enemy' who betrays our love, and we continue to love him still more deeply, then pain is born in us. In an ethic without pain we love our fellow only as long as he is worthy of our love; then, when he is no longer worthy, we drop him and forget him. There is no constancy in

---

[12] Luther, Heidelberg Disputation, thesis 26.

such love."[13] This last sentence is especially insightful when it comes to marriage. Lack of constancy throws everything out of whack. Whenever one party in a couple suspects that conditional love is at work, defensiveness and stubbornness abound. True love opposes this and begins with the premise that since love wasn't dependent on individual performance in the first place, it can't be lost. Fortunately, Kitamori explains, the bonus to all this is that "love of the unlovable when we are absolutely consistent in it, displays the power to transform the unlovable into the *lovable*."[14] Forgiveness depends entirely on this way of thinking, which is foolishness to the world's wisdom. Let us endeavor, therefore, to be holy fools.

This way of thinking, this commitment to *agape* within a marriage, involves *passion* in the fullest sense. We often claim to be "passionate" about someone we love. The Latin word *passio* means "suffering." It carries with it a sense of having to endure pain. In the middle ages, forms of the word *passio* came to mean "deep desire" but also the Passion of Christ—that is, his redemptive suffering. Surviving marriage, similarly, includes both the cultivation of deep desire and a heroic commitment to suffering together, all for the sake of love.

Guest Contribution: Debi Winrich, "Forgiveness in Marriage"

Mawidge ... mawidge is what bwings us togewer today ...
—The Impressive Clergyman, *The Princess Bride*

If you've never seen the film *The Princess Bride*, I say, first of all, shame on you. Get yourself to your favorite movie-streaming site and view it. Stat! Second, the esteemed Impressive Clergyman

---

[13] Kitamori, *Theology of the Pain of God*, 93.

[14] Ibid., 94.

with a speech impediment "that would stop a clock"[15] opens up a dialogue about marriage. If indeed marriage brings a man and woman together, what in the world keeps them together? I have a few hard-earned thoughts on that subject after forty-one-plus years of marriage.

Twice in my sixty-three years I've been confronted—at a whole new level—with how disgustingly selfish I am: the first was getting married and the second was becoming a mother. I know both relationships have many purposes, but I think God additionally uses both to show us who we really are.

I'll start backward with my journey into motherhood. It's October 8, 1981. You remember that year: MTV was launched, the first case of AIDS was found in Los Angeles, Ronald Reagan was president, Lady Di married Prince Charles (by all accounts at the time, the wedding of the century), and most important to me, I became a mother.

Picture this: I'm standing in my bathroom stark naked with my deflated belly sagging from the recent birth of my first son of three. I now have breasts for the first time in my life. Let's just say they are no longer concave. My head is cradled in my folded arms, resting on the chest-high bathroom counter. I am crying like a baby. I know this because I had just given birth to one and had already become an expert on the sound of infants testing their lungs. In walks my mother, who had come from a long distance to witness the birth and help with the initiation. The following exchange was a life changer for me.

"What's wrong?" she cried.

"I can't do it. It's too hard!" I cried.

"You have no choice, you big boob! YOU HAVE TO!" she firmly stated.

She always called my brother and me *boobs* when we were growing up. It was code for "big baby." What she didn't know was that I was actually crying about the fact that (1) my breasts hurt because they were stretched beyond capacity and (2) I was having

---

[15] William Goldman, *The Princess Bride* script, 1987—Shooting Draft, http://www.imsdb.com/scripts/Princess-Bride,-The.html, accessed March 1, 2017.

a hell of a time inserting a suppository in my derriere (when you push during a birth for two hours, you need those). But I knew in my heart and soul what she actually meant.

There was no turning back; cats were out of bags, the toothpaste was now tubeless, and the Genie bottleless. My newborn son was here to stay. I was a mother forevermore and responsible for another human life. Good Lord! I was an indispensable life source for all my baby's needs. I would be the person needed to feed and clothe and mentor this tiny, helpless creature for the next eighteen or so years. God had called me to be a mother. My life was no longer about me. It was now about someone else: my son. If I reneged on my end of the deal, he would die. He would have to become first above all else.

Now let's rewind things six more years back to my wedding day. Marriage, too, foists upon you the stark truth that daily life is no longer about you. That became a school-of-hard-knocks reality as the years passed. My husband and I were (and still are) Christians, but our Christianity then involved the notion that our lives and behavior would get better and better because we made every effort to please God. However, when conflicts began to emerge and our spouse was not meeting all our personal needs, we became oft-embroiled in the battle of the egos: wife versus husband. As the years ticked by, I knew one thing about myself: I wasn't actually getting better, kinder, or more obedient to God. Oh, sure, I'd improve at times, but sooner or later I'd slip up and I'd be back to square one. My sin did and still does run deep. It is unfathomable.

It was not until I'd been married more than twenty years that I came to a Christian tradition that explained my daily struggles. If you read the seventh chapter of Romans, you find the apostle Paul talking about his battle with doing the things he knows he should do but failing miserably. He describes a person who seems to have two people battling inside him. I came to know the term for that. It's fancy and it's Latin: *simul iustus et peccator.*

This phrase, a slogan born out of Martin Luther's sixteenth-century Reformation, simply means that I am simultaneously a sinner and a saint. I'm a saint only because I have been given the righteousness of Christ to cover me. I am no longer judged by my *inability* to do what is right. Jesus took that with Him to the cross. And I now wear His perfect ability to keep the law, removing the onus put on me to be perfect and to do all that is required of me. But that sinner in me keeps coming up for air to plague me every day. If that's what was happening to me, I realized, it was also happening to my husband. And if I had been unequivocally forgiven for Christ's sake, despite my inability to please God, I then could and should forgive my husband. It sounds too simple. But that is the essence of the Gospel. Jesus took our place on the cross and continues to do so every day. God isn't mad at me, for Christ's sake (Rom. 8:1). Indeed, just this morning my pastor reminded me that I am "blood-bought and covered."

So two decades later, I tell this story to those who will listen: Every day, without fail, I rise in the morning, giving thanks for another day of breath, and I forgive my husband. Has he done anything yet to warrant my forgiveness? No. But he most certainly will. He's so predictable that way. And, every day, as my husband rises, he gives thanks for another day of breath and he forgives me. I have not done anything yet to warrant his forgiveness, but I know I will—probably in the first phrases I utter as my feet hit the floor. It's inevitable. But it's OK. Don't think for a minute that I am bragging or proud of my penchant for sin or making light of the fact that I fall daily. But because I am relationally right with God, I am free to get up, dust myself off, and try again to do the right thing. I'm not condemned, and I'm not paralyzed. I'm rejoicing in God's unmerited gift of forgiveness.

So my husband and me? We have each other's backs—because Jesus has ours.

I have a dear pastor friend who once told me that when he officiates at weddings, he tells the soon-to-be husband and wife to look closely at each other and know "that standing before you is the one person who will sin against you more than any other person on the planet for the rest of your life." Oh, that all pastors would speak this truth! This forgiveness that my husband and I practice is something I call pre-emptive forgiveness. It's akin to what God did for us: "But God shows his love for us in that while we were yet sinners Christ died for us" (Rom. 5:8).

Hey, but why did I tell my motherhood story first?

Here's why: We need to look at marriage as seriously as we look at having children. Like a child, marriage is a gift to be guarded and protected. When that little one comes into the world, he or she does so into the arms of someone who has his or her back. And there is no turning back. Remember the silly toothpaste metaphor? It is (or should be) a permanent state. You can't stop being the parents. You can give up your rights (God forbid!), but you will always be the blood parents of this child. In some Christian traditions, infants are baptized; in others they are "dedicated." In either case, they often include a vow to raise the child with the creeds and catechism of the church. It is a beautiful ceremony not unlike a wedding. And like the baptism of a baby, marriage is, as some traditions would say, a sacrament, which signifies God's grace or unmerited favor—a gift, if you will, as children are a gift from the Lord (Ps. 127:3). As with children, this gift must be cherished, nurtured, washed, fed, educated, sometimes coddled, praised, sometimes laughed about, hugged, sometimes disciplined, lifted up, rescued, and—*most importantly*—both recipients of the gift of marriage must *forgive the other just as a parent always forgives a child*. This looks a lot like our relationship with our Maker. In fact, marriage is the mirror image of the relationship Christ has with His bride, the church. It is the cornerstone upon which everything that comes after rests. It is a safe place to be who we are. But we must all the while remember that we won't be perfect at this forgiveness thing. That sinner still in us will fail at it miserably and often. But know for certain that tomorrows bring new mercies and more days to forgive and be forgiven: "The steadfast love of the LORD never ceases, his mercies never come to an end; they are new every morning; great is thy faithfulness" (Lam. 3:2–23).

> Forgwivness . . . Forgwivness is what keeps us togewer.
>
> —Debi Winrich (on a good day)

Call the Thing What It Is

Is your marriage struggling? Then admit it. Admit it to yourself and your spouse. Unfortunately, when things go badly, the worst thing we can do in a relationship is to deny the reality of our situation. In most cases, it's important to admit you're unhappy when you're unhappy. This requires a safe context of grace and trust, of course. It requires a deep connection to *agape* as the bedrock of a relationship. Otherwise, such honesty can backfire. After all, in a relationship based on transaction, law, and scorekeeping, admitting anything negative gets interpreted as an act of aggression.

Luther's Heidelberg Disputation (1518) thesis 21 is helpful here: "A theology of glory calls evil good and good evil. A theology of the cross calls the thing what it actually is." In marriage, we usually want to pretend everything is OK, especially on social media or when having dinner with other couples. We think that if there is anything off, we will be seen as spiritual failures. But with the understanding of grace, so important to Luther's way of thinking, we are free to diagnose and address the troubling parts of marriage. Indeed, couples who practice this type of calm honesty when experiencing injustice have a better chance of enjoying a long and satisfying marriage.

I'm no marriage counselor. What I'm talking about here is a theological frame of reference that has been important for my own marriage and the marriages of close friends with whom we've discussed these ideas. However, if your marriage is in extreme crisis, I must refer you to the most important scholar on the subject of marriage and divorce: John Gottman. He has several books based on extensive university research. Pretty much anything he has published can be helpful. He shows that couples who fight aren't necessarily in a dangerous or unhealthy situation. Sometimes not fighting at all can mean the relationship is dead. The most important question for Gottman is, *How does a couple fight?* And then, *How do they work to repair the relationship?*[16]

Of the several factors that can destroy a marriage, he identifies *defensiveness* as one of the greatest threats. He goes so far as to call it one of the "Four Horsemen of the Apocalypse," alongside criticism

---

[16] John Gottman et al., *10 Lessons to Transform Your Marriage* (New York: Random House, 2007).

(making a global attack on a partner's personality or character), contempt (relating to a partner with hostility and disgust), and stone-
walling (when a partner withdraws from a conversation). Here's
Gottman's definition of defensiveness: "These are counterattacks people use to defend their innocence or avoid taking responsibility for a
problem. Defensiveness often takes the form of cross-complaining or
whining." Defensiveness, for our purposes, is the opposite of "calling
a thing what it is" and is an Old Logic behavior. In biblical terms, it is
an attempt to stitch fig leaves together to hide our shame rather than
letting God clothe us in his own righteous sacrifice. Defensiveness is
a sign we aren't surfing the Tao. It's a sign, on the contrary, that we
are operating in terms of law and transaction.

The legal concept of marriage is terribly dangerous. Consider
the common phenomenon of celebrities embroiled in scandal. In
almost every case, the celebrities begin with a bold denial of having done anything wrong. Later, their handlers and lawyers instruct
them to remain silent, to avoid self-incrimination. Nothing can be
gained in a legal sense, their thinking goes, from saying they did
wrong. Eventually, they might issue a formal apology if they think it
can get the media or a potential litigant off their backs. But admitting
you were wrong up front can also serve as evidence against you in a
law court. So there we have it: is our relationship best understood as
taking place within a courtroom or is it a holy and romantic covenant? If it takes place in a courtroom, we're doomed.

I once heard Paul Zahl say something like while it is true that
the primary mark of a Christian community should be love for one
another (John 13:35), a community saturated in gracious love—the
genuine Christian community—also should be notable for its ability
to be the first to confess when it is wrong. I think he is spot-on with
respect to the way we *should* relate to each other and to the culture at
large. We are a community that both confesses the truth about God
and also confesses the uncomfortable truth about ourselves. This
gives permission to everyone involved to be honest and seek healing.
I can't commend Zahl's book *Grace in Practice* highly enough. His
opening paragraph in the chapter "Grace in Marriage" is insightful:

> The feelings leading to marriage are aroused by the physical and
> romantic ecstasy resulting from being discovered, in one's true

hidden existence, by another person. This is the thesis concerning grace in relation to marriage: Being known in weakness is the origin of marriage. Marriage, in other words, depends on a theology of the cross rather than a theology of glory. If you are married or were married, remember the origin of your marriage. The root and fountain of the relationship was the discovery by another of your true but hidden self. You disclosed yourself. The disclosure sure lit a fire that gave off a lot of heat. A "purely" sexual relationship did not have this fire. But the sexual relationship that accompanied the disclosure did. It led to your desire to be married.[17]

By being naked and not ashamed, marriage is, in a way, a map back to the bliss of Edenic relationships. Grace creates space for *intimacy*, which Zahl defines as "when I know somebody else as they really are."[18] Indeed, Zahl's connection between the gracious vulnerability in marriage and the delight of physical sexuality is precisely what true *sexiness* is all about.

Now, those familiar with the twelve-step community know that the first step in recovery is to *admit that you have a problem*. Failure here leads to ultimate failure in the pursuit of sobriety. The same principle holds true for troubled marriages. Far too often, couples keep insisting that all is well, but meanwhile, they try to salvage their marriages at such points by making another baby or buying a more expensive house. Often all this comes on the eve of a nasty divorce.

Vulnerability is terrifying and difficult. Moreover, couples in failing marriages who depend on a courtroom model for relating sometimes soon find themselves hashing out their differences within an actual law court, mired in the details of divorce proceedings. If your relationship lives by the legal sword, you are likely to see it die by the legal sword. In such cases, vulnerability can be a bad strategic move. Admitting fault can lead to concrete financial loss, especially in states where divorce courts take fault into consideration.

There's an alternative, however. If divine grace undergirds our marriages, there is room to be laid bare, though that is never entirely

---

[17] Paul F. M. Zahl, *Grace in Practice: A Theology of Everyday Life* (Grand Rapids, MI: Eerdmans, 2007), Kindle Loc. 1819–20.

[18] Ibid., Kindle Loc. 1846.

a comfortable experience. Grace creates a safe space in which we can be honest. Grace establishes a relationship strengthened by trust. This trust can't be a naïve sense that a partner will never let us down. Rather, it depends on a cosmic trust, which depends on God. As Lao Tzu rightly said, "Without fundamental trust, there is no trust at all."[19]

Therefore, remind yourself and others that relationship score keeping is a losing endeavor from the perspective of the New Logic. Paul writes that love keeps no record (λογίζεται/*logizetai*) of wrongs—that is, true love isn't in the business of keeping a log. It covers over or casts out offenses rather than using them for relational ammunition. There's even a more audacious way of applying this concept, according to Micah Bournes; in his blues song "No Record of Right," he suggests that even keeping score of our own contributions to a relationship can be unhealthy:

> You goin' off on a rage
> Throwin' your good in my face
> Screamin' that I don't remember all your patience and grace
> Yeah I made some mistakes
> But it's easy to see
> I'm not the one forgettin' how you used to love me
>
> All that good you was doin'
> All them gifts that you gave
> Didn't know that they was credit you would try to exchange
> Didn't know that they was weapons you would use for my shame
> Didn't bother keepin' score
> 'cause it wasn't a game
>
> Love keeps no record of right
> If you think I owe you somethin'
> this whole thing is a lie
> We was s'pose to be forever
> Why you keep your receipts
> I don't care how much it cost you
> Now I know it was cheap

---

[19] Lao-Tzu, *Tao Te Ching*, trans. Stanley Lombardo and Stephen Addiss (Indianapolis: Hackett Classics, 2011), 22.

Just how many thank-yous do you think you deserve
Your generosity seems a little perverse
If love is what you givin' don't be holdin' it tight
And don't you have that left hand keepin' track of the right
Is this what you wanted
Your praise in a song
Is this what you wanted
A round of applause
Here goes your attention
There go your reward
Now the whole world know that your love is a fraud

Love keeps no record of right
If you think I owe you somethin'
this whole thing is a lie
We was s'pose to be forever
Why you keep your receipts
I don't care how much it cost you
Now I know it was cheap

I don't owe you nuthin' baby
True love is always free
True love is always free

Of course, we do have obligations in our vocations. In a moral sense, we are obligated to care for our spouses and to protect our children from harm. The problem is with the business of moral accounting. It is wrongheaded and—despite all our efforts to hoard relational wealth—leaves our marriages bankrupt.

Guest Contribution: Stacie Mallinson, "Praying for Marriage to My High School Sweetheart"

I was seven years old, looking out the upstairs window of my Lake Forest, California, bedroom. I saw the perfectly manicured yards of the typical Southern California cookie-cutter homes of all my neighbors, I saw the street filled with shiny white trucks and SUVs, before I peeled myself from the window and began making my bed. A flood of questions came to me: "Why do I live in this house? How is it that I live in this house, in this city, with my parents? Who am I? What am I supposed to do with my life? What does all this mean?"

Throughout the years, I've found myself buying into what I thought was involved in achieving the American Dream. In this version, success was finding a husband, getting married, getting a nice house and two shiny cars of my own, and having a decent savings account to afford having and supporting children. I planned on two to be exact: the first a boy and then a girl. If the second was a boy, then I'd go for number three to try to have a girl; but if I didn't have a girl, *then* I'd call it quits. I was convinced that it was too expensive to have four or more children and still have the rest of the American Dream. After all, I saw how much my parents struggled to support my three sisters and me.

At fourteen, I found the boy of my dreams. He was smart and handsome and had lots of charisma and passion. I was immediately attracted to him; there was something about him, I don't know what it was, but I "fell in love." I actually prayed to God, saying, "Dear God, please let me marry Jeff. I'll do anything if I can marry him, even if it's the worst thing for me, please let me marry him." At sixteen, we started dating. I couldn't believe it! My dreams were coming true; God answered my prayer! I knew I wanted to marry him. He was the piece I needed to begin the path of success toward my American Dream.

During the four years of dating, I found myself getting upset every time he didn't fit into my neat little package. Why didn't I get flowers on this particular Valentine's Day; that's what the man does when he loves his woman, right? Why is he leaving me to go to college in Colorado? In my understanding, the man doesn't part from the woman he loves for any reason; he would stay right by her side . . . after all, if he leaves, maybe somebody else would steal her away. Anyway, even though he didn't completely measure up to my expectations, all in all, he was a good guy, a superintelligent hard worker. Even though he wasn't perfect, I thought he loved me. So we pushed on to the next step: marriage. Of course, in my mind, once we were married everything would fall into place and my American Dream would be a reality. Wrong!

I see the same Facebook anniversary posts we women create all the time. We write how there have been good and bad times, but if we had to do it all over again, we'd still choose our husbands. There isn't anybody we'd rather do life with, and we profess our undying love. We talk up our family's successes. We have nice pictures of expensive houses and possessions. The sad part is that maybe later that same year, or perhaps several years down the road, we often come to find that these marriages are falling apart. Why?

Through pondering this phenomenon, and also through the course of my own romantic life, I think about the times I've pondered divorce. Usually it's because the particular dream I had hasn't become the reality. Life is hard. We get stuck in the same old fights, and nothing seems to get better. Is this my reality? Is this the life I want for myself? Hell no!

Oh, but the kids, I can't leave because of the kids. I want what is best for them. So I plow on, trying to will myself into making my husband and my relationship better. Maybe I won't say anything this time when he messes up. I'll bite my tongue because that's what true love is. Forgiving his faults, not letting it get to me, not losing my cool, and putting up with all his imperfections. That is love. Once again wrong! That's not love; that's self-righteous indignation. In such cases, we get to despise our spouses *and* congratulate ourselves for putting up with the jerks.

The Bible says that the man should leave his mother and father and be united to his wife, and the two shall become one flesh (Gen. 2:24). Think about that: the two shall become one. Not two separate people trying to get through this life by getting around the obstacles created by the other, not trying to achieve one's own version of the dream. "One flesh" means that you need to work together as one. This is the only way we can hope to fulfill our marital vocations, our callings in life.

In this case of marriage, our calling is to be one. I realize that when I want to accomplish something in practical life, I get the right tools together and utilize the correct part of the body to make it happen. If I want to get across the street, for example, I don't do a handstand and expect to navigate across using my hands and arms. I use my feet and legs. In addition, the hands don't say to the feet, "That's not fair; you get to be the one that touches the ground and gets us across the street." Instead, you are grateful for your feet, if you are lucky enough to have them, to get there efficiently. Similarly, if you see your relationship as two who are joined as one, you don't begrudge a talent when it is not yours personally. When this talent is in the other person, we shouldn't just try to stay out of the way; instead, we should actively encourage and foster that talent. In terms of the original metaphor, perhaps you use hands to put on shoes so the feet can do the work they need to. With this approach to things, I now see the real love my future husband was showing me when he moved to Colorado. He temporarily moved away so that he could get a degree that would ultimately help support the family and help us achieve our God-given vocations, as we were to become united as one flesh. I now believe this mutual support is far more important than the dream I originally envisioned at age seven.

As I look at my own life and the lives of so many of the women around me, we often understand some of what our men want to do or need to do to fulfill a calling or put a roof over our heads and the heads of our children; yet, for some reason, we wives have a tendency to get selfish and forget about being one flesh, and we start to think of how our needs are not being met as individuals, or our troubles become overwhelming compared to what we imagine our husbands are suffering. Consequently, we feel the need to stop them from what they are doing so they can come help us. Rather than being complementary, we put our hands in the way of our husbands' feet, causing them to trip and delaying and possibly injuring both parties in the process. Of course, the same could be said of our men doing something like this to us women, but I'm not talking to the men right now. I'm talking to the ladies. If you love your man, you'll stop tripping him and instead work with him to cross the street as one.

Perhaps this illustration will help explain what I mean by "tripping your man." In our family, we jokingly label things as

"Daddy's fault." Let me explain why. The plight of the man, at least in my culture, is a difficult burden, and there has been a lot of change lately with respect to gender roles, but the husband still tends to carry a great weight of responsibility; he is still seen by most as ultimately responsible for taking care of his family, which especially entails providing a house for them to live in and making sure that house is filled with all the necessities and the extras.

Even if Mommy works and brings in a significant portion of the household income, society still often suggests that Daddy is responsible for making sure the children have access to the proper health care, schooling, and opportunities that they need to be successful. Therefore, we expect the man to go out and make the money or whatever it takes to procure these "necessities." The size of the house, whether big or small, we in my family (in jest) label as "Daddy's fault." The type of car we drive and whether it runs properly? Daddy's fault. If the car is cheap and embarrassing, that is to Daddy's shame. If he spent too much on a car, perhaps as part of his midlife crisis, the resulting financial difficulty is also Daddy's fault.

Is it all really "Daddy's fault?" Yes, to the extent that all parents serve as world creators and sustainers, perhaps at a subconscious level, for their families. But in another sense, it isn't his fault, and this is the tragedy. There are all sorts of sociological and economic factors involved in worldly success, and these are often beyond his control. But do we women and society look at our men and size them up as to what their value is as men by how nice our cars are or how nice our houses are? Sadly, I think we too often do. So our men go out and try to find a way to support their families so that they can have comfort in the fact that their families are not left wanting. But then, when our men are spending their time and energy to keep their families happy and well-fed, we wives often start to complain: "You're not spending enough time with me" or "You don't play with the kids enough or help me take care of them."

Now, I'm willing to reconsider the optimal gender expectations in contemporary society. But we women can't have it both ways. Men can't be in two places at once; they are either out making money or spending time at home. Of course, there needs to be a balance between work and home, but what we should keep in mind is that we need to have realistic expectations. Sometimes, in order for your man to complete the calling of your one flesh, it will require that he spend time away from you and the kids. For example, if he is a doctor, I need to understand that he may stop in the middle of anything, any family time, and go help somebody in need. I shouldn't just avoid stopping him; I need to *encourage* him to go, and I need to feel his pain when he can't be around to experience and enjoy this family time that he works so hard to facilitate. Therefore, when he comes home, I shouldn't give him the cold shoulder for not being with the family. I need to draw him into my arms and thank him for what he does to take care of us and others in this world and recognize his pain for having to work that hard. Recognizing his sacrifice, which it is, helps me appreciate all that he does and makes me want to help take care of him by doing whatever I can to ease his burden in this life.

This being said, going with my earlier analogy of walking, true love doesn't just stay out of the other's way; it recognizes the pain of the feet, the blisters, the burden of carrying the weight of the rest of the body to reach the destination. It involves compassion for our husbands and a desire to assuage their pain. Too often, I find that I myself, as well as others, get into the habit of disdaining and belittling my man—sometimes in his presence, but more frequently behind his back. Consider changing course on this, for when your man feels your support, compassion, and ultimately your love, it's like magic. His strength and stamina increase, and he is able to joyfully contribute his part to what your one flesh needs to fulfill in its God-given purpose. I've come to find my original version of the American Dream to have been mistaken and materialistic. That said, I've seen firsthand that supporting rather than belittling a husband has a way of leading to financial benefits too. Anyone who is being supported rather than beaten down, encouraged rather than belittled, will be more effective and upbeat in his or her vocation. This produces real-world success. I'm not as interested in those material things anymore, but it's worth noting that by easing up on the demands for those things, they tend to come more easily.

In short, I believe that the secret ingredient to a successful, loving marriage is this: to understand and take on the plight of another. That is what God did for us. He had compassion and freely gave the gift of His Son, Jesus, so that we could be healed. He loved us. We, in turn, love others (1 John 4:7–21). Because God first loved us, we can know true love. Notice that God didn't just forgive us; He didn't just stay out of our way. He loved us even while we were running willfully toward our impending doom. Because of Him, we are saved, and through Him, it is possible for us to fulfill our God-given purpose, our one-flesh vocation. It is possible to love with a true love, the love that comes from God.

Stacie Jerk Chain

I very much appreciate Stacie's sentiments above, especially the generosity of seeing the unique burden many men have, one in which they are both despised for the privilege of being males and yet despised when they are unable to achieve the traditional benefits of that privilege. I think that has a lot of explanatory power regarding the anxiety of men, often in their late fifties, who find that changes in technology and global economics have put them out of rewarding employment. Imagine a man who's built his whole life around a career—one in which he was incredibly successful—but whose industry has made him obsolete. He may have studied hard in school, gone into work when other guys would have called in sick, and taken advantage of opportunities for continuing education. But nothing prepared him for the reality of losing his work, looking like a failure to his wife, and having to tell his kids that they might have to move out of the house they call home.

Similarly, consider a guy who cashed in all his savings to try to get out of a job where he seemed to be spinning his wheels, moving nowhere. Maybe he had a steady income, but he had to work late with little hope of promotion. So he decided to invest in a hoagie shop. He did his research. His sandwiches are great. His marketing is professional. It's just that, as it turns out, he didn't fully understand the traffic patterns in town, and the place he was leasing just didn't bring walk-in customers. I've seen this particular situation many times. Often these people never really figure out why their businesses failed. Just as often, I can see the implicit or explicit expressions of disdain on the part of their spouses. Dad needs to take a risk, but risks are just that: not guarantees. Sometimes the father is indeed on a foolish path (read John Steinbeck's *East of Eden* and consider one man's attempt to break into the refrigerated shipping business), but the paths that make people rich also often appeared foolish at the time. So who's to know? And if a fellow *doesn't* take a risk and remains financially stagnant, that often becomes part of his shame and sorrow.

Perhaps you think the scenarios I just described are not worthy of sympathy, maybe because you think it's all just a result of the bad karma white guys have coming to them, or maybe because you think the assumptions about gender roles involved in this pain are obsolete, If so, I encourage you once again to consider Stacie's main point: truly listening to the pain of one's spouse is at the core of marital success. Listening to pain doesn't necessarily vindicate the other spouse's point of view; it only validates and recognizes the reality of the experience. Sometimes just knowing that someone sees your pain is enough to help you move forward in life.

So now, let me briefly return the favor and try to understand some of the pain with which my wife and other women I know have to deal. Wives are often called, or at least they were a generation or two ago, *a ball and chain*. This could mean that a woman distracts a man from floating up spiritually to the heavens. It could mean that a woman keeps a man from having fun in this life. In any case, it reflects a sense that a wife is often there holding her husband back. Stacie has described how this works, negatively, in many instances. But I believe there is also a sociological and biological reason for this sense that wives tend to shackle their husbands.

In my family, we have another shopworn phrase, besides "Daddy's fault." It has to do with a common pattern we have when leaving the house: "the Stacie jerk chain." Stacie almost always circles back to the house just as we are walking out the door. Usually, we're already running late and urging her to please get in the car. Stacie is quicker in this regard than my own mother, but she's still slower than the boys and I are when it comes to getting on the road. The Stacie jerk chain is like the chain on a dog that gets too excited, lunges forward, but forgets the length of the chain attached to his collar. Thus as he's eagerly running in a direction, the chain jerks him back abruptly. The Stacie jerk chain is thus like an invisible chain pulling me or the kids back into the house after we thought we were ready to get on the road.

I used to give Stacie a hard time for this phenomenon. But then I learned something about male and female behavior after I joined the Snohomish County Mycological Society in Washington State. This is a society of professionals and amateurs who are interested in the collection and study of mushrooms. If you live near such a group, I highly recommend connecting with it. It's great camaraderie, you'll learn about your local wildlife, and most importantly, you'll learn how to harvest some of the most valuable and tasty mushrooms on earth. Go to the grocery store and you might find one or two relatively tasteless varieties. Go get involved in a mycological society, and you'll be able to get your hands on the delightful chanterelles, morels, and creminis. The best mushrooms force us to go back to our ancestral patterns and forage once again, since they are either unavailable at the grocery store or too expensive at specialty markets.

What I learned from a talk at the mycological society was that researchers were tracking the GPS patterns of men and women as they went out searching for mushrooms. What the journal articles claimed seemed instantly plausible, for I recognized that Stacie and I routinely took different paths when mushroom hunting. I always stayed on the move. I hiked farther, faster, higher, trying to find big scores. Stacie, on the other hand, didn't go as far; was exhaustive at checking for hidden gems; and found a greater variety of edibles. According to one study, our different approaches to foraging stem from the division of labor among our ancient ancestors.[20] Over time, women became better at jobs related to gathering stationary plant food, while men became better at tracking down moving animals. Thus when modern couples forage, the men are often eager to take risks and cover greater territory, looking to find unpredictable food

---

[20] Luis Pacheco-Cobos, Marcos Rosetti, Cecilia Cuatianquiz, and Robyn Hudson, "Sex Differences in Mushroom Gathering: Men Expend More Energy to Obtain Equivalent Benefits," *Evolution and Human Behavior* 31.4 (2010): 289–97.

sources. Meanwhile, the women are reluctant to move too quickly away from potential sources of food nearby. This also means that when our female ancestors gathered food, they consumed fewer calories in the process, leading to a greater net contribution to a family's nutrition when it came to gathering. Meanwhile, men were important to the family in obtaining big scores of protein because their long treks and risky hunts turned up migrating animals.

This all may seem like irrelevant trivia. But I think it is at the heart of things. Though Stacie might get frustrated at my lack of attention to detail, my impatience when leaving the house, and my tolerance of investment risk, these may well be hardwired into my mind by ancient necessities. Likewise, while I get frustrated that she can't get out the door quickly, she is following her female ancestors in attending to details that I might miss. Just this month, for instance, her "frustrating" behavior of Stacie jerk chaining me has led to (1) not leaving the house without our NFL tickets, (2) not forgetting to pay the fee for our boat slip when I was desperate to start our trip to the mountains, and (3) finding a gift certificate that we had misplaced.

Recently, after considering all this, I asked Stacie to think about embracing the advantages of her disposition (and understanding my own) but doing so with a greater awareness of the root issues. What if our different approaches to things could become a balancing act instead of a game of tug-of-war? In such a case, I might learn gratitude for her diligent attention to detail and avoid treating every case of her precision as nagging or shackling me. Likewise, she might learn to recognize that my lack of attention to detail was not a sign of disregard for the home and its inhabitants but rather part of my natural desire to track down important resources. In such a balance, we might see our marriage like the Tao's yin and yang: a balance that enables proper cycles of existence. We've only just begun to experiment with this new way of thinking. For now, I'm going to stop thinking about the Stacie jerk chain and cultivate gratitude for the Stacie *anchor*.

Let Your Spouse Have Friends and Adventures

In my experience, one of the most unfortunate aspects of married relationships is the way in which one spouse traps the other into a daily routine where he or she can't escape to explore personal interests or have time alone. This is especially a problem after retirement, when not even work can insert itself to give couples a break from each other. For this reason, it is important for couples to establish, early on, a commitment to not only *allow* the partner to cultivate friendships but also *encourage* such friendships in others.

After all, selfish, suffocating love is not really love at all. It's interested in seeking its own gratification. It may look to ourselves or even others as if our jealousy is a sign of devotion. But it is a sign of erotic narcissism. Trapping a person to ourselves hardly ever works well in the long run, but the sin involved is sin against New Logic love itself. Søren Kierkegaard understood this well when he wrote, "You, husband, do not lead your wife into the temptation of forgetting to love the neighbor because of you; you, wife, do not lead your husband into this temptation! The lovers no doubt think that in erotic love they have the highest, but this is not so, because in it they still do not have the eternal secured by the eternal."[21] True love provides us an infinite well of love. We spill this love out to the world indiscriminately. Thus when we refuse to let our spouses spill love out through volunteerism, friendships, or travel, we betray the fact that we aren't tapped into true love in the first place.

Sometimes I've found that when one partner committed a grave sin against the other early in the relationship, this results in a life of restrictions. If there's been an affair, for instance, the cheater loses travel privileges and must remain perpetually watched. If one partner got into financial trouble early on, he or she might have to explain every little purchase for the rest of the couple's lives together. As understandable and common as this sort of response is, it is a terrible idea. It can lead to resentment and a sense of being trapped at best and clandestine, dangerous activity at worst. Grace doesn't mean we are to be stupid, be permissive, or ignore warning signs. But grace does entail letting forgiven spouses live normal, free lives.

---

[21] Søren Kierkegaard, *Works of Love* (Princeton, NJ: Princeton University Press, 2013), 61.

Is Marriage a Sacrament?

Medieval Catholic theology emphasized the importance of seven sacraments, one of which was the sacrament called holy matrimony. After the Reformation, however, Protestants typically limited the number of sacraments to two: baptism and Holy Communion. The number of sacraments is a human construct, so the official list isn't as important as it might seem at first. As a Protestant, I believe that we can benefit from thinking of marriage as *sacramental*. That is, we need not think of it as an official sacrament, and by no means do I think it merits points in heaven or time out of purgatory. But it is, nonetheless, something that—like a sacrament—offers a physical sign and token of God's grace.

This is not an original thought of mine. For instance, according to Miroslav Volf, although sexual intercourse can be a selfish act at times, "sexual union can be a sacrament of love—not just a sacrament of human love, but also a means of expressing and mediating divine love. Pleasure—pleasure of the soul no less than of the body!—given to the other and for the other's sake *is* then a pleasure received. And a pleasure received by the other is, almost paradoxically, a pleasure returned to the giver."[22] Similarly, according to Robert Capon, romantic desire for beauty in another person resembles what goes on in the Lord's Supper, especially in its ability to help provide a reminder (*anamnesis*) of the New Logic of grace:

> [It is] an *anamnesis* of a love that had already called me and of a home that had already borne me. [*Anamnesis*] by the way, is the Greek word used by the New Testament in recording Jesus' command at the institution of the Eucharist. . . . "Remembrance," however, is too weak a translation to convey its force: since orthodox Christians have always held that Jesus is not just mentally remembered in the Eucharistic rite but really present in the power of his death and resurrection, the word *anamnesis* conveys the idea of something in the past that is also an ongoing fact in the present. It indicates not merely an intellectual representation of a previous event but an actual *re-presentation—a making present once again* of the event. Even our first romantic

---

[22] Volf, *Free of Charge*, 70.

event, therefore, is precisely an *anamnesis*. . . . It is a making present again of our deep Home in the Bed of the Trinity; second, and more immediately, it is also a representation, a sacramental manifestation, of our earliest home here—of the home into which we were literally and historically born.[23]

I've found this to be true not only for the couple involved but for those around them. Whenever Stacie and I are in a good place, living with the New Logic, we find that other couples, children, and even strangers become intrigued. In a world of transactional, legalistic marriage, folks sometimes approach us and try to understand how we could have been married for so long, had so many challenges in our relationship, and yet interact joyfully with one another. For us, the answer is that we often forget the New Logic, so we work constantly to return to it and to practice the art of *remembering* the infinite love of God.

This remembering in marriage sometimes takes the shape of sexual intercourse. Healthy married sex represents a sign of overall well-being, integrating spirit and body. According to Paul Fairweather,

> When the body is resymbolized so that its powers correspond to positive image states, then sexual behavior is experienced as the completing of body-Being unity. The body comes alive. In this experience of unity, sex has taken on a new meaning for the participant, and the compulsive syndrome has fallen to the wayside. The meaning of sex has shifted away from sex as an act to discharge a sexual tension which is related to unpleasant introjects. Instead, it has become an ultimate expression of the unity of one's own body with its ground in Being. The sexual act has become transformed into an expression of human love and affection. Sexual release is integrated with encompassing personal emotions. As a result, it is experienced as comforting and fulfilling and having cosmic significance. In this integrative context, the choice to have sex is a personal one in which the individual is affirming his unity with nature. This free choice which is constituted by the positive image state does not

---

[23] Robert Farrar Capon, *Health, Money, and Love: And Why We Don't Enjoy Them* (Grand Rapids, MI: Eerdmans, 1990), 120–21.

become a means of "proving" closeness where closeness may be in doubt. Rather, it is a choice within the context of bodily comfort, bodily affection, bodily acceptance, and bodily love. It is the conscious affirmation of organic being.[24]

Put another way, sexiness is about saying yes to God's gift of existence. The sexual act is about rejoicing in God's gracious gift of life.

Eastern Orthodox Christians maintain, with Roman Catholics, that marriage is a sacrament. However, they also believe that it is dissolvable in certain circumstances. Partly, this is because the Western church has typically operated in terms of legal, contractual terms. Thus the East thinks of marriage sort of like a mirror of a spiritual reality in the heavens, sometimes even using Trinitarian terms for married relationships. Orthodox laypeople can have as many as three marriages.[25] I assume this is because if you are on your fourth marriage, *you are probably the problem* and ought to figure out what's wrong within your soul before going out and disrupting other people's lives. In any case, I dig how the Orthodox theologian Kallistos Ware talks about the sacramental nature of marriage in his tradition: "Marriage, the 'sacrament of love,' is a direct expression of our human personhood according to the image and likeness of the Holy Trinity. Formed as an icon of the Trinitarian God, the human person is made for mutual love; and that means, first and foremost, the love between man and woman."[26] In most Orthodox marriages, the couple gets crowned. I dig that tradition a lot more than the unity candle. Instead of two individuals extinguishing their individuality into one flame, the image in the East is of a daughter and son of heaven crowned as part of the Royal Priesthood, "called out of darkness into light" (1 Pet. 2:9). The couple then is welcomed into a life of mutual sexual gift-giving, in which sex is not only an act of obligation, meant merely for procreation, but is also an opportunity for the experience of spiritual wonder. According to Ware,

---

[24] Paul Fairweather, *Symbolic Regression Psychology* (New York: Irvington, 1981), 68.

[25] Kallistos Ware, "Marriage and Divorce—an Orthodox Perspective," in *A Textbook of Christian Ethics*, 4th ed., ed. Robin Gill (London: Bloomsbury, 2014), 32.2.

[26] Ibid., 32.1.

> We Orthodox have always felt unhappy about the ruling given by the Holy Office at Rome in 1944 that the "primary purpose" of marriage is "the generation and bringing-up of offspring," and not mutual love. . . . In the words of an Arab Orthodox bishop, Metropolitan George Khodre, "Marriage has no other end than that the husband and wife prepare for the coming of God." "The union between husband and wife," writes Father John Menedorff, "is an end in itself; it is an eternal union between two unique and eternal personalities. From this it follows that, even when God does not grant the gift of children, a marriage may still exist in its true fullness."[27]

If you, like me, are in a Protestant tradition, I suggest we remain free to borrow this sublime concept concerning marriage as the preparation for the coming of God's kingdom. After all, the "Great Exchange" or marriage metaphor was important to Luther's understanding of salvation: in the marriage, we, as brides of Christ, become co-owners of the divine blessings, and our groom (Jesus) takes on our debts.[28] Therefore, in marriage, we can celebrate the mutual *agape* and *eros* in married sexual union. This also creates a beautiful space for potential children to learn the language of the New Logic. Our families, in such cases, become embodied witnesses to God's alternative kingdom.

No Strings Attached?

When I was teaching virtue ethics in China, I tried to create definitions for key virtues that also introduced idioms from American English. For the virtue of love, I created a poster that read, "Give kindness to others with no strings attached." The first time we read it out loud, the American team had to stifle their laughter. In today's debased culture, especially online, "no strings attached" (NSA) is code for a casual sexual hookup with no expectation of a relationship.

---

[27] Ibid., 32.12–13.

[28] Luther explores this theme throughout his treatise *On Christian Liberty* and in "Instructions to the Perplexed and Doubting, to George Spenlein, April 8, 1516," *Luther: Letters of Spiritual Counsel*, ed. Theodore G. Tappert, Library of Christian Classics, vol. 18 (London: SCM Press, 1955), 110.

It refers to a desire to have a meaningless experience of sexual gratification without worrying that a lover will become a threat either to one's freedom or to the stability of a preexisting marriage.

Of course, there is a vast difference between the decadent understanding of "strings" and the Christian sense of "stringless love." Indeed, there exists both a good and a bad version of NSA romance.

> *Vicious NSA*: No commitment, not even the mention of love, emptiness
>
> *Virtuous NSA*: No transaction, unconditional love, deep fulfillment and peace

Virtuous, Christian NSA love treats our act of love as a pure gift, not a legal exchange. Our giving comes from the eternal source of the divine love-giver, not through a calculation of any return on investments.

But what about marriage and monogamy? Often Christian advocacy of monogamy comes across—and is, admittedly, often intended—as a way of keeping people in line, ensuring that no one has too much fun. Isn't monogamy a "string" to tie us up? No, I prefer to think of it as a rope, the sort of rope rock climbers use to scale treacherous mountainsides. We secure these ropes to one another for our mutual survival. In marriage, we snap on our respective carabineers because we have deep concern for and trust in our partner. Without this, we go it alone, to our own peril.

For too long, we in the church have emphasized that people need to be monogamous—or else! A better approach is to recognize that people need the comfort and security of monogamy and that people touched by the New Logic of the Gospel experience a deep need to share God's *agape* with someone. Monogamy isn't, therefore, primarily a restriction to limit our fun. It's a sexy promise to endure a life of difficulties in the name of eternal love itself. Some will object here and point to evidence from human physiology and psychology that suggests that our ancestors were naturally promiscuous. Indeed, there is compelling anthropological evidence for this, and it is accessibly set forth in Christopher Ryan and Cacilda Jethá's *Sex at*

Dawn: How We Mate, Why We Stray, and What It Means for Modern Relationship (2012). The authors argue that we have a built-in biological need for nonmonogamous sexual release. I think, on a naturalistic level, this is probably true. But it isn't the whole story. I believe that grace can help us transcend nature or perhaps invite humanity to a newly created nature. In this new creation, we offer the gift of unconditional, monogamous love. If this is contrary to our base behaviors, how much more beautiful and miraculous is its attempt? When this love is a reality in a marriage, it leads us to the most holy of nuptial mantras: *I need you. I need you. I need you.*

This need is neither one of dependency nor one of obsession, nor one of suffocating desire to keep someone all to ourselves. We need the other person, who is a conduit of God's grace. When we are in danger of falling from emotional precipices, we *need* our beloved. Monogamy is a promise that we will not let someone down, no matter how grumpy or unfulfilled we happen to be that day. Monogamy, therefore, isn't so much a burdensome command as it is an invitation to delight in the gracious presence of love itself. So be compassionate to each other. The journey will likely be difficult for all of us, and there's no need to ignore this reality. But do you want a partner for mutual protection and encouragement on the road? If so, and if you are currently married, skip through this odd existence arm in arm with your frustrating yet delightful partner. Have a little fun along the way.

Lamentation along the Way

The hardest thing about surviving marriage is managing our responses to the frustrations inherent in almost every step along the marital journey, at least in our penultimate lives. If we are fortunate, we might learn to surf the Tao on occasion. We might find ourselves enjoying the love of our spouses as both of us are prayerfully mindful of the New Logic. Let's stick with the language of the Tao here, since it carries the meaning of being indefinable and almost impossible to hang onto. Blissful spiritual experience, like genuine romantic love, is inherently transitory; it escapes us almost as soon as we notice it's there. Thus there are really only two places you'll find yourself on this journey for most of your life:

A. Frustrated because you are on the way to the Tao of love,
but you haven't experienced it yet

B. Frustrated because you once experienced the Tao of love,
but now you seem to have slipped back into your old
transactional ways

In other words, you might find yourself in condition A, in which
you are frustrated with your marriage and perhaps also angry
with your spouse that you have not yet learned to surf the Tao
together. You do not have an experience of married ecstasy to rely
on. You see others at least sometimes experiencing something
you've yet to encounter. You may have had sex, but you haven't
experienced *sexy* yet; you haven't *made love*. So when you hear people talk or act as if they've got a deep connection, it only makes you
envious. You might, however, find yourself in condition B—which
is where Stacie and I find most of our relationship trouble these
days. We know better. We remember the beauty of living in nontransactional, sympathetic, *agape* ways. And then we act in petty
Old Logic ways. The fact that we know better makes us angry with
ourselves and sometimes furious with each other. I don't mention
this to discourage you. I mention it to encourage you to go easy
on yourself and your spouse. It is nearly impossible to remain in
a state of saintly love. We can only learn what it looks like, repent
when we neglect to surf the Tao, and get back to seeking sexy love
once more.

How to Shoot at Somebody
Who Outdrew You (Divorce)

Well, maybe there's a God above
But all I've ever learned from love
Was how to shoot somebody who outdrew you
It's not a cry that you hear at night
It's not somebody who's seen the light
It's a cold and it's a broken Hallelujah
—Leonard Cohen, "Hallelujah"

Before considering the tricky topic of divorce, consider the following four theses, which I believe are at the core of understanding the reality about marriage and its potential dissolution:

1. Everybody is broken.
2. Everybody is redeemable.
3. Not everyone is redeemable *by you.*
4. Yet love hopes all things and thus is never quick to give up on the possibility of God's gift of death and resurrection, even for a troubled relationship.

These four theses guide my understanding of the question of divorce. For all the idealistic stuff we've explored together, we must still reckon with the grim reality that many marriages end tragically. Sometimes one spouse wants to stay in a relationship, but the other simply will not. Other times a spouse is abusive or abandons his or her partner. The aftermath is often a sort of total war in which finances, children, extended family, friends, pets, and the couple all suffer. There are rarely any winners. This is because, in our broken world, broken people end up in broken relationships and break a lot of their own stuff in the process of breaking up.

How should we think about divorce, therefore, from the perspective of the New Logic of God's kingdom? The answer is both complex and simple. It's complex with respect to the tangled circumstances of human sinfulness. It's simple in the sense that Jesus is clear on this topic. Nevertheless, understanding the nature of His teaching on the matter can help us make sense of not only divorce but also the nature of sexiness itself. Consider the following exchange between the Pharisees and Jesus:

> And Pharisees came up to him and tested him by asking, "Is it lawful to divorce one's wife for any cause?" He answered, "Have you not read that he who created them from the beginning made them male and female, and said, 'Therefore a man shall leave his father and his mother and hold fast to his wife, and the two shall become one flesh'? So they are no longer two but one flesh. What therefore God has joined together, let not man separate." They said to him, "Why then did Moses command one to give a certificate of divorce and to send her away?" He said to them, "Because of your hardness of heart Moses allowed you to divorce your wives, but from the beginning it was not so. And I say to you: whoever divorces his wife, except for sexual immorality, and marries another, commits adultery." (Matt. 19:3–9)

While we often think of the Pharisees as extremists or legalists and contrast them with a *nice* Jesus, the Pharisees were, in actuality, known for being *liberal* on the question of divorce. They wanted to make it easy for a man to dispose of his wife without too much hassle. They wanted to do this *and also treat it as lawful.* Jesus wouldn't go along with them in this but rather insisted on a higher standard. As Robert Capon explains,

> Jesus is nowhere near as tough on the subject of adultery as he is on marriage. With the scribes and Pharisees who were chafing at the bit to stone the woman taken in adultery, he *cranked down* the crime: "C'mon, fellow," he said, "she's just another sinner. If there's anybody here who's not a sinner, let him throw the

first stone." And when they all had the good grace to walk off in disgrace, he said to the woman, "No takers, eh? Well then, I don't accuse you either. Go on home and be a good girl." But with the same bunch of upright types who had unuprightly figured out Eight Ways to Divorce Your Wife Without Breaking the Torah, he *cranked up* the requirements of matrimony. "Can't you boys read?" he asked them. "You never saw that 'one flesh' stuff in Genesis? You think your wife is hard to take. Divorce her, and you'll really be in deep trouble."[1]

It's important to recognize the context and the implications of divorce in Jesus' time.[2] First, notice how the Pharisees asked the question from the husband's perspective. They wanted to know, essentially, if a man gets tired of his wife, for whatever reason, can he trade her in for a new one? Once we realize this, we can see that even an atheist should recognize the injustice involved here. This sort of divorce could relegate a "discarded" woman to poverty or prostitution. Divorce, in such a situation, could place a woman in the category of the widow or orphan, the most vulnerable members of first-century Near Eastern society. In other words, Jesus' condemnation of divorce was, in a sense, a matter of justice, not prudishness.

Second, Jesus recognized that in a civil context, even Moses could grant that such a deed might be permissible, given our current fallen condition. But He refused to accept the idea that this is the way people of the New Logic should think about love. Because marriage ought to be based not on transactional concerns or economic value but rather on the unlimited and unconditional love of God, the idea that there could be any real *reason* for divorce is based on a false premise about holy love. There is no quid pro quo reason for loving. Therefore, there is no quid pro quo reason for not loving.

Third, the rest of what we know about Jesus helps us realize that the way to love those who experience broken relationships is not to

---

[1] Robert Farrar Capon, *Health, Money, and Love: And Why We Don't Enjoy Them* (Grand Rapids, MI: Eerdmans, 1990), 115–16.

[2] My friend Steve Byrnes offered the following helpful explanation of Moses on divorce: "The other aspect of all this is that, if the only allowable 'out' was the death of the spouse, well then! That could be arranged through a simple accusation of adultery. Recognizing their hardness of heart and wanting to protect those weaker citizens, Moses' provision of divorce at least allowed women to live after the dissolution of a marriage."

say that divorce is good but rather to recognize it's sinful reality and yet love those who have been marred by sin. While the Pharisees wanted to go soft on sin, they were typically hard on sinners. Jesus, on the contrary, was relentless in His condemnation of sin but scandalously merciful toward sinners. This is why He was misunderstood, as He himself noted: "For John came neither eating nor drinking, and they say, 'He has a demon.' The Son of Man came eating and drinking, and they say, 'Look at him! A glutton and a drunkard, a friend of tax collectors and sinners!' Yet wisdom is justified by her deeds" (Matt. 11:18–19). This is at the heart of what Martin Luther recognized as the distinction between Law and Gospel. Forgiveness implies prior condemnation, not compromise. Instead of making the Law easier in order to meet its relaxed standards, the Gospel gives us the assurance that under the cloak of Christ's righteousness, we can take a serious look at our behaviors, recognize our failures, and begin to practice virtuous habits in our relationships.

I wish I had heard this Law-Gospel approach to divorce in my high school years. Back then, in my conversionist evangelical circles, it was common for people to brag about how they had enjoyed many sexual exploits, along with drugs and rock 'n' roll. This became part of their wild "testimony." They *used* to do those things, but then they became believers and were freed. Meanwhile, I noticed people in the congregation who lived under a terrible cloud of shame: they might have only had two sexual partners in their lives—their first and second spouses—but because of a rigid adherence to Jesus' explicit teaching, they were considered somehow unworthy of full status as members of God's kingdom. Meanwhile, I noticed that other, progressive congregations, in an effort to make things comfortable for potential new members who were divorced, opened their doors by relaxing the Christian principle of 'til-death-do-us-part matrimony.

I'll leave it to biblical scholars and pastoral counselors to help you work through all the fine points regarding whether a situation justifies divorce, or whether a divorced and remarried person should receive communion, or whether a divorced person can be a pastor. Here I simply want to point out that it is possible for Jesus to be uncompromising about God's call to committed love and also willing to embrace those who have somehow failed at or been failed by human love. Indeed, that's how true Christianity works.

A gracious attitude to marriage recognizes that *everybody is broken*. This means that, to leave a spouse because he or she has faults is incompatible with the Gospel's New Logic. Marriage provides a framework in which two broken people help support and heal each other. By not worrying about score keeping, spouses can recognize shortcomings in their partners and yet assure them that they are willing to work together to become the best people they can be.

A gracious attitude recognizes that *everybody is redeemable*. Granted, not everyone will respond to a gracious invitation from unyielding love, but the New Logic sees no reason to write someone off, even when he or she has established a pattern of failure. Love keeps no record of wrongs (1 Cor. 13:5). Love believes all things (1 Cor. 13:7). Love presses on in hope, despite the odds. Love is beautiful, therefore. Through prayer and commitment, spouses often discover that breakthroughs happen even with the most troubled partners. When they do, the delight and joy is beyond compare in this life. As Jesus says, "Just so, I tell you, there will be more joy in heaven over one sinner who repents than over ninety-nine righteous persons who need no repentance" (Luke 15:7).

The problem is, after a time, you might find that *not everybody is redeemable by you*. This reality shouldn't be invoked casually, but it remains worth considering. Of course, in the strict sense, *no one is redeemable by you*. That requires God's supernatural intervention. But even in a practical sense, there are situations that require strength or training beyond an individual's natural ability. If a spouse is physically dangerous, threatens the children, or is gripped by a long-lasting and powerful addiction, it might be possible that even if he or she wants to stick it out, more evil than good would come of it. The love of God is infinite, but sometimes our ability to channel that love, or to tolerate exposure to danger for ourselves and our children, is not. In such cases, one might have to tragically choose between the lesser of two evils. We would not say that the action taken is ideal, holy, or good. We could only say that we believe it was the right choice and ask God's forgiveness for whatever part we played in the dissolution.

Before entertaining the idea that a spouse is beyond reconciliation, we must return once more to the love theology of Paul in 1 Corinthians 13:7. There, we remember that love always hopes and thus perseveres. Thus even with the most frustrating partners, if believers give up on a relationship, they do this not gleefully but rather with recognition of the tragedy of the matter. This is because *love hopes all things and thus is never quick to give up on the possibility of God's gift of death and resurrection, even for a troubled relationship.* For this reason, divorce is best understood not as a "good" act but rather as an act of last resort.

Luther on Divorce

By the time of the Reformation, the medieval church had made it abundantly clear that marriage was indissoluble. But the Reformers, to one extent or another, recognized that there might be some circumstances where, after trying to establish reconciliation, divorce might be permissible. The Lutherans and the Genevan Reformed tended to agree that adultery and desertion might justify a divorce. The first point was already established by Jesus (Matt. 9). The latter point was a matter of compassion. Without modern tracking mechanisms, men could simply skip town and leave a helpless and impoverished woman to fend for herself. Divorce allowed such women to seek more stable arrangements. Luther, despite advocating for forgiveness and patience, eventually included other possible grounds for divorce, including the physical inability to consummate a marriage on the part of one or both parties and intractable unwillingness to engage in sexual intercourse. The point in all this is that at least some broken circumstances, for those early evangelicals, made divorce a lamentable but potentially legitimate option. If so, since a possible ground for divorce doesn't *require* an offended party to obtain a divorce, the question remains whether a particular divorce might be a relatively just option.

Just War Theory Applied to Divorce

What I'm suggesting here is analogous to the old tradition called "just war theory." The idea of a just war is something of a misnomer. "Just" implies holiness, goodness, and righteousness. War is always tragic. In this tradition, if a Christian goes to war responsibly, it is never conceived of as ideal, but it is due to the hardness of human hearts. As Lutheran virtue ethicist Gilbert Meilaender rightly says, "The evil deed can still be done in such a moment as an act of trust, but only if this prayer [of Augustine's: 'Deliver me from my necessities.'] is also uttered. It can be done not with a 'good' conscience, but with a 'comforted' conscience."[3] Thus what we are after here might best be called *justifiable*, rather than *just*, divorce theory.

By applying just war criteria to divorce, we might arrive at healthier deliberations for ourselves and those we care about. Just war theory seeks *ius ad bellum*, which refers to ethical considerations (*ius*, or justice) leading up to (*ad*) war (*bellum*). There are also criteria for *ius in bellum* (right conduct in war). Let's apply these to the question of whether one might rightly consider divorce in a particular case. These criteria should not be used in a manner whereby we determine that we *have* to get divorced; rather, they should serve as questions to ask to process all the issues involved in a troubled marriage. In the New Logic, even when there are *reasons* for a divorce, a loving partner might wish to overlook transgressions just as God does for us: "Above all, love each other deeply, because love covers over a multitude of sins" (1 Pet. 4:8 NIV).

Ius ad Bellum

1. Just Cause

This criterion asks whether the reason for going to war is just. Just as we ought not to declare war for immoral or evil reasons, in marriage, divorce ought not to be sought for petty or vindictive reasons. Likewise, it should not be pursued for selfish ends. For instance, seeking divorce to escape the commitments of family life is unjust, but we might rightly consider it to protect the lives of our children.

2. Comparative Justice

This criterion asks whether the wrongs committed by an offending party outweigh those inherent wrongs that will be if the offended

---

[3] Gilbert Meilaender, *Faith and Faithfulness: Basic Themes in Christian Ethics* (Notre Dame, IN: University of Notre Dame Press, 1992), 107.

party instigates a battle. In the context of marriage, we almost always find that both spouses have a part to play in the breakdown of a marriage. Abuse, abandonment, and infidelity are thus comparatively worse than constant quarrelling. This criterion is least compatible with the New Logic, in that it is usually a matter of score keeping. It should only be applied, therefore, as an exercise in which we consider the relative weight of the offending partner's offense.

3. Competent Authority

This criterion makes more sense in actual war: it asks whether the authority (a president or parliament) is constitutionally authorized to declare war. However, one might apply this criterion, in a way, by seeking the advice of a pastor, mediator, or marriage counselor. Especially when children are involved, couples do well to seek an outside opinion to determine whether the marriage is merely going through a tough, stressful phase or whether things have broken down beyond repair. Often only an external party can help us make that sort of determination.

4. Right Intention

This criterion asks whether the stated reasons for going to war are the real reasons or good reasons. Applied to divorce, we should not pretend that we are seeking a divorce because of a partner's adultery when we are actually interested in gaining assets for ourselves or in order to free ourselves to pursue our own extramarital romantic interests.

5. Probability of Success

This criterion asks whether the toll of war will be in vain; the lives lost on both sides of a war should be spared in cases where nothing can be accomplished but loss. Applied to divorce, the cost of a divorce should be considered. For instance, even when a partner commits adultery, the offended partner should consider staying in the relationship if the well-being of children will be severely damaged by divorce. In terms of the initial financial cost of divorce alone, the legal cost of severing ties in the United States is typically $15,000 to $30,000.[4]

6. Last Resort

This might be the most applicable criterion: in war, it forces a nation to consider all alternative options before engaging in war. In a marriage, the New Logic calls us to do everything we can to maintain the relationship, pressing on until we find that the injustices involved are irreparable.

7. Proportionality

This criterion asks whether the potential gains from war are comparable to the inevitable losses involved. Applied to divorce, we should ask whether the offenses of a spouse are worthy of the drastic measure of severing the relationship.

Ius in Bello

Once battle has begun, just war theory (*ius in bello*) also directs how combatants (or, in our current context, spouses) are to act or should act.

1. Distinction

In war, we ought to be careful to direct violent acts only toward enemy combatants. There is an incredibly important analog here in divorce. Too often, one spouse or both will use children, friends, and extended family as pawns in their bitter disputes. This is to be avoided, especially with respect to children, even when manipulating children would result in beneficial custody outcomes. Unless abuse or endangerment (due to mental illness, reckless lifestyles, or addiction) is involved, offended partners should encourage and help facilitate a healthy relationship between children and both parents.

---

[4] Lisa Magloff, "The Average Cost for Divorce," LegalZoom, http://info.legalzoom.com/average-cost-divorce-20103.html.

2. Proportionality

This type of proportionality asks combatants to ensure that the damage done to the enemy does not outweigh the advantage gained by an action. In divorce, this means we should not be overly severe. This is all too often where divorces become unnecessarily vicious. What might start as a relatively amicable divorce can easily descend into total war, with excessive destruction for all involved. Perhaps the saddest way things become *disproportionate* in a divorce happens in conservative Christian communities: given the negative view of divorce in Christianity, those who determine they must sever their relationship too often feel the need to exaggerate or lay out *all* the sins of the other person. This tactic will always be with us to the extent that there are divorce courts. But it should not be necessary for one spouse to thoroughly destroy the reputation of the other to ensure that the community of faith remains ready to care for and love them.

3. Military Necessity

Actions in combat need to truly aim at a just end to the conflict. In divorce, one or both parties too often will prolong a bitter legal battle or make the ex-spouse suffer. Even with the worst offenders, the New Logic of the Gospel calls us not to inflict harm for harm's sake. Actions should only be taken that serve to protect one's self and children from harm, not to exact revenge.

4. Fair Treatment of Prisoners of War

Captured or surrendering combatants should be treated fairly and never tortured. Likewise, in the context of divorce, family members, friends, and even offending ex-spouses themselves should be spared from cruelty and vengeance. Mercy ought to prevail, even with the most loathsome ex-partners and their allies.

5. No Means *Malum in Se* (Evil in Themselves)

Warring parties must not employ weapons or methods that are evil in themselves, such as systematic rape or chemical warfare. In divorce, we must resist temptations to act illegally or immorally toward the ex-partner.

All this means that those who have encountered and are committed to *agape* love might rightly decide to end a married relationship in extreme cases, but—even then—he or she will not cease to love. In other words, if we decide to seek divorce as a last resort, in order to avoid greater evil, our aim isn't supposed to be about winning or losing; rather, it should be a matter of quarantining unhealthy individuals from our lives for a time. That is, in a proper divorce, we should be seeking to remove ourselves or our children from harm. We are free, then, to love and even seek the healing of an ex-spouse. This is because we quarantine even beloved family members or pets when they have contracted dangerous, infectious diseases.

Hopefully, even when there might be good earthly reasons for a divorce, we will seek divine, *agape* love to work miracles. Too often, divorce is a misguided attempt to base a loving relationship on something unstable and fleeting, the result of disconnection from eternal love itself. As Miroslav Volf writes, "Untethered from God, self-giving love cannot stand on its own for long. If it excludes God, it will destroy us, for we will then deliver ourselves to the mercy of the finite, and therefore inherently unreliable, objects of our love."[5]

Indeed, in the name of traditional morality or family values, some discover a painful paradox: by elevating the expected benefits of marriage too highly, by demanding a sort of perfection, and by ending a marriage as soon as a justifying offense is uncovered, marriages are ruined. Robert Capon says as much when he writes, "If I had to assign a single, overarching cause to the high American divorce rate, it would be our refusal to throttle, or even to question, the religion of marriage. Our marital breakups are almost always seen by us—after a few token apologies for our own (pardonable) shortcomings—as due to our partners unpardonable offenses against

---

[5] Miroslav Volf, *Free of Charge: Giving and Forgiving in a Culture Stripped of Grace* (Grand Rapids, MI: Zondervan, 2006), 103.

the god of matrimony."[6] In other words, by living in a legalistic world that is unmerciful toward those who screw up, "pure" people often can become more responsible for their divorces than those who end up sinning. This is true especially when people are quick to divorce because of infidelity. We are *free* to divorce in such cases, but we are by no means required.

Natural Law, Nonmonogamy, and Infidelity

There is a great deal of confusion in religious circles about what is called *natural law*. Today, this term typically calls to mind the laws of the physical universe. Originally, it referred to the moral law that was—whether by reason, observation, or intuition—accessible to all people, even those ignorant of God's revelation. Natural law is thus the law above human laws. By appealing to natural law, for example, prosecutors at the Nuremberg trials were able to convict Nazis who had committed atrocities that were technically legal because the Nazis passed unjust legislation in Germany.

Many traditional Christians today turn to natural law in order to demonstrate that behaviors like nonmonogamy or same-sex marriage are not only unbiblical; they are unnatural abominations. The danger of such reasoning, however, is that the biological world as it is might suggest that we are physiologically prone to nonmonogamy. Christianity teaches that we have been alienated from nature and God through the Fall. Thus we need not look to nature as it is but are called to transcend it through grace. Looking to the natural world as it is, therefore, cannot bring us to an understanding of the way the world *should be*. As Meilaender explains, thinking of natural law in the wrong way can be unhelpful for true sexiness:

> One way [of thinking about natural law] begins by noting that the "natural" may refer to what we regularly observe in the world. That is, it may be essentially a descriptive category. Acorns grow into oaks. Only societies with the courage to defend themselves survive. In this sense what is natural is simply what we see happening regularly around us. . . . Thinking of the natural law in this way gives rise

---

[6] Capon, *Health, Money, and Love*, 133.

to an ethic that makes survival central and that describes the basic conditions necessary for any community to function effectively and survive. Natural law presents us with hypothetical imperatives prescribing the minimal requirements for social survival.[7]

As well-meaning as this approach might be, it has many unfortunate side effects. For instance, Thomas Aquinas believed that monogamy is an obligation of natural law for humans, partly because of the inferior spiritual and intellectual abilities of women:

> Again, we must consider that in the human species offspring require not only nourishment for the body, and in the case of other animals, but also education for the soul. For other animals naturally possess their own kinds of prudence whereby they are enabled to take care of themselves. But a man lives by reason, which he must develop by lengthy, temporal experience so that he may achieve prudence.... Moreover, a long time is needed for this instruction. Then, too, because of the impulsion of the passions, through which prudent judgment is vitiated, they require not merely instruction but correction. Now a woman is not adequate to this task; rather, this demands the work of a husband, in whom reason is more developed for giving instruction and strength is more available for giving punishment. Therefore, in the human species, it is not enough, as in the case of birds, to devote a small amount of time to bringing up offspring, for a long period of life is required. Hence, since among all animals it is necessary for male and female to remain together as long as the work of the father is needed by the offspring, it is natural to the human being for the man to establish a lasting association with a designated woman, over no short period of time. Now, we call this society *matrimony*. Therefore, matrimony is natural for man, and promiscuous performance of the sexual act, outside matrimony, is contrary to man's good. For this reason, it must be sin.[8]

There is, however, a deeper type of "natural law" according to Meilaender. It's a natural law considered from an eternal

---

[7] Meilaender, *Faith and Faithfulness*, 118.

[8] Aquinas, *Summa*, 14.8.

perspective. Thus "in seeking moral knowledge we might begin from a quite different sense of the natural: not what we regularly observe all around but the development appropriate to a particular kind of being."[9] In other words, the New Logic points us not to our fallen nature but to the sort of human nature God originally intended for us.

Not only is natural law difficult to understand and apply—especially in our age in which human behavior has become increasingly complicated as we study the ways in which biology, psychology, and societal influences interact within each of us—but natural law remains a form of *law*. This means that while it is able to condemn us, it has no ability to transform us. Thus while Christian laity and pastors keep hearing the rules, they also keep committing adultery. Often these cases become public scandals in which sinners addicted to *other* types of sin love to pile condemnation on those caught in the scandals. While this may seem to be an expression of holiness, it usually emerges from the old misguided logic of karma and transactionalism. As Capon writes, "Hardly anyone can resist the temptation to put the arm on adulterers—to urge them to stop enjoying all those surmised pleasures and be miserable like the rest of us. We may cloak our urgings with calls to repentance, but what we really object to is the unfairness of God in letting sinners get away with sin."[10] The takeaway here is that while Christians are right to uphold the radical commitment and astonishing sexiness of committed, lifelong monogamy, we do well to check our own legalistic indignation. The grace of Christ is sufficient even for adulterers, even for adulterers who have cheated on us. Thus while we are freed by grace to sever a relationship because of infidelity, we are also freed to overcome infidelity with grace and heal a wounded marriage. This can only come when we allow the law not only to condemn our partner's infidelity but to confront our own self-righteous indignation. To explain, I've invited my wife, Stacie, to share a relevant story.

---

[9] Meilaender, *Faith and Faithfulness*, 123.

[10] Capon, *Health, Money, and Love*, 111.

Guest Contribution: Stacie Mallinson, "Gospel-Law-Gospel"

One day, while at a theological conference, I found myself sitting in a small, no-frills side room of a church. I never thought that would be the beginning of one of the most transformative moments of my life. Our close friend Dan van Voorhis spoke publicly for the first time about his battle with addiction, to a room full of people, on the six-year anniversary (to the day) of his sobriety. At the end of his message, there was hardly a dry eye in the room.

What was so powerful about this message was that Dan had the courage to be vulnerable, to remove the fig leaves that we typically use to hide our shame, and he gave expression to the raw reality of his sin and suffering. We need Christian communities—the church—to be places where we experience gracious support and can be honest in this way. I must admit that sometimes, in my darkest moments when sin is thick and closing in, the last place I want to turn to is the church. But it *should* be the first place I turn. What I witnessed in Dan's classroom was a glimmer of what church can be at its best. It was encouraging to see that Dan wasn't scoffed at. Instead, those who heard his story embraced him with love and acceptance. There was healing—the kind of healing that only the Gospel can bring. Many who witnessed this began to sense that they too could begin to let their guard down.

With the safety and freedom of the Gospel as our conference's backdrop, the Law was ironically able to do its proper surgery on me. I had the space to take a long, hard look at my own life and behaviors. I don't have the same struggles as Dan. No, my sin was more deeply hidden, beneath the appearance of righteousness. And that made it more insidious. Through the words of keynote presenter David Zahl, I learned about another type of sin. See, I was going about life with my "correct" and "only" way of doing life, and when everybody else did it "wrong," I felt justified in my judgment of them—after all, I was doing it "right." I learned about the sin of self-righteous indignation and how hurtful and destructive that sin can be to those around me.

During this past weekend, I wasn't left alone with the Law and the painful experience of recovering from its surgery. That would have kept me in the same spot where I'd started, trying to be righteous through my own self-reflective effort. Instead, I needed to be reminded yet again of the forgiveness that Christ achieved on the cross for this sin too! And I was fortunate to have this echoed in a very real way through the love and forgiveness that my husband extended to me. Through this, I discovered the healing power of a pattern of Gospel-Law-Gospel. I'll leave it to pastors to consider whether this has any bearing on a sermon. But it seems to be important for the general way in which Christians relate to one another. Perhaps one has to be able to feel safe enough to remove the fig leaves, to be naked before God and our brothers and sisters in Christ, and then, when others freely tell us about forgiveness, allow the Gospel to mend us again.

All this helped me better understand something that occurred through a blog called *The Jagged Word*[11] during the week before the conference. It seems that a good bit of anger got stirred up by a recent post Dan wrote about our need to be respectful of women in conservative Christian communities. Since I know him well and know his heart, I understood that he was trying to continue a process of self-reflection. This had been a theme of his podcast during that Lenten season. At first, I wondered why his ideas came across to some not as liberating but rather as an attack on our shared values. But later I had the privilege of having two powerful conversations that helped me process what might be at work here.

The first conversation was with a dear female friend of mine in reflection on a presentation by Elyse Fitzpatrick that "women's ministry" is too often about "how to fold the perfect napkin." My friend explained that there is often excessive law in women's ministry—how to keep the perfect house, how to make the perfect recipes, how you can be a perfect mother *and* a great volunteer. Such talk can feel suffocating, especially when it looks like other upstanding women in the church seem to be able to do it all.

---

[11] http://thejaggedword.com.

This made me wonder whether some women might have thought Dan was suggesting *yet one more* area in which women need to be perfect. (I'm not trying to rehash that past debate; I'm just trying to provide my own reflection.) Some might have heard him saying that *in addition to* your vocation as a wife and mother, you can be a career woman too, which would become just one more thing to add to an already exhausting list of duties without anything or anyone getting freed. But what if we women apply Luther's paradox about the freedom of the Christian man in this way: *"A Christian woman is a perfectly free queen of all, subject to none. A Christian woman is a perfectly dutiful maidservant of all, subject to all."*

In other words, what if we are freed by the Gospel to be the women we're called to be? What if we can do this according to our unique vocations—callings that might change during different stages in life? In my case, this liberty meant I was free to set aside my career for a season in order to enjoy enriching time with my growing children. This was true even when my husband's female colleagues might dismiss me as insufficiently self-actualized. But I was and am free to discover ways in which to follow other callings, as I'm now able to work part time with a nonprofit organization that I love dearly.

The second remarkable conversation that helped me make sense of things was one I had with a complete stranger. She approached me out of the blue to talk about Christ while my husband and I were at a public musical event. This is something that almost never happens to me. She told me her story of how she recently left her physically abusive husband and the guilt she was wrestling with, but she knew she had to leave for her own safety. She explained that she wrestles with something else as well. She wants to be a godly woman. She wants to fulfill her calling to pattern her life after biblical teaching. Yet she needed to know she was free to get out of a dangerous situation. Moreover, she struggles because she has always wanted to be a mechanic, and that desire to work with her hands has not left her. It would be inappropriate to ignore the various ways in which an individual's unique situation requires a pastoral response. Nevertheless, as we all discuss gender roles, we would do well to remember that we're dealing not with abstractions but with real—and sometimes quite complex—human lives. In the case of this young woman I met, I realized that she didn't need to stay in a situation where her husband knocked her teeth out, just so she could earn points with God. Others need to hear that they are also free to be mothers and wives without feeling inferior to other women in professions outside the home. The message needs to keep each audience and individual in mind.

When our conversations about the tricky matters in life start with the freedom of the Gospel, we can then begin the process of learning what that means in our various vocations. In this light, our vocations don't become burdensome but are joyful. Maybe I've got this all wrong. I often do, but one thing I do know is that through the grace of God, I have been afforded the space to identify and expose my own debilitating sin and subsequently have been reminded of the healing power of the Gospel. The whole process allowed me to experience the joy of sharing that same love with my neighbors.

We are forgiven. The Law continues to perform surgery on us. We begin to recover from that surgery when we are reminded of the Gospel of forgiveness in Christ. The blood of Christ, as it turns out, is sufficient to cover even the sins of self-righteously indignant wives and mothers. Thank God!

The Real Problem with Divorce

We have already seen that divorce can be a problem because it can lead to injustice. In many cultural contexts, it can leave a vulnerable wife in a precarious financial situation. It can deeply harm children. It can disrupt communities. Moreover, to the extent that divine sexiness in marriage channels *agape*, or unconditional love, divorce usually reveals that we are living in a world of *conditions* and legal transactions. Think about it: lawyers and courtrooms get involved in divorce proceedings. There is nothing gracious or holy about divorce.

Divorce often stems from a misguided expectation that we should demand perfect fulfillment from a spouse. When that doesn't happen, we often feel justified in acting with cruelty or disregard. C. S. Lewis suggests that the problem with divorce is that it seeks to put sexuality in a different category from everything else in life. He writes, "The sexual motive is taken to condone all sorts of behaviour which, if it had any other end in view, would be condemned as merciless, treacherous and unjust."[12] In other areas of life, people expect us to keep our promises. With love and marriage, however, many people assume that when the flame of romantic feelings dims, it's perfectly acceptable to break our promises. Lewis writes,

> The idea that "being in love" is the only reason for remaining married really leaves no room for marriage as a contract or promise at all. If love is the whole thing, then the promise can add nothing; and if it adds nothing, then it should not be made. The curious thing is that lovers themselves, while they remain really in love, know this better than those who talk about love. As Chesterton pointed out, those who are in love have a natural inclination to bind themselves by promises. Love songs all over the world are full of vows of eternal constancy. The Christian law is not forcing upon the passion of love something which is foreign to that passion's own nature: it is demanding that lovers should take seriously something which their passion of itself impels them to do.[13]

In other words, the Christian Tao of marriage is not something foreign to our noblest human desires. Rather, it reflects a commitment to our highest longings and a hope that the infinite power of God can free us to become who we truly want to be. Therefore, while we ought to have compassion and mercy for those whose marriages unravel, we should never assume the perspective of the world's logic—namely, that marriage is only to remain intact when our spouses are able to provide enough return on investment for us to keep our promises. New Logic love is patient; it waits until the end of time for our spouses to become their glorified, risen selves.

---

[12] For the whole, worthwhile argument, see C. S. Lewis, "We Have No Right to Happiness," in *God in the Dock* (Grand Rapids, MI: Eerdmans, 2015), 354–62.

[13] C. S. Lewis, *Mere Christianity* (New York: HarperOne, 2001) 107.

Your Root Problem Might Be Boredom

Before people contemplate getting a divorce, they should ask themselves whether the real problem isn't boredom. Sure, we pretend that we're upset about some way in which we've been wronged. Or we think we found our real soul mate in someone else. Or we think we are biologically incapable of monogamy. But most often, the problem is much more mundane.

Now, I agree with Søren Kierkegaard's understanding of the subject (as discussed in his famous 1843 book *Either/Or*): boredom is a sense of emptiness and meaninglessness. Doesn't that make perfect sense, given the ground we've covered together thus far on our quest for erotic virtue? Somehow, when disconnected from the New Logic, sexual activity turns out to be hollow. When this is true, the personality, attractiveness, or sense of humor in a spouse can only delay the inevitable. This is why, no matter how interesting and glamorous a Hollywood couple might be, even they eventually grow tired of each other's nonsense and in fact seem to divorce more quickly and frequently than the rest of the population.

Once a person moves on to a new sexual partner, or even a new spouse, if he or she still lives under a cloud of meaninglessness, he or she will soon grow tired of that new love interest too. This cycle is incessant, unless someone wakes up and repents of shallow marriage in the first place.

Kierkegaard explains that boredom is dreadful because it takes away even pain's motivation to change one's course of life for the better. Boredom, in this way, is not idleness or stillness but, like the vice of sloth, involves despair of meaning and hope. In situations of boredom, we frantically try to inject entertainment of any kind. We seek diversions. These may start out as innocuous hobbies. We might overspend, overwork, or obsess over the neighbor's barking dog. When that gets boring, we might turn to an affair. Surely that, we think, will bring back our youthful lust for life. But even the returns on an affair involve diminishing returns over time.

Thus Kierkegaard suggests that some sort of spiritual awareness is the only real remedy for boredom. He writes, using a pseudonym, "And what could divert me? Well, if I managed to see a faithfulness that withstood every ordeal, an enthusiasm that endured everything, a faith that moved mountains; if I were to become aware of an idea that joined the finite and the infinite."[14] Note the biblical imagery packed into this dense line. But note especially the idea that the Tao of love, located in Jesus Himself, is the junction between divine and human love and connects *agape* with *eros*. Kierkegaard suggests, then, that a remedy for boredom is not frantic activity but rather stillness or mindfulness of what is already in one's midst.

If this sounds too theoretical, Kierkegaard provides the practical example of crop rotation. By cultivating the same crop in the same soil, year after year, the soil's nutrients become depleted. But cultivating different crops each year allows the soil to recover and remain fertile. If we keep moving to new soil but practice the same misguided farming strategy, we will do little more than deplete the resources of all the fields we till. We can apply this to marriage neatly. Like it or not, the intense flame of passion involved in the early stages of a relationship inevitably diminishes over time. When this happens, we might be tempted to find a new intense romance. But after a few romantic tragedies, we will soon find that the whole thing becomes boring. The solution, then, is to rotate the crops, not change the field. Applied to marriage, we should become mindful within our current marriage of the joys and resources present, and we should cultivate new interests and experiences as a couple rather than move on to a new partner.

This has been incredibly helpful for Stacie and me. We treat our expedition in life as one great adventure with various unique chapters, but we explore together. For instance, one of the best boosts to our relationship was a weekend motorcycle safety class we took. Even if you never plan on riding a motorcycle regularly (Stacie hasn't ridden, apart from on my pillion, in years), there's something invigorating about the challenge of going from little or no knowledge of motorcycling to being able to ride over a 2×4 plank at speed. Similarly, there have been periods when we got into geocaching, bird-watching, and wild mushroom hunting. Sometimes we grow tired of these pastimes, but we do so together, and then we find new interests together. So again, if possible, rotate the crops; don't move to a new field.

---

[14] Søren Kierkegaard, *The Essential Kierkegaard*, 4th ed., Kierkegaard's Writings, ed. Howard V. Hong and Edna H. Hong (Princeton, NJ: Princeton University Press, 2000), 43.

Before it's too late, if you are married but the relationship has now become dreary, consider trying to kindle an original flame of *agape-eros* in your marriage. Find new things to explore. Don't just seek petty diversions; seek deeply moving activities. I don't suggest this to be pious: consider traveling abroad for a service project, or consider becoming regular volunteers at a local charity. Get outside yourselves, and love the world together, and some of that unconditional love you're pouring out to others might just splash back onto your own relationship.

Grace after Divorce

While the medieval Catholic Church prohibited divorce, Luther believed divorce could be legitimate as a last resort, when there was adultery, impotence, unwillingness to have intercourse, or desertion. Moreover, he believed that the offended party should be allowed to remarry. Such a position has nothing to do with a belief that marriage is unimportant; rather, it is born of a spirit of graciousness. Fidelity, commitment, and intimacy flow from the New Logic. But so does a willingness to embrace people who have not lived up to their own standards. Grace empowers sustained marriage; it also covers those who have become divorced. We love to point out categories of people who are especially sinful and loathsome. Whatever we think about the ideal, however, we ought to bring grace to those who have been divorced. If you have been divorced yourself, there's grace for you too. Dust yourself off. Seek a life of reconciliation and peace, and then seek virtuous ways to love anew. This need not involve racing headlong into another romantic relationship. Just as we observed with respect to teenagers, for older adults who've endured a divorce, worth and fulfillment do not depend on sex.

Now You Never Show
It to Me (Sex and Aging)

There was a time you let me know
What's really going on below
But now you never show it to me, do you?
And remember when I moved in you
The holy dove was moving too
And every breath we drew was Hallelujah
—Leonard Cohen, "Hallelujah"

There's an evil I have seen under the sun. It prompts me to laugh and weep simultaneously: while adolescents often fight against libidos that are too strong, driving them to sexual encounters they know aren't good for them, older adults desperately wish to augment their libidos, hoping to please their partners through sustained sexual performance. I've known young Christian couples who were plagued by the guilt of premarital sex, only to grow up plagued by guilt for not having frequent enough—or vibrant enough—sexual encounters. While the angels chant laments for a young woman who thinks she can only guarantee her value by sexualizing a relationship, they intone a similar tune for the aged man who thinks he can only guarantee his value by maintaining an erection. From start to finish, the tragedy of our sexual lives is that we tend to think of sex not as a free dance but as a matter of obligation and exchange. Love for performance. Beauty for value. Prowess for honor. This is the way of the world, and it is dreary.

Granted, in today's rapidly changing society, this picture I've painted is not *always* the case. As we've seen, young people who find comfort in the digital world are delaying sexual intimacy. Advances in the health sciences are allowing older people to remain sexually active much longer than they once did, and there are many accounts of retirement homes being hotbeds of promiscuity. Nonetheless, many still live with a sense of frustration that their physical bodies are out of sync with their wishes.

Performance anxiety and decreased desire for sex in old age should point us back to a fundamental principle of erotic virtue: sexiness does not depend on intercourse. There is a sexiness that transcends physical contact. Just as sex is not the basis of a relationship in youth, sex is not the basis of a mature relationship. Despite what medieval Catholic theology thought about sex being for procreation only, the New Logic of grace offers the freedom to continue enjoying sexuality, but it in no way *demands* that we do so. Too often, our relationships remain transactional, conditional, and oppressive.

True sexiness is about resting secure in a love that is guaranteed and energized by an infinite source, requiring no individual performance whatsoever. The New Logic of grace frees us from treating sex as a currency with which we can buy true love and relational security. Just as sex is that *to which* youthful sexiness points for an adolescent, sex is also that *from which* we can derive peace and joy in old age. It's a mark of romantic bonding, and it is intended to bring about families and connectedness. In maturity, we remember when physical and spiritual intimacy intersected, when the "holy dove" was dancing in time with our holy movements, intertwined with our beloved's body. Even as our eyes dim and our bodies become frail, we remember the sexy hallelujah, and we cuddle in the peace that surpasses all understanding.

I've found that older couples who get this are the sexiest folks on the planet. I especially dig it when they walk past me at the harbor or on a hike, holding hands, with similar sweaters. Mature love is like fine wine; young love is more like a shot of Fireball liquor. This is because, while puppy love can be fun and intense, the most exquisite love rests in the *history* of a relationship.

Love Is in the History

My own marriage has by no means been an ideal model for couples to emulate, at least not until recently. If I were to list the top three moments in which I was at the precipice of despair, each would relate to a moment of turbulence in my relationship with Stacie. But this same, often-strained marriage remains one of the most cherished blessings of my existence on this earth. Why? Because love is in the history.

Fidelity over the long haul may seem tedious at times. But in retrospect, it is our greatest treasure. After decades of marriage, Stacie and I will encounter other people who may be better looking, more interesting, more famous, or wealthier. But none of these others will have shared the adventures we've had with our spouses. These people will not have the depth of shared experiences. This Christian call to long-suffering fidelity is not some tragic hero's burden. It is a witness to divine love itself. Ethicist Gilbert Meilaender expresses this well: "Our task is nothing less than this: to achieve within human life the love that is a dim reflection of the life of God."[1]

And what is God's way with humans? It is historical. It isn't perpetual ecstasy; rather, it involves long periods of wandering through wastelands. In such difficult times, we turn to the way God has been there for our ancestors and for us. Thus for ancient Israel, God was not an abstract, philosophical concept. He was the God of Abraham, Isaac, and Jacob—a God who shared a story with the ancestors. In times of bondage and slavery, the people of God remembered the Passover, the time when God brought his people out of captivity and into the Promised Land. This is expressed in the rather gloomy Psalm 39, which starts with deep groaning but takes comfort in God's history:

> Hear my prayer, O Lord,
>   and give ear to my cry;
>   hold not your peace at my tears!
> For I am a sojourner with you,
>   a guest, like all my fathers. (v. 12)

Thus just as we are pilgrims and wayfarers in this life, our relationships will never be perfect. But they can always be interesting, hopeful stories.

---

[1] Gilbert Meilaender, *Faith and Faithfulness: Basic Themes in Christian Ethics* (Notre Dame, IN: University of Notre Dame Press, 1992), 48.

Most importantly, Christians take comfort in the history of Jesus, who, when on the cross that "Good" Friday, cried, "My God, my God, why have you forsaken me?" (Ps. 22:1). The person Christians claim was actually God in the flesh had a moment when He seemed either nonexistent or absent. And yet at that time when all seemed lost, the time when even the faithful disciples seemed to despair of God's presence, God was working more powerfully than ever for the redemption of the world. When believers don't immediately *feel* God's love, they can be reminded that these feelings are often unreliable. From this history, we trust that in any moment of agony, God is in fact alive and at work in our story.

When the original feelings of infatuation and outward signs of love change over time, we often misinterpret this as a sign that love is dying. We need not panic in such cases. Likewise, we don't need to try to relive those outward signs, forgetting to attend to the romance itself. Robert Capon explains this phenomenon well:

> They [the couple] sense that the signs of the romantic vision (the walks on the beach, the phone calls, the dinners in candlelit restaurants—all the blinding newnesses that once were) are slipping away from them; so they begin the fruitless effort to "put back the romance" in their relationship by putting back the particular details through which they first caught the vision of the romance. But it never works. It was the vision that generated the significance of the details, not vice versa—just as it is faith that discloses the bread and wine, not vice versa. And so all their efforts at conjuring—at making a religion of the details of romance—do nothing but saddle them with the old, ineffectual burden of religious observance. The resumption of beach walking, phone calling, or dining by candlelight—the offering of renewed sacrifices to the details of romance—can no more take away the old sins that have returned to bedevil the relationship than could the blood of bulls and goats. Once again, it is the vision that led to the recognition of the details; if the vision is going to be recaptured, it can only be caught by following the laws of the vision, not the laws of the details.[2]

---

[2] Robert Farrar Capon, *Health, Money, and Love: And Why We Don't Enjoy Them* (Grand Rapids, MI: Eerdmans, 1990), 126.

This doesn't mean that we should avoid finding enriching activities to share; rather, we are free to find new adventures and interests. These should flow from the nature of the relationship and personal interests at the time. For example, picking up a new shared interest in bird-watching might be sexier than buying racy lingerie in order to "spice things up."

More Human than Human: Transhuman Sex

Instead of trusting in the natural arc of organic life, we often try to manipulate and improve on it. There's nothing inherently taboo or sinful about using technology to extend or improve our lives. The same goes for our sexual lives. We are free. But like so many human endeavors, our efforts are often misguided or rooted in a false understanding of what abundant, happy life is all about.

These are strange times with respect to bioethics. Technology has allowed us to extend life significantly, at least by modern standards.[3] Scientists and futurist thinkers are increasingly arguing that superlongevity, and cybernetic transcendence of death are just around the corner. Many traditional Christians agree that the vocation of medical professionals is to heal and support life—so much so that they even advocate extension of life in the midst of diminished life quality, cognitive impairment, and cost. However, these same Christians also tend to insist that to extend life beyond its "natural" limits is a dangerous act of "playing God." In other words, we instinctually assume that to end life by withholding medical intervention might be allowing a physician to *play God* but simultaneously worry that if this same physician is too successful at prolonging life, or at least consciousness—perhaps for a few centuries—this would once again involve *playing God* in a dangerous manner.

The movement at hand, one that has its own think tanks (and even a political party), is called *transhumanism*, or H+.[4] The

---

[3] I'm convinced that hunter-gatherer life was happier and healthier for a variety of reasons, two of the most important being a varied diet and a strong, supportive, and sharing community. Older reports of short lifespans in ancient societies of this type tend to be skewed by higher rates of infant mortality.

[4] When people first hear about transhumanism, they sometimes scoff, thinking it is little more than science fiction. But there is now a growing body of serious literature on the topic.

movement's three main objectives are superlongevity, superintelligence, and super-well-being. These objectives are interrelated. For instance, if we live longer, we will want to live happier lives, free from cognitive deterioration (superintelligence) and with mental and physical health (super-well-being). The technologies involved are manifold and include hormonal therapies, mechanical technologies, and pharmaceutical enhancements.

The ethical dilemmas transhumanism poses for society are precisely the sort of conundrums in which virtue ethics becomes useful. Clear rules elude us here. Instead, we need to discover what authentic human existence is all about. We need to decide what kind of people and what kind of society we hope to cultivate. This is a crucial task as we face the unintended consequences of exponential technological development. For instance, if sexuality is the basis of human happiness, then we will want our ability to function sexually to keep pace with our ability to augment longevity.

Perhaps the most important immediate concern for Christians is the way in which Christians are (and will increasingly will be) singled out as obstacles to progress. That fits well with the atheists' secular myth: the idea that the more advanced our culture becomes, the less it will need the superstitions of religion. We have advanced, so the secular narrative goes, from animism, to polytheism, to henotheism, to monotheism, to deism, and finally to atheism. We are grown-ups now, and we need to seek more concrete answers to our existential questions. Our biggest question is how we might overcome death. If, in fact, there is a chance that we can live incredibly long lives, with brains tied into the digital world and pain eliminated by medicine and genetic engineering, this looks a lot like the goal of eternal life, or heaven. It is a secular eschatology with the promise of a *tangible* kind of salvation.

Now, when we get the scent of immortality (or something close to it), panic sets in. We ask, who might thwart this opportunity for life beyond death? Ah, that's the tricky part! Who will hinder secular salvation? Religious people in general and Christians in particular!

One might begin to examine the topic by consulting *The Transhumanist Reader: Classical and Contemporary Essays on the Science, Technology, and Philosophy of the Human Future* (Chichester, England: Wiley-Blackwell, 2013).

After all, conservative Christians tend to oppose embryonic stem cell research and often meddle in secular science education, particularly as it relates to the science of origins. In other words, if science holds the key to our salvation, and Christians obstruct science, then Christians must be neutralized in this path to materialistic immortality.

It is premature to argue that faithful people *should* oppose all transhumanist research and development. After all, in our various vocations, we are called to act as the face of God for the world. Thus it is possible that a Christian, as a scientist, might virtuously pursue technology that can help people live longer, happier lives. Nonetheless, we have an opportunity here. Instead of trying to put societal cats back into the bag, we have a chance to keep evil cats from getting out of the bag in the first place. Even secular thinkers recognize the potential dangers of transhumanism.

Arguably, drugs like Viagra and Cialis, along with synthetic testosterone replacement therapies, are examples of transhumanist endeavors. Again, under the banner of unconditional love, we are free to use such technologies to enjoy life together, especially in contexts where medical or psychological conditions hinder the sexual function of people who are at an age during which one would otherwise be sexually active. Most of us aren't Amish when it comes to technology. But we must all be thoughtful about the ways in which our technologies control us or—as in this case—feed into unhealthy, oppressive expectations.

Sometimes, however, there is something unhealthy behind the marketing and popular demand for sexual enhancement technologies: the denial of death and an oppressive need to *perform*. Lao Tzu says, "Only those who don't strive after life truly respect life."[5] I apply this to sexuality as we age this way: by making an idol out of extended sexual performance, we fail to treasure it for what it is—a part of the beautiful experience of biological existence. We respect it because it is not all there is. It is a gift from and manifestation of eternal love. By trying to make temporal, physical experience immortal, we give it both too much and too little significance. We

---

[5] Lao-Tzu, *Tao Te Ching*, trans. Stanley Lombardo and Stephen Addiss (Indianapolis: Hackett Classics, 2011), 94.

value it too highly when we act as if it is the supreme asset of a relationship, something we must not lose unless we are willing to lose the relationship itself. We undervalue it when we think of it only as a biological or mechanical act.

Before debating the fine points of sexual enhancement technologies, we would do well to address expectations, demands, and resentments in our sexual relationships. Technological sex surrogates threaten to bypass the important process of relationship healing. It is tragic that some have wiped out so badly when trying to surf the Tao that they've arrived at a state of erotic despair. But I'm convinced that the New Logic can transform even our most deadened relationships. It's at least worth a try before turning to sex with robots.

Interestingly, the philosopher Slavoj Žižek turns things upside down—with respect to the relative priority of human touch versus mechanized sex—when he jokingly describes his perfect first date. He says he would dig it if he met a woman, went to her apartment, and brought a synthetic vagina with him. Then she could get out a dildo. They would then turn both battery-powered, vibrating sex toys on and connect them together. They could then let the devices worry about the sexual performance while they could get to know each other intimately. He explains, "We have a nice talk; we have tea; we talk about movies. I talk with the lady because we really like each other. And, you know, when I'm pouring her tea, or she to me, quite by chance our hands touch. We go on touching. Maybe we even end up in bed. But it's not the usual oppressive sex where you worry about performance. No, all that is taken care of by the stupid machines. That would be ideal sex for me today."[6] In other words, even an atheist philosopher can recognize something important to embodied, Christian sexuality: that spiritual and emotional intimacy is far sexier than mere physical gyrations. Moreover, delicate touch and deep conversation are more appealing than any method of "spicing things up" in bed will be for mature lovers.

---

[6] Colin Marshall, "Slavoj Žižek Explains What's Wrong with Online Dating & What Unconventional Technology Can Actually Improve Your Love Life," *Open Culture*, December 1, 2015, http://www.openculture.com/2015/12/slavoj-zizek-explains-whats-wrong-with-online-dating.html.

Virile, Heterosexual, Christian Dudes

Often in conservative evangelical America, Christian piety gets associated with active sexual lives. This is especially true for men in these traditions. They brag about how much sex they have with their wives, how vigorous it is, and how satisfying they are. This proves that they are masculine, fulfilling God's ideal, and thus thoroughly heterosexual. They rule the home with biblical, masculine authority, and they convince themselves and others of this rule through routine, mandatory intercourse.

I'm rarely proud or envious of such folks. Sex with one's spouse costs nothing and reinforces intimacy and strengthens relational bonding. Touch is good for us emotionally. But there's a dark side to thinking that it *has* to be frequent and lively. For one thing, I suspect that some aren't telling the truth. That's sad. For another thing, I'm worried that they aren't having enough fun with sex. Unable to grapple with their own erotic fatigue, they either fake passion or strive restlessly to cultivate it in themselves. Perhaps they, in turn, place heavy demands on their wives, who must remain sexy in a worldly sense. (This comes up occasionally in such circles, which also often speak of the spiritual and moral importance of being fit and healthy.) It suggests to other couples that they are failing if the act of intercourse ceases to be a daily routine.

There are times when, as a free partner in a marriage, I do believe we should get over ourselves and make love for the sake of our partner. Especially if it's been a while, there's nothing wrong with eating kale because it's good for you, and there's something even better about making love as a gift to a dear spouse who would enjoy the gesture. But rote, obligated, demanding sex is as unsexy as just about anything.

I'm glad that most Protestants have moved beyond the medieval Catholic idea that sex is only for the purpose of procreation. We're free to enjoy embodied love, and we're free to express it frequently. But that doesn't mean we should now place ourselves into the chains of expectations to sexually perform when we are exhausted by our hectic lives. Moreover, as a practical matter, such pressure to perform can itself be a possible cause of male erectile dysfunction. Stress—and performance anxiety can be a terrifying stressor—produces a fight-or-flight response in the body, releasing stress hormones like epinephrine and norepinephrine, which constrict blood vessels. Erections, of course, depend on blood flow and expanded blood vessels.

So we need to give our partners a break. Long days at work, screaming kids, illness, sleeplessness, and emotional swings can make sexual activity burdensome. If we love each other, we should cultivate relationships in which we are able to be vulnerable, open, and honest. That is precisely the sort of relationship where intimacy is possible. Granted, we may encourage our spouses to seek medical or psychiatric attention if they experience a radical drop in their sex drives. But we should never make sexual performance the primary litmus test to determine whether our partners love us. Moreover, when women and especially men are unable to be sexually intimate, this does not mean they necessarily find their spouses unattractive or unworthy of love. There are all sorts of other factors, including nicotine, caffeine, chronic depression, and cannabis. It is great to explore the causes of sexual dysfunction in an individual, but this need not be conducted in a state of panic.

Often I've heard from wives that social media generates deep anxiety about their performance. They see other Christian women online, bragging about their wonderful relationships, their beautiful and smart children, the financial success of their husbands, and the perfect organic dinner they created. They don't see the imperfections, fights, failures, and messy homes, since few take photos of such negative things to post online. After too much time on social media, many of these same women end up shutting down their accounts for a time to preserve their sanity. I suspect this is also a problem for men, though they don't indicate they are suffering in this way as often. Just as a conservative Christian woman might feel performance anxiety about her cooking, decorating, and parenting, a conservative Christian man who wants to feel successful in business and the bedroom can experience sexual difficulty. Feeling like a failure can disrupt the relaxed intimacy of a good relationship and kill a couple's sex life for good.

Perhaps, instead of flailing about, we might first seek fundamental peace. Taoist philosopher Chuang Tzu thought our incessant striving was a problem for contentment in general:

We cling to this body
That we are given.
We rush through our lives
Helter skelter,
Clashing with this,
Bowing to that.
We race like a wild stallion,
Which nothing can impede.
Should we not be pitied?
Working and striving
And wasting our vital energies,
Exhausting ourselves.
Finding no comfort or peace,
And not even able to derive
The slightest satisfaction
From our achievements.
Is this not tragic?
Should we not be pitied?[7]

In other words, the tragedy is that even if our constant striving for sexual fulfillment were to produce regular and frequent sexual intercourse, we very well might find ourselves unable to enjoy the act in its fullness. We need to rest, and spoon-cuddle, and watch a good movie, and do this without burdensome expectations. When we do, we just might find that our freedom *not* to have sex results in a more active sex life. In my own experience, I'd wager that I've actually enjoyed intercourse more often on nights when Stacie and I decided to just cuddle. When we plan on sex, we often end up falling asleep. Sex is best when it's play, not when it's work.[8]

---

[7] Chuang Tzu, *Chuang Tzu* (Chicago: Cloud Hands Press, 2015), Kindle Loc. 571–73.

[8] As a side note, several pastors have mentioned to me that one of their newest pastoral concerns is the number of elderly divorcees, widows, and widowers who are remarkably promiscuous. Sometimes elders form committed relationships, but for financial reasons (e.g., a Social Security paycheck will go away if they marry), they remain unwed. Other times, they enjoy their later years without commitment. In such cases, these individuals are able to extend sexual activity through hormonal and pharmaceutical enhancement. Strangely, I'm told that even when these individuals are otherwise conservative and religious, they somehow feel at liberty to act according to their desires, while they meanwhile lament the immorality of young-adult premarital sex. Changes in human longevity and the nuances of the economy will require further study and contemplation. Nonetheless, a

Likewise, when we fail to live up to our own ideals, and perhaps even find the embers of our libido (or the libido of our partner) turning to ashes, we ought not to become overwhelmed with resentment, self-loathing, or frustration when we find the embers of our libidos (or the libidos of our partners) going to ashes. It happens, and it's part of life: from dust you come, and to dust you shall return. The death of the libido need not always be lamented. As Plato, using Sophocles, illustrates in his *Republic*, freedom from the tyranny of the libido can produce new opportunities for elderly humans:

> "How do you feel about sex, Sophocles? Are you still capable of having sex with a woman?" He replied, "Be quiet, man! To my great delight, I have broken free of that, like a slave who has got away from a rabid and savage master." I thought at the time that this was a good response, and I haven't changed my mind. I mean, there's no doubt that in old age you get a great deal of peace and freedom from things like sex. When the desires lose their intensity and ease up, then what happens is absolutely as Sophocles described—freedom from a great many demented masters. However, the one thing responsible for this, and for one's relationship with relatives as well, is not a person's old age Socrates, but his character.[9]

Indeed, people have long lamented that their youthful erotic drives were too strong and got them into trouble until a point when they became too weak. This is tragic unless we learn to be honest, on both ends of the life arc, about where our bodies and minds are pointing us. Through cultivating virtue, we ought to then adjust our behaviors and daily routines to compensate. There's a time for everything under the sun. Be at peace with the season in which you find yourself.

---

fundamental Christian principle is as important here as it is in late adolescence: whatever the circumstances, we ought to understand who we are and who we want to be for others. Just as a young person should be respectful and heroic toward a boyfriend or girlfriend, the elderly ought to treat their romantic partners with respect and dignity, always looking out for their best interest.

[9] Plato, *Republic*, 1.329c–d.

Grace and Humor: Powerful Medicine
for a Mature Relationship

C. S. Lewis had it right when he observed that both uptight Christians and atheists like Sigmund Freud take sex way too seriously and, in so doing, take all the joy out of it. They can't laugh about it. Thus as we deal with our topic, it's good to remember that there is something hilarious about our simultaneously tragic and comedic erotic quest. I've had to remind myself of this fact throughout the writing of this book. I've needed to take myself and my own high-minded ideas with a grain of salt—which of course means you should do the same—and I've also needed to recognize that many will deny that surfing the Tao is as powerful as I think it is to transform our erotic lives.

The New Logic is foolishness to a world addicted to reciprocity, transaction, and achievement. But that's what Lao Tzu said would always be the case for our species. He wrote, "The great scholar hearing the TAO tries to practice it. The middling scholar hearing the TAO, sometimes has it, sometimes not. The lesser scholar hearing the TAO has a good laugh. Without that laughter it wouldn't be TAO."[10] To apply this to our erotic quest, those ready for the journey just get busy trying it out in all their relationships, however imperfectly. Others find it helpful here and there, though they are inconsistent in their application. Perhaps, for instance, they have great love for divorced people and recovering alcoholics, but not so much love for coworkers who have a different opinion about the direction in which the business should go. But isn't this whole tragic stumbling and flailing about worthy of an occasional laugh?

Martin Luther used humor to reinforce the preeminence of grace within relationships and the church.[11] He wrote, for instance, "I resist the devil, and often it is with a fart that I chase him away. When he tempts me with silly sins I say, 'Devil, yesterday I broke

---

[10] Lao-Tzu, *Tao Te Ching*, 54.

[11] The following section was adapted from my paper "Flatulence before Flagellants: Luther's Use of Humor as Theological Pedagogy," presented at the AAR-Rocky Mountains/ Great Plains Region Meeting, March 28, 2008.

wind too. Have you written it down on your list?'"[12] This represented a response to *anfechtung* (spiritual anxiety) that differed from his prior method: self-flagellation (whipping oneself to avert the wrath of God). There are many quotations like this. His irreverent ethos is evident in a letter to his friend Jerome Weller: "Sometimes we must drink more, sport, recreate ourselves, aye, and even sin a little to spite the devil, so that we leave him no place for troubling our consciences. . . . What other cause do you think that I have for drinking so much strong drink, talking so freely and making merry so often, except that I wish to mock and harass the devil who is wont to mock and harass me."[13] Such playfulness helped communicate his theology of the cross. Eric Gritsch rightly shows how Luther used humor to attack intellectual and ecclesiastical tyrants, to provide an eschatological response to the terrors of life, and to reflect the paradoxes of a simultaneously saintly and sinful existence.[14] Most scholars who study the concept of humor identify three models. The first is the *superiority* model, associated with Thomas Hobbes, whereby one defines humor as the phenomenon of suddenly and gleefully viewing someone or something as inferior. It is the sort of thing bullies use on the playground. The second is the *incongruity* model, associated with Immanuel Kant and Søren Kierkegaard, where humor is defined as the juxtaposition of two related but inconsistent realities. The third is the *relief* model, associated with Sigmund Freud, which considers humor a way to release repressed psychic energy.

Luther's anti-institutional use of humor employs the superiority model, since he could use it to turn the ecclesiastical hierarchy upside down. In a sense, he invited his students to stand with him and peer down at a lower level of the world in which bishops, scholastics, and donkeys all wallowed in their own feces. Superiority humor *can* make a downtrodden individual or community the butt of its jokes, but it can also work for liberating purposes when the

---

[12] Table Talk no. 122 (1531), *Luther's Works*, vol. 54, ed. Theodore Tappert (Philadelphia: Fortress Press, 1967), 17–18.

[13] Letter to Jerome Weller, November 6, 1530, quoted in Darrin McMahon, *Happiness: A History* (New York: Grove Press, 2006), 171. This is left out of the American edition of Luther's correspondence, and it would have come at the very end of the first volume or the very beginning of the second. I wonder if this is intentional.

[14] See Eric W. Gritsch, *The Wit of Martin Luther* (Minneapolis: Augsburg Fortress, 2006).

seemingly stronger is shown to be the weaker. But Luther used more sublime humor than mere ridicule of his opponents.

Relief humor occurs during Luther's bouts with *anfechtung* or when counseling those who were downcast. This humor served to provide a psychic release for Protestants still struggling with a sense of fear—instilled through the late medieval penitential system—that merely trusting in Christ would not remove their sins or that their abandonment of the old church would send them to hell. Luther's fart jokes could help such people experience the release from condemnation offered by the Gospel, and thus it was an important aspect of Luther's ethos.

The most important comic form for Luther is incongruity humor, since it enabled him to convey his cross-shaped theology. The cross involves paradoxes in which the foolish shame the wise, the weak overcome the strong, and the lost will be found. Theologies of the cross thus involve a recognition of the ways in which the world is oddly not the way it ought to be. Thus, according to Lutheran sociologist Peter Berger, this sort of humor is a "sign of transcendence," whereby an individual is able to look beyond immediate instances of suffering.[15] For Berger, as long as we "can still laugh at [ourselves], [our] alienation from the enchanted gardens of earlier times will not be complete"; humor allows us to bear suffering through a hope that those enchanted gardens will be restored.[16]

The best text to convey Luther's understanding of the theological role of humor is his commentary on Genesis 42–45, which includes a story in which Joseph plays a prank on his brothers, who don't recognize him in his new, powerful government job. Even though they had sold their younger brother into slavery, Joseph gave them grain. But he had something valuable placed in their bags so he could pretend to arrest them. When the joke gets too rough, Joseph reveals himself and expresses his forgiveness. Some patristic commentators, especially Augustine, struggled to answer whether Joseph's ruse, which includes deception and temporary anguish for the innocent family members, was appropriate for a biblical hero.

---

[15] Peter Berger, *Redeeming Laughter: The Comic Dimension of Human Experience* (New York: Walter de Gruyter, 1997).

[16] Ibid., 215.

But Luther insists that Joseph's actions are not only allowable; they also express a spiritual maturity, marked by grace. Luther uses this narrative as an occasion to contrast his movement's ethos with that of his opponents. He writes,

> I have often pointed out, and it must always be inculcated, that the Holy Spirit records humorous and inconsequential matters about such great patriarchs, whereas He could choose very weighty and sacred subjects. . . . An ignorant and carnal reader, who thinks that those matters are of no importance, is easily offended and is surprised that they are read in the church of God and that the Holy Spirit wastes time and effort in relating such nonsense. Why does He not set forth the wonderful stories of monastic fastings and the stoical and Spartan austerity of iron men, as the Carthusians want to be regarded? As though there could be important doctrine in ludicrous and worthless things! They also dispute whether this game, which Joseph plays, is pleasing to God or what impelled and inspired him to do so. But I reply that this is done by Joseph and recorded by the Holy Spirit in order that we might learn the right way to live before God.[17]

In other words, the natural life, for a child of a loving father, is filled with playfulness. Luther believed that the Roman Catholic monks' "flagellations, fastings, and all kinds of torments of the body" represented a false humility in stark contrast to that of the biblical saints, who transcended their "most grievous troubles" by displaying robust faith. Luther claimed that monks thought Joseph's behavior was "puerile" because it "conflict[ed] with their self-chosen righteousness."[18]

Defying an ascetic (body-denying) ideology, Luther insists "this game which Joseph played with his brothers was a very pleasing spectacle to God." For Luther, our lives are a kind of game played by the Creator; though our lives include times of suffering, they exist in expectation of the eschatological self-revelation of God, who, like

---

[17] Martin Luther, *Luther's Works, Vol. 7: Lectures on Genesis: Chapters 38–44*, ed. J. J. Pelikan, H. C. Oswald and H. T. Lehmann (Saint Louis: Concordia, 1965).

[18] Ibid.

Joseph, can see that our temporary incongruities will become the stuff of a great cosmic comedy. Luther writes that in the eschaton, God will declare, "I am the Lord your God. Hitherto I have treated you just as if I wanted to cast you off and hurl you into hell. But this is a game I am wont to play with My saints; for if I had not wished you well from My heart, I would never have played with you in this manner." As Gritsch rightly observes, "According to Luther, poetry, music, and humor are better means to express God's love of the sinner in Christ than logic."[19]

What is communicated through humor is the idea that a community or couple is serious about grace. Under the law, we try to hide our sins and can't reveal them to tell a joke. But with the New Logic, humor becomes evidence that one trusts in forgiveness enough to permit self-criticism. Humor says that everything is, in the deepest sense, all right. Couples should of course avoid demeaning or dismissive jesting. But when they are able to have fun and joke about their history together, it is often a sign that they are confident in the mutual forgiveness that keeps their relationship safe.

Robert Capon, through a fictional voice, suggests that mature romance is often the best laugh of all: "It's not just youth that's wasted on the young. It's romance. They moon their way through it as if it were some kind of church service or patriotic duty. Nosir! Give me two forty-five-year-olds in love any day. More fun than a barrel of monkeys."[20] He goes on to explore the ways in which this is not always apparent to us. Nonetheless, he is on to something, especially when we recall the ways in which disconnection from the Tao leads to protocol, propriety, and dreary obligation. He explains that "with romance: if you focus on the details of the experience—if you give all your efforts to preserving them as they were in their first, gorgeous appearance—you find yourself drifting away from the substance of the experience."[21] In other words, we should avoid trying to simply re-create the outer trappings of young love and instead learn to embrace the new forms of connection and affection we develop as we age.

---

[19] Gritsch, *Wit of Martin Luther*, 83.

[20] Capon, *Health, Money, and Love*, 99–100.

[21] Ibid., 125.

Conclusion

I've argued in this chapter that we should not put pressure on ourselves or our spouses to perform sexually when their libidos run low. And just as intimacy in early relationships is not to be identified exclusively with sexual intercourse, this should still be the case in old age. Intimacy must remain. Intercourse is something you are free to enjoy but not enjoined to perform. This doesn't mean we shouldn't, within reason, try to do our part to meet our partners' sexual needs when we can, even if it takes effort. And that effort most likely includes living active, healthy lives; staying active is sexy and prolongs one's sex life. Stop living, lounge about at home, and you will slow down. So to stay sexy, don't retire selfishly; it could kill you indirectly as you become sedentary and disconnected from people. It's healthier to get out into the community and spill out love in your final decades. For this reason, I intend to live passionately and be with others until I can't get out of bed. I just need to avoid getting on my wife's nerves when the kids move out, and I need to stay focused on surfing the Tao. Throughout the whole thing, I plan to focus more on pouring out the infinite love of God to my ever-expanding family and focus less on keeping my youthful good looks, horde of riches, and sexual prowess.

Even Though It All Went Wrong (Erotic Healing)

And even though it all went wrong
I'll stand before the Lord of Song
With nothing on my tongue but Hallelujah

—Leonard Cohen, "Hallelujah"

There are likely some of you kind readers who have succeeded in failing at every step along the erotic journey. Perhaps you ignored true love and sought only casual encounters, sexualized your relationships too early, had a few marriages end in divorce, and abandoned the spirit of gentleness toward your current spouse in your old age. Or perhaps you only screwed up in a few areas, but that still haunts you. If only, you wonder, if only you could have thought through the ideas we've explored together *before* it all went wrong, then maybe things would be different. That might be true. But in another sense, your brokenness and emptiness are gifts. It's hard to recognize this when it comes to sexual sin, because sex is so closely bound to personal vulnerability, emotion, and feelings of shame.

Nonetheless, you didn't design the secret chord in the first place, and you didn't compose the divine harmony. The Lord of Song did. So stand before that Lord and sing of your sorrow. If you don't have the words, consider Psalm 51:8:

Fill me with joy and gladness;
let the bones which thou hast broken rejoice.

It isn't that we should encourage folks to behave in destructive ways in order to find spiritual insight. Rather, we must learn to use, and allow God to redeem, our preexisting pain and brokenness to level us. It is through this spiritual death that we are disabused of our false sources of comfort and are ready to drop our self-righteousness. By passing through this death, through this total judgment of our self-ish selves, we are finally ready to understand the power and importance of resurrection. Through this process, we come with fewer self-justifying words, fewer theories, and fewer distractions. Nothing remains on our tongues but "Hallelujah."

Mary and Martha

I've come to consider the meaty part of the Gospel according to Luke—the teachings of Jesus recounted in the chapters between the birth narrative and the passion narrative—as the most important treasury for understanding the New Logic. That the Incarnate One entered the world at Christmas and that this same Lord died and rose again are of course central to Christian teaching. But we too often skip from the beginning to the end without attending to the powerful teaching of the Messiah. Among other things, I believe a key theme in Luke is that of religion as a human impulse to obsessively keep one's house clean.

In Jesus' day, this is precisely what the Pharisees were after. If they could just get people to follow the Law, they thought, God would bring about his kingdom. Israel would be set free from Roman oppression, and a new Davidic rule would commence. In other words, they believed that God wouldn't show up unless they cleaned the house first. This caused them to naturally conflict with Jesus, who claimed He was the God *who already had arrived*. Since they refused to accept that their religious housecleaning was unimportant, they failed to recognize the one who was the way, truth, and life.

We find an intimate illustration of this addiction to housecleaning in the story of two sisters. I find that this subtle encounter holds the key to understanding the overarching point in the rest of the book about the nature of spiritual housecleaning. Luke recounts the following encounter between Jesus and these women:

> Now as they went on their way, he entered a village; and a woman named Martha received him into her house. And she

had a sister called Mary, who sat at the Lord's feet and listened to his teaching. But Martha was distracted with much serving; and she went to him and said, "Lord, do you not care that my sister has left me to serve alone? Tell her then to help me." But the Lord answered her, "Martha, Martha, you are anxious and troubled about many things; one thing is needful. Mary has chosen the good portion, which shall not be taken away from her." (Luke 10:38–42)

Martha represents a typical religious inclination. It is well intentioned and recognizes the importance of the presence. But it gets distracted by the "many things" and thus fails to listen properly to the One present, the "only one" thing needed. Those "many things" here are not worldly, sinful things. They are religious things. They are good and proper in their own way, but religious distractions remain distractions from the Tao of Jesus.

How lamentable is it that the people who are named after this Jesus so often fail to internalize the message? Jesus becomes an abstraction. In turn, people become abstractions. This causes us to treat people who fall into erotic vice as political issues rather than fellow wayfarers in a strange and perplexing land. All of us, at least at times in life, exist in a painful tension between biology and spiritual values, hormones and holy longings. Riddled with guilt, we seek to stitch our religious fig leaves together; we seek to hide our nakedness and shame. We focus on establishing a long list of rules about what to touch and what not touch, what punishments are suitable for those who violate the principles of erotic virtue, and what penance we can perform to expunge our erotic guilt. But Jesus invites us to "choose what is better," as Mary did. And what is this? Listening to the Word Himself.

Note that Mary isn't performing a work of "worship" in this account. She is not serving Jesus here. She is allowing herself *to be served* by the bread of life—which is the New Logic that flows from the mouth of the embodied God. With this, the rest will be made clean in their time. Martha has things backward: we don't clean up our act so God can show up; rather, we let God show up so He can clean up our act.

Thus we can stand before the Lord of Song precisely because we come before Him empty. We sit at the Master's feet. We breathe.

We pray. We heed. We are healed even after it all went wrong; more precisely, we are healed *only* after our best efforts go wrong. This is because death through the condemnation of the law leaves only one path to life open: the Gospel.

Luke's account of this Gospel has a lot to say about getting the spiritual house in order. Today, the Western church is in conflict because of the dissonance between its sexual ethic and the world's sexual ethic. This leads many to focus on sweeping out those who have failed in the quest for erotic virtue, but this misses the point. I think the following are the particularly helpful points of this encounter for us to consider and apply:

1. *Jesus has arrived in God's house even though we often fail to recognize Him.* Jesus' first words in Luke occur when he was twelve. His parents lost track of him, only to find him in the Jerusalem temple, conversing with the religious teachers. When they show up to retrieve the boy, He says, "How is it that you sought me? Did you not know that I must be in my Father's house?" (Luke 2:49).

2. *Even when Jesus shows up in the house, He is found unacceptable by the housekeepers.* Thus Jesus said, "No prophet is acceptable in his own country" (Luke 4:24). This is because religious folks develop their own expectations of what God wants. When His way conflicts with theirs, they reject the Way.

3. *Jesus came not to cast sinners out of the house but to invite them in.* He says, "Those who are well have no need of a physician, but those who are sick; I have not come to call the righteous, but sinners to repentance" (Luke 5:31–32). Repentance is an awakening, a change of perspective that the New Logic of Jesus creates in a person.

4. *The house of God is a safe place of refuge for God's people even though it appears to be a house of many rules.* This is so important that even seemingly unlawful things become acceptable in the New Logic. Thus Jesus says, "Have you not read what David did when he was hungry, he and those who were with him: how he entered the house of

God, and took and ate the bread of the Presence, which is not lawful for any but the priests. . . . The son of man is lord of the Sabbath" (Luke 6:3–5).

5. *The house of God offers a tap with inexhaustible forgiveness; we drink this and dispense it to others.* Thus Jesus explains, "Be merciful, even as your Father is merciful. Judge not, and you will not be judged; condemn not, and you will not be condemned; forgive, and you will be forgiven; give, and it will be given to you; good measure, pressed down, shaken together, running over, will be put into your lap. For the measure you give will be the measure you get back" (Luke 6:36–38). We aren't to pour out grace in a measured way; rather, when we spill it out without spiritual stinginess, we find that it floods the world with the New Logic, and this flood of grace heals.

6. *The house of God can be cleansed not by self-righteousness but by a process of personal self-diagnosis and repentance, which can allow us to help bring our neighbors to a place of healing.* Jesus submits the following humorously tragic image: "Or how can you say to your brother, 'Brother, let me take the speck that is in your eye,' when you yourself do not see the log that is in your own eye? You hypocrite, first take the log out of your own eye, and then you will see clearly to take out the speck that is in your brother's eye" (Luke 6:42).

7. *The house must be built on the foundational rock, which is Christ.* Nonetheless, we tend to want to build the house on our own imagined but weak foundation. When this happens, the floodwaters come, and the "ruin of that house [is] great" (Luke 6:49).

8. *The music in God's house involves the devastation of the Law and the new life of the Gospel, but religious people don't really care for that music.* Jesus compares those who fail to heed the unwavering ethical call of John the Baptist and who resist the unwavering forgiveness of his own kingdom to children singing in a marketplace: "'We piped to you, and you did not dance; we wailed, and you did not weep.' For John the Baptist has come eating no bread

and drinking no wine; and you say, 'He has a demon.'
The son of man has come eating and drinking and you
say, 'Behold, a glutton and a drunkard, a friend of tax
collectors and sinner!' Yet wisdom is justified by all her
children" (Luke 7:31–35). The religious tend to resent the
strenuous call of John and resent the freedom of Jesus.
They want some artificial, human way, which is light on
ethics but intolerant of the broken.

9. *The door to the house is open to sinners when Jesus is truly
   present.* For this reason, despite the shame of a woman
   "who was a sinner," she came to Jesus' feet, washed them
   with her tears and hair, and anointed his feet with oil. This
   woman gets it and thus comes rushing in, even while the
   religious man scorns her for her shame and scorns Jesus
   for not acknowledging it (Luke 7:36–48).

10. *When Jesus casts out our monsters, we are to return and tell
    the story of our healing, even when it frightens or offends.*
    After casting out Legion from a possessed man, Jesus tells
    him, "Return to your home, and declare how much God
    has done for you" (Luke 8:39).

11. *God's house is not fixed in a physical location, but it is the
    house in which you find yourself.* Jesus says, "And whatever
    house you enter, stay there, and from there depart. And
    whenever they do not receive you, when you leave that
    town, shake the dust from your feet as a testimony against
    them" (Luke 9:4–5).

12. *The house of God is owned by a loving father.* Thus when
    we come to the house from a long journey, even in
    our tattered garments, we will be invited in. Jesus says,
    "Ask, and it will be given you; seek, and you will find;
    knock, and it will be opened to you. For every one who
    asks receives, and he who seeks finds, and to him who
    knocks it will be opened" (Luke 11:9–10).

13. *Strong men who seek to protect the purity of the house
    through their own strength will fail.* Jesus uses this illus-
    tration: "When a strong man, fully armed guards his own
    palace, his goods are in peace; but when one stronger
    than he assails him and overcomes him, he takes away his

armor in which he trusted, and divides his spoil" (Luke 11:21–22). In other words, in our well-meaning attempts to guard the house of God through power and armor, these attempts—especially when they take the form of institutions and contempt for sinners—end up becoming tools unworthy of our trust.

14. *Similarly, even when we think we've cast out all the unclean spirits from the house, if we don't let the Word occupy it, it once again becomes infested by spiritual monsters.* Jesus says, "When the unclean spirit has gone out of a man he passes through waterless places seeking rest; and finding none he says, 'I will return to my house from which I came.' And when he comes he finds it swept and put in order. Then he goes and brings seven other spirits more evil than himself, and they enter and dwell there; and the last state of that man becomes worse than the first" (Luke 11:24–26).

15. *The true house of God becomes a venue for a banquet that is open to the beautiful losers, not those whom we admire or who have something to offer us.* Jesus says, "When you give a dinner or a banquet, do not invite your friends or your brothers or your kinsmen or rich neighbors, lest they also invite you in return, and you be repaid. But when you give a feast, invite the poor, the maimed, the lame, the blind, and you will be blessed, because they cannot repay you. You will be repaid at the resurrection of the just" (Luke 14:12–14). By way of application, we are to turn the house not into a selective, dignified networking event but into a spilling out of true gift giving.

I share all this to drive home a point that is all too often lost on churches: the house is not an institution that we need to protect, cleanse, or dignify through our own effort. It is a banquet house, where those in need of healing come to sit at Jesus' feet, hear His Tao, and practice gift-giving with each other. This means it is a place open even to those who've failed in the quest for erotic virtue. They aren't supposed to get cleaned up before they sit down at the banquet. The banquet, on the contrary, is provided for them and their healing.

This means that while Christian communities have a legitimate calling to cultivate a unique sexual ethic, this is not primarily accomplished by keeping people out of the house of God. There are times for church discipline, especially when abusive or destructive behavior would otherwise seem to be winked at by the community. Nonetheless, the church's concern for purity should emphasize the safety of the place, in terms of its staff and especially its pastors. That is, people in need of erotic healing need to trust that they are coming to a place that will not victimize or manipulate them further. But they should also know that they are loved when they show up with their emotional and spiritual wounds. They should know that the purity of the church is precisely about having a place where spiritual surgery can take place without further infection, not a place where naughty people are kept out in the first place. In other words, the church should be a safe place for healing the sick, not a place that quarantines or excludes them.

Throughout Jesus' teaching, we find that the law, on its own, is unable to heal our relationships. Even though what it demands is good and true, commands do not come with the power to obey them. Moreover, those who try to fix relationships by the law alone will make matters worse. "The law," Gerhard Forde writes, "even the law of God, 'the most salutary doctrine of life,' is *used as a defense against the gift*. Thus, the more we 'succeed,' the worse off we are. The relationship to the giver of the gift is broken."[1] In other words, religious housecleaning gets in the way because we begin to depend on the success of our own cleaning efforts.

Occasionally, folks will say that the way of Grace leads to failure. They can point to folks who declare their trust in the abundant mercy of the divine and yet fail to live virtuous lives. Sure, there are many such cases among mortals. Nonetheless, I remain committed to the cause of Jesus against the Pharisees, of Paul against the Judaizers, and of Chuang Tzu against the legalists, when the Chinese philosopher writes,

How can it be
That they appear with their rituals

---

[1] Gerhard Forde, *On Being a Theologian of the Cross: Reflections on Luther's Heidelberg Disputation, 1518* (Grand Rapids, MI: Eerdmans, 1997), 27.

And do-gooding,
Their squares and plumb lines,
Their glues and varnishes
To alter the world
Rather than to abandon all of this
And to lose themselves in the Tao
And to dwell in Virtue.
There is no need to be confused.
Small confusions may cause us to lose the way.
Large confusions may cause us to lose ourselves.
For ages now all of those aspirations
To be good and to do good,
To be kind and generous
Have only caused them
To lose their way
And to lose Virtue itself
In the pursuit of these empty forms.[2]

I'm not insisting that Chuang Tzu understood the Tao in precisely the way Mary heard it from the lips of Jesus. What they have in common is important, however. The rituals, attempts to control the world, petty confusions, and endeavors to self-justify through good works distract people from the source of virtue. What is needed is attention to the one thing that matters.

For Shame

Speaking this way causes some to think that the New Logic is permissive and encourages shameful behavior. This is entirely untrue. The New Logic involves utter judgment. This is because forgiveness implies judgment and defenselessness, not explanations and excuses for moral failings. However, recognizing these failings is the beginning of restoration, not despair. Nonetheless, people remain afraid of the freedom of the New Logic and accuse those who adhere to it of being particularly sinful and dangerous. Martin Luther addressed this matter directly in a letter to George Spenlein:

---

[2] Chuang Tzu, *Chuang Tzu* (Chicago: Cloud Hands Press, 2015), Kindle Loc. 2666–81.

Learn to praise him and despairing of yourself say "Lord Jesus, you are my righteousness, just as I am your sin. You have taken upon yourself what is mine and given to me what is yours. You have taken upon yourself what you were not and have given me what I was not." Beware of aspiring to such purity that you will not wish to be looked upon as a sinner, or to be one. For Christ dwells only in sinners. This is why he descended from heaven, where he dwelt among the righteous, to dwell among sinners. Meditate on this love of his and you will discern his most precious consolation.

If you firmly believe this as you ought . . . receive your untaught and hitherto erring brothers, patiently help them, make their sins yours, and, if you have any goodness, let it be theirs. This is what the Apostle teaches, "Receive one another as Christ has received you to the glory of God" (Romans 15:7) and again "have this mind among you which is yours in Christ Jesus . . ." (Philippians 2:5).

Cursed is the righteousness of the man who is unwilling to assist others because they are worse than he is, and who seeks to flee them and forsake those whom he ought now to be helping with patience, prayer, and example. If Christ had desired to live only among good people and to die only for his friends, for whom, I ask you, would he have died or with whom would he ever have lived?[3]

Here we see that instead of trying to clean house, lest God and others accidentally associate us with sinners, we are called to radically take the sins of our neighbors onto ourselves, as if they were our own. When we do this, we demonstrate our unwavering confidence in the power of grace. If we simultaneously seek virtue and allow others to think we're vicious in the process, those who see this will realize that we take the divine promises seriously. And they will run to us because we have found peace and security in the sacred cloak of God's righteousness and healing.

The way of grace, as liberating as it is for the one who follows it, provokes intense anger from many religious observers. Yet we need not fret over the fact that we, as Jesus' Tao surfers, will be despised

---

[3] Luther, *Luther's Works*, vol. 48, ed. J. J. Pelikan and H. T. Lehmann (Saint Louis: Concordia, 1986), 12–13.

and misunderstood when we embrace those who have failed miserably. We should expect that people who assume only forgivable people are eligible for forgiveness will have a hard time accepting the way of indiscriminate embrace. The religious will not only misunderstand us but will also dish out condemnation, as Kazoh Kitamori puts it: "We may appear to be spineless when we forgive and embrace those who should not be forgiven. This very shame constitutes our pain."[4]

It is painful to love the unlovable, but it is also a delight to bring people from despair to the chorus of *hallelujah*. Unfortunately, until we confront our own failings, experiencing judgment and forgiveness, we won't be able to share forgiveness with others. Jesus is consistent on this. If we want to heal, we need to seek prior healing. This is because, in removing the shame of others, we find ourselves terrified that our own cloaks of self-righteousness will be removed along the way.

To my *own shame*, I recently realized I was ashamed of an older female relative in my family. We'll call her Cora to preserve some anonymity.[5] She died several years ago. I went to the funeral, but for reasons I didn't understand at the time, I felt ashamed of her. Like all of us, she caused her share of harm to others occasionally during her life. Long before I was born, Cora went to a conservative Christian college. She met lots of young Christian men, some of whom were preparing for seminary. I don't know exactly what happened to her at college, but I believe she was thrown out for a sexual indiscretion. From what I can tell, this was an unwanted encounter imposed on her by an undergraduate man. After she left the college, she went on a long journey away from the faith of her youth. Cora got into new age spirituality, crystals, and psychics.

At her funeral, I confess I was a bit ashamed of her. I thought it was because I was embarrassed at her rebellion against the truth, against kindness toward her own family at times. In retrospect,

---

[4] Kazoh Kitamori, *Theology of the Pain of God: The First Original Theology from Japan* (Eugene, OR: Wipf & Stock, 2005), 120.

[5] I'll leave out her exact identity and change a few details for anonymity. I might have misheard this story over the years. And I can no longer check with my relative. Regardless, the story is a common one, and the point remains that we often tend to shame victims, even victims who are close to us. I also reserve the right to combine two similar stories from my family into one for readability and brevity.

however, I have a greater shame that I, symbolically, joined in the long history of religious men who, seeking to hide their own failure to oppose a culture of injustice against women, refuse to recognize that we are often implicated in the shame of hiding injustices against young women. What's worse, we have a tendency to treat a person who's been harmed as the cause of the problem. We scapegoat them, cast them out, and get back to the safety of a house that is purified from sinful women. I've not done any of this directly. But remember that there are bad things we have done and bad things we have left undone (we call these "sins of omission"). We must repent of both types of sin. This book represents a call to all to address the problem of coercive sex in earnest and a desire to rectify a problem within religious culture. We must do this even if we are accused of being social justice warriors and of "virtue signaling" to score points with progressive friends. I'm calling not for more rhetoric but rather for leaders in schools, colleges, and universities to take their vocations seriously and refuse to sweep injustice under the rug in order to keep a school's image intact.

At Cora's college, I believe that hypocritical religious men exiled a young woman in her shame rather than bringing her under the healing cloak of God's grace. The shame wasn't hers, but it was made hers. And she was sent out like a scapegoat to carry shame out of the community. She kept it with her. The college was only one instance among many wherein the quiet struggles of women are ignored. Silence in such cases can be toxic. If nothing else, this book represents a resolute commitment to listen closely to the voices of all who cry out, to those in misery, and especially to those whose sexual histories make us uncomfortable. I'm sorry if I offended you with an opinion here or there in this book. Forgive me for the places where I may have been mistaken or insensitive. But that's part of what I want to get past: sometimes the subject of sexual ethics is so filled with virtual land mines that we refuse to address the subject altogether. While avoiding perplexing topics might provide a sort of comfort for professors, pastors, and other leaders in the community, we need to give each other the grace to hash all this out, in the open when possible. Otherwise, the hushed tones of the discussion make it harder to hear what's going on and harder to speak with a prophetic voice.

I refuse to be another religious professor, in a long line of religious professors, who is unwilling to expose erotic tragedy to the light, where healing can begin. On the contrary, I'm committed to the idea that the days of burying our erotic traumas should be put behind us. We should repent of the ways our predecessors blamed sexual victims for their trauma. Moreover, we should commit ourselves so sincerely to the New Logic of grace that we remain unafraid to discuss candidly the various struggles almost every embodied being faces, from puberty to old age.

Sometimes it's hard to convince religious people to change their approach to sinners in their midst. I suspect this is because they worry that if they admit they had been doing it wrong, they will be unable to bear the weight of guilt—of the damage they've done to people in the past. If our hostile approach to broken people in the past has driven them from the fountain of mercy and healing, we would have to admit this guilt, and we think we'll be unable to bear it. But there is grace even for those who got it wrong: grace is inexhaustible. It is an attitude and not a limited resource like petroleum. I heard David Zahl once contend that, while it is true and biblical that Christians will be known for their love, it would be magnificent if Christians also became known in our day as the people who were the quickest to admit that they were wrong. He wasn't advocating false modesty; rather, he was observing that those who really get the gist of the Christian message realize there is nothing to fear in honest confession. *Agape* love is not conditioned on what we do right, and it will not be taken away because of what we do wrong. Realizing this produces freedom to change course. We lose nothing in God's eyes, under the cloak of Christ's grace. But by losing our false self-righteousness, we gain something: the ability to begin healing the world.

Back to Cora: I admit I was wrong about her in several ways. I've been thinking a lot about her recently, especially after I invited a university student named Julia Cornish to write about her experiences with sexuality and the church. A couple weeks after Julia gave me the piece, I was traveling, hours away from home, and I accidentally passed the place where Cora's funeral was held for the first time since the service took place. Julia's situation reminded me that we all have a chance to get it right where our predecessors got it wrong. Julia is a twenty-one-year-old literature student at Concordia University, Irvine. I invited her to tell something about her own story, in her own words, and without editing on my part. As with all my guest contributors, I wanted to get someone who had a slightly different angle than mine rather than someone who would merely represent what I already wanted to say. Here is what she offered, and I thank her for it.

Guest Contribution: Julia Cornish, "My Experiences with Sexuality and the Church"

I have never been able to reconcile the relationship between my sexuality and my spirituality. From an early age, I was told that these were in fact irreconcilable—at least outside of marriage. The summer before I began sixth grade, every girl in my church went to a girl's weekend retreat in the mountains and came back with a purity ring and a bond that seemed to last through high school graduation. I didn't know what that meant, and now looking back, I'm fairly sure they didn't either. My liberal European parents, however, would not have it. I was not allowed to go, as much as I begged them to let me. When I showed up at youth group the Wednesday after the retreat, I had no purity ring and consequently no friends.

I grew up in an ELCA Lutheran church in southern Orange County, and just like every other teenager, I went through my phases of loving and hating the church, but my parents decided that I was only required to go to church until I completed my confirmation. After that, my faith was my call. In my sixteen-odd years of going to that church, I never heard of a conversation taking place about sex. There was no room for curiosity. When sex came up, it was immediately shot down with "sex is for marriage" and a few judgmental looks. There was no preparation for what happens once you're a partner in a marriage. There was no discussion of how to deal with desire or how to have God be a part of your sexuality. As a result, I learned that God and my sexuality could not exist in the same place.

Maybe it's because of my religious upbringing, but my sexual experience has always been a battle fought like World War I. It's a battle of territory, standing my ground, and seeing how much it's going to take to keep the boundaries where they are by fending off any advances. I am in a constant state of self-defense. This has been my experience in any sexual situation, consensual or not. Whether I was in that situation with someone I loved or someone I had no intention of sharing it with, it has always been up to me to decide the stopping point. That determined stopping point is typically met with resistance and guilt.

Ultimately, I feel as though my religion and my personal experience have taught me the same thing: that my sexuality is not my own. My church taught me that my sexuality should be essentially nonexistent until I'm married, and then it exists only in the possession of my husband. My experience taught me that I was selfish, that I was not giving enough if I was not giving everything. This is where my conundrum lies, because I know that this is not what God wants for me.

While my past gives me reason to be a victim, I choose not to see myself that way. I don't ignore what has happened to me, but I choose every day not to let it define me. In my experience, allowing these circumstances to define me only allows fear and confusion to permeate into every facet of my life. Choosing instead to be who I am despite what has happened to me makes me feel like I finally have some control. I am better than what I have been conditioned to know about my sexuality. It is my own, but it will take the rest of my life to feel comfortable with it, figure out what I am OK with, and proceed in a happy and healthy sexual relationship. I ask God for guidance in this.

I don't expect a full and complete recovery at any point in my life, but I do know that I'm not making a journey to healing alone. I don't know what it will take to find peace, but for now, the comfort of God's presence in my life feels like enough. I'm not currently engaging in a sexual relationship with anyone. The idea of starting all over with someone, telling them all this, and then trying to engage . . . it feels daunting. But I take that as an indication that I'm not ready to start over yet. God has perfect timing, so I don't need to be in a rush.

Naked Judgment and Forgiveness at the Banks of Lethe

Healing erotic failure and trauma involves a distinctly Christian understanding of forgiving and forgetting. This has been developed extensively by Miroslav Volf.[6] For Volf, there is an important difference between forgiveness and disregard. For example, "it is *morally wrong* to treat an adulterer and a murderer as if they had not committed adultery and murder—more precisely, it is wrong to treat them that way until the offenses have been named as offenses. That's why such offenses should not be disregarded, they should be forgiven."[7]

As I've mentioned already, forgiveness implies judgment. If I were to forgive you for wearing the shirt you're wearing, you might take offense. "What about my shirt requires forgiveness?" you might rightly ask in the face of such an offer. Therefore, whether the erotic vice is located in our selves or in those who have harmed us, it is vital that we identify the sin or vice for what it is. Too often, the Christian community is confused on this point. It ignores predatory behavior and manipulation under the guise of Christian forgiveness. The better way is to respond to injustice with righteous indignation, especially on behalf of those who are easily manipulated or coerced.

Nonetheless, following judgment of injustice, we forgive others as we have been forgiven. This is no easy task, and it might take a lifetime to fully embrace. When it comes, however, this experience of releasing resentment, of forgiveness in the deepest sense, is not only healing for our enemies; it is healing for ourselves. It frees us from the natural tendency to cloak ourselves in our victimization; it sets us free from mental loops in which we dwell on injustices as if these have become our badges of honor or our very identities.

Christian forgiveness is freeing because it doesn't wait for our traumatizers to cry hard enough, recognize our suffering explicitly enough, or change their ways to make them safe enough to be around. Rather, forgiveness arises from a supernatural spiritual heroism. As

---

[6] Miroslav Volf, *The End of Memory: Remembering Rightly in a Violent World* (Grand Rapids, MI: Eerdmans, 2006).

[7] Miroslav Volf, *Free of Charge: Giving and Forgiving in a Culture Stripped of Grace* (Grand Rapids, MI: Zondervan, 2006), 168.

Robert Capon explains, "Forgiveness is not a reaction to something else. It is the beginning of something new."[8] We cannot demand that others who have been traumatized do this when they are not ready. However, we can model lives of releasing resentments and invite others to try the same, even in difficult situations.

Volf describes Christian forgiveness using Dante's picture of the afterlife, as found in the final part of the *Purgatorio*. He uses Dante's imagery to describe the process of remembering, forgetting, and remembering anew. In canto 31, Beatrice leads Dante to the bank of the river of forgetfulness called Lethe. Dante, standing there, is judged. He reflects on the ways in which he himself has failed in love. There, he beholds Beatrice radiating a beauty that exceeded anything she displayed in earthly life, and she was there with the "Grifon, which is Christ, one sole person in two natures." Of that moment, he writes, "The nettle of repentance stung me so fiercely, that the thing that drew me most to love of it, of all other things became most hateful to me. Such great remorse gnawed at my heart, that I fell, stunned, and what I became then she knows, who gave me cause."[9] This is judgment. It is unpleasant but cleansing. It is like private confession, where a confessor vows to bury, forget, and cast out, in a ritualized manner, the memory of sins confessed.

In his description of Lethe, Dante draws here from the old pagan Greek idea that in the course of the transmigration of souls (something similar to Hindu concepts of reincarnation), memories are erased before souls return to new bodies in the world. But as a Christian who does not hold to reincarnation, Dante adds a second river, Eunoë, which is the river of "good knowing."

> And Beatrice said: "Perhaps some greater care, that often robs us of memory, has dimmed the eyes of his mind. But see, Eunoë, that flows from there: lead him to it, and as you are used to do, revive his flagging virtue." . . . Reader, if I had more space to write, I would speak, partially at least, about that sweet drink, which would never have sated me: but because all the pages determined for the second Canticle are full, the curb of art lets me go no further. I came back, from the most sacred waves,

---

[8] Ibid., 209.

[9] Canto 31, stanza 90.

remade, as fresh plants are, refreshed, with fresh leaves: pure,
and ready to climb to the stars.[10]

Here Dante re-remembers the past in a redeemed form. The past sins
and pains become part of a story of reconciliation that revives virtue;
it is sweet and restorative to contemplate. It prepares us for spiritual
transformation, or a sense that we might be ready to "climb to the
stars." In other words, in the New Logic, even broken love becomes
restored, because the final cosmic chapter is exceedingly beautiful.
Applied to our quest for erotic virtue, the process here involves three
steps: (1) recognize your sins and the sins against you for what they
are, (2) let go of the resentment and self-loathing that those remembered sins stir up in you, and (3) when you are emotionally and spiritually ready, begin to re-remember past vices and victimizations in
light of God's redeeming narrative. This leads us to the concept of
Christ's recapitulation of the human story.

Recapitulation

Cicero once said, "Gratitude is not only the greatest of the virtues,
but the parent of all the others." Saint Paul said that the greatest of
the theological virtues is love (1 Cor. 13:13). These two sentiments
need not cause a conflict between love and gratitude, since, as Luther
taught, gratitude flows from our encounter with the good news that
love is at the center of God's cosmic story. My colleague, psychology
professor Dr. John Lu, tells me that the process of listing the things
for which we are thankful is one of the best ways to increase our
happiness. Though it sounds cliché, the advice to "count your blessings" works best when we go beyond simply saying or thinking we
are thankful for the many good things that come our way in this life.
It involves seeing all of our lives, even our struggles, in light of our
promised, blessed *last chapter*.

God isn't in the business of going back in time to eliminate
our traumas. Our scars remain, just as the scars in Jesus' hands and
side remained after his resurrection. God *is* in the business of doing

---

[10] Canto 33, stanzas 103–45.

something even more astounding than raising pain: He redeems it by drawing it into His grand story.

Irenaeus of Lyons, a second-century theologian, can be of service in this process. He famously explored the way in which the work of Christ *recapitulates* the human story. *Recapitulation* means "rechaptering." The Latin word *caput* literally means "head," but it also can refer to a chapter *heading*. Accordingly, God doesn't go back and change the content of our past life chapters, but He is masterful when it comes to providing new meaning to those past experiences, including our traumas. Drawing from classical rhetoric, Ephesians 1:7–10, and Paul's description of Jesus as the "new Adam" in Romans 5:12–18, Irenaeus spoke of the work of Christ as a retracing of our failed steps. Adam fell in the Garden of Eden; Jesus was faithful in the Garden of Gethsemane. Adam encountered spiritual death in the Garden of Eden, and Jesus conquered death, which the angels announced at the Garden Tomb. Humans were barred from the Tree of Life (Gen. 3:22) in Eden, but Jesus died on a dogwood tree to become—Himself—the life-giving fruit and welcome us back to communion with Yahweh. In other words, in God's consummation of things, He takes control of the story's climax and provides new, redemptive meaning to all the mess we've made of the narrative. Jesus retraces our steps and does it all right. Through unity with Christ, we are made heirs to the riches of His successful journey. Thus even though it all may have gone wrong, Jesus sets it all right.

How does this relate to us? We sometimes want to be thankful only for the pleasant parts of our personal narratives. We sometimes resist being thankful for individuals in our lives who have provided us many good things but have been flawed and incomplete and have caused us harm. Try this thought experiment: list the major chapters in your life up to today. Give them full titles. For me, one chapter might be "1986: The Year a Crazy Christian School Broke My Spirit." Another might be "2008: The Year I Lost My House because I Changed Jobs during the Housing and Financial Crisis." A third might be "2017: The Year Authoritarian Church People Attacked Me for Trying to Be Faithful in My Christian Vocation." Note that we have a psychological tendency to remember the painful stuff and forget about the positive moments. But now, consider two more chapters: "AD 33: The Year Christ Flipped the Cosmic Script" and "The Last Chapter of the World: When Death Was No More." The last book of the biblical canon describes the last chapter of the cosmic narrative:

> And I saw the holy city, New Jerusalem, coming down out of heaven from God, prepared as a bride adorned for her husband; and I heard a loud voice from the throne saying, "Behold, the dwelling of God is with men. He will dwell with them, and they shall be his people, and God himself will be with them; he will wipe away every tear from their eyes, and death shall be no more, neither shall there be mourning nor crying nor pain any more, for the former things have passed away." And he who sat upon the throne said, "Behold, I make all things new." Also he said, "Write this, for these words are trustworthy and true." (Rev. 21:2–5)

Do you believe this, really? It's a bold claim, after all. It sounds naïvely optimistic. It seems too good to be true. But what if it *is* true? That would change everything. If the last chapter is beautiful, it redeems all the old ugliness. If the last chapter recovers the truth about our humanity, it flushes out the resentment of all the inhumanity we humans inflict upon each other. If the last chapter is good, it gives the bad new meaning. We can recognize this phenomenon when we are engrossed in a good novel. If the story has a happy ending, then the struggles in the middle chapters, while not things we celebrate, become part of the richness.

It's hard to write or speak this, because some will think I'm after the theology of glory offered by well-meaning Christian counselors (like Job's counselors) who want to try to find a silver lining in all of life's horrors. That's not what I'm talking about at all. It isn't that we must call evil good. It's that God is powerful enough to transform evil into good through His infinite love.

For this reason, I'm able to retitle chapters from my own past: "1986: The Year I Found a Sense of Purpose: To Study Theology and Liberate the Spiritually Wounded." Likewise, another new chapter heading might be "2008: The Year I Reconnected with Lutheran Higher Education." A third chapter might be "2017: The Year I Learned to Let Go of My Ego and Found the Courage to Speak Out for Goodness, Truth, and Beauty, without Fear." The title changes make all the difference.

These titles only work, however, if the last chapter is as blessed as promised. If there's nothing beyond this mortal coil, then who cares what I sensed in grade school, and who cares about Lutheran thought? But I am confident that all manner of things shall be well in the end for those who do not run from the New Logic. Perhaps, at the great Wedding Supper of the Lamb, you and I will clink our glasses together and share in a toast to the weird twists and turns of this life. In the meantime, a toast to you and those you love. May you and I continue to let go of all our resentments and cling fast to the blessings we have received. May you, in your romantic relationships, let love reframe your sometimes painful history. May you see your life in the light of the perspective of the beatific vision for which we hope in the last chapter. For, as Capon writes, in God's cosmic story, "tragedies, without ceasing to be tragic, are converted into amazing grace."[11]

According to Søren Kierkegaard, this last-chapter rescue is not a case of easy deus ex machina, a literary device in which characters get saved from an impossible situation through the rescue of someone or something outside the system. Rather, it is a case in which, at the end, it will be revealed that God's love was with us since the foundation of the world. Kierkegaard writes,

> Humanly speaking, consolation is a later invention. First came suffering and pain and the loss of joy, and then afterward, alas, long, long afterward, humanity picked up the track of consolation. The same is true of the individual's life: first comes suffering and pain and the loss of joy, and then, afterward, alas, sometimes long, long afterward, comes the consolation. But Christian consolation can never be said to come afterward, because, since it is eternity's consolation, it is older than all temporal joy. As soon as this consolation comes, it comes with the head start of eternity and swallows up the pain, as it were, since the pain and the loss of joy are the momentary—even if the moment were years—are the momentary that is drowned in the eternal.[12]

---

[11] Robert Farrar Capon, *The Fingerprints of God: Tracking the Divine Suspect Through a History of Images* (Grand Rapids, MI: Eerdmans, 2000), 43.

[12] Søren Kierkegaard, *Works of Love* (Princeton, NJ: Princeton University Press, 2013), 64.

Jesus' New Logic was in, with, and under the creation, since the beginning. We just couldn't see it. Our consolation comes from the final realization that a loving heavenly Father had our best interests at heart in the beginning, cares for us as we are now, and remains committed to our healing forever: world without end.

Everything's Going to Be OK

A while back, on the Virtue in the Wasteland podcast, Dan and I explored antiwisdom and spiritual depression (especially Ecclesiastes, Job, and Psalm 39). Shortly after this, we started exploring the joy and peace that passes all understanding (Phil. 4:7), and I started ending the show with the phrase "Everything's going to be OK" (#EGBOK). This soon became the unofficial tagline for the show. But it has often been misunderstood. It's not a trite, naïve refusal to recognize suffering or impending earthly doom. It's not a denial of judgment, especially since one of the reasons things will be OK is that divine justice will set wrongs to right. It is an eschatological position, and it is the key to erotic healing. Only if we recognize that God has things under control, that the divine plan will set things right, *whatever that will mean*, can we trust in God's surgery on us. Even when it hurts, we can be vulnerable and ready for the painful process of self-examination and repentance—*even when it hurts.*

This refrain, "everything's going to be OK," is in one sense an allusion to our podcast's patron poet, T. S. Eliot, whose poem "Little Gidding" includes the line "And all manner of thing shall be well." Eliot was appropriating the words of the English mystic Julian of Norwich, who wrote, "And this way our good Lord answered all the questions and doubts that I would bring forth, saying in an entirely comforting manner: I may make all thing well, I can make all thing well, I will make all thing well, and I shall make all thing well; and you will someday see for yourself that all manner of thing shall be well."[13] When asked how this could be, given the orthodox Christian teaching on final judgment and hell, she says God responded, "That which is impossible to you is not impossible to me: I shall keep my

---

[13] Julian of Norwich, *Revelations of Divine Love*, chap. 31. I have updated the spelling and some of the vocabulary for clarity.

word in all things and I shall make all things well. Thus I was taught, by the grace of God, that I should steadfastly remain in the Faith as I had previously understood it, and therefore that I should firmly believe that all things shall be well, as our Lord revealed at the same time."[14]

Perhaps Isaac the Syrian (613–700) helps explain a way in which inexhaustible divine love and the concept of hell are compatible:

> As for me I say that those who are tormented in hell are tormented by the invasion of love. What is there more bitter and violent than the pains of love? Those who feel they have sinned against love bear in themselves a damnation much heavier than the most dreaded punishments. The suffering with which sinning against love afflicts the heart is more keenly felt than any other torment. It is absurd to assume that the sinners in hell are deprived of God's love. Love is offered impartially. But by its very power it acts in two ways. It torments sinners, as happens here on earth when we are tormented by the presence of a friend to whom we have been unfaithful. And it gives joy to those who have been faithful. That is what the torment of hell is in my opinion: remorse. But love inebriates the souls of the sons and daughters of heaven by its delectability.[15]

Now, I have no evidence to prove that the vision Julian saw was from God or that Isaac the Syrian's opinions are the precise way to understand the nature of hell. Moreover, my religious tribe is particularly skeptical of extrabiblical revelation, so I won't press these ideas too forcefully. But I cite these passages from Julian and Isaac because they reflect the way in which Dan and I have used this idea. We don't know *how* everything will be OK, and we know that things look pretty grim at times. But the all-powerful, all-loving God of the

---

[14] Ibid., chap. 32.

[15] This text is adapted from Hilarion Alfeyev, *The Spiritual World of Isaac the Syrian*, Cistercian Studies 175 (Kalamazoo: Cistercian Publications, 2000). Some will accuse Isaac of being overly gracious. But his words resonate with Paul's: "For we are the aroma of Christ to God among those who are being saved and among those who are perishing, to one a fragrance from death to death, to the other a fragrance from life to life. Who is sufficient for these things? For we are not, like so many, peddlers of God's word; but as men of sincerity, as commissioned by God, in the sight of God we speak in Christ" (2 Cor. 2:15–17).

universe will not let us down. This is a theological commitment from which we should not waver. It is a commitment to the belief that the New Logic is the ultimate logic of the universe and that old karmic thinking will eventually dissolve away. As Revelation 21:4 says, "he will wipe away every tear from their eyes, and death shall be no more, neither shall there be mourning nor crying nor pain any more, for the former things have passed away."

After we started our #EGBOK refrain, Dan and I started to see it echoed all over the place, especially with artists who had experienced loss and renewal. Bob Marley sang, "Don't worry 'bout a thing, 'Cause every little thing gonna be all right."[16] Teegarden and Van Winkle wrote similar lyrics, covered by the Temptations: "As long as I've got shoes to put on my feet, and food for my children to eat, everything is gonna be alright, be alright."[17] Australian songwriter Xavier Rudd sings, "If I'm bringing my soul to ya, bet ya money there's a reason I believe. Building with a rusty hammer, standing strong in the things that I've seen. If I'm bringing my soul to ya, coming at you with truth in my eyes, building with a rusty hammer, strong feeling everything gonna be just fine."[18] Melaena Cadiz sings, "Wreathed in chatter strung with flickering lights. Keep repeating 'it'll be alright.' This is the shape of things. The joy and ache of things."[19] These lines all resemble the chorus to the eternal song, undergirded by the secret chord. Many if not all those who repeat phrases like this haven't a clue why or how things will be set right, but that doesn't mean they aren't sensing something legitimate. I believe they are sensing the faint rumor of the Logos (however muddled for them) within the very design of all things.

I first came across the profound significance of this idea of the world's final OK-ness in the work of Lutheran sociologist Peter Berger. He writes,

> A child wakes up in the night, perhaps from a bad dream, and finds himself surrounded by darkness, alone, beset by nameless

---

[16] From his song "Three Little Birds."

[17] From the song "Everything Is Going to Be Alright."

[18] From his song "Rusty Hammer."

[19] Melaena Cadiz, "The Shape of Things."

threats. At such a moment the contours of trusted reality are blurred or invisible, and in the terror of the incipient chaos the child cries out for his mother. It is hardly an exaggeration to say that, at this moment, the mother is being invoked as a high priestess of protective order. It is she (and in many cases she alone) who has the power to banish the chaos and to restore the benign shape of the world. And of course, any good mother will do just that. She will take the child and cradle him in the timeless gesture of the Magna Mater who became our Madonna. She will turn on a lamp, perhaps, which will encircle the scene with a warm glow of reassuring light. She will speak or sing to the child, and the content of this communication will invariably be the same—"Don't be afraid—everything is in order, everything is all right." If all goes well, the child will be measured, his trust in reality recovered, and in this trust he will return to sleep.

All of this, of course, belongs to the most routine experiences of life and does not depend upon any religious preconceptions. Yet this common scene raises a far from ordinary question, which immediately introduces a religious dimension: *Is the mother lying to the child?* The answer, in the most profound sense, can be "no" only if there is some truth in the religious interpretation of human existence.

. . . To become a parent is to take on the role of world-builder and world-protector. . . . "*Everything* is in order, *everything* is all right"—this is the basic formula of maternal and parental reassurance. Not just this particular anxiety, not just this particular pain—but *everything* is all right. The formula can, without any way of violating it, be translated into a statement of cosmic scope—"Have trust in being."[20]

Now, there's no need to stay in the realm of speculation. We will have to wait until we encounter eternity to know precisely what it holds for us. In the meantime, in this penultimate life, we must cling to the promises of the New Logic and rest in these alone for our certainty and peace. As Luther wrote in *Heidelberg Disputation* (1518) thesis 26, "The law says, 'do this,' and it is never done. Grace says, 'believe this,' and everything is already done."

---

[20] Peter Berger, *A Rumor of Angels: Modern Society and the Rediscovery of the Supernatural* (Garden City, NY: Doubleday, 1970), 54–55.

Christians assert that everything *is* OK because everything is already done through Christ who cried, "It is finished," on the cross. This means that the table is prepared for you. There's nothing you can do to earn this complete gift. The only danger is if you push it away, reject it, and instead rest on your own moral bean counting, intellectual achievements, or some other artificial game that strikes your fancy.[21] Taste and see that the Lord is good. So breathe, son or daughter of heaven. Rest for a moment. Quiet yourself. Listen to the secret chord that resonates through the cosmos, the chord God struck before the foundation of the world, amplified for men and women in the life of Christ and reverberating in the love Christians pour out, overflowing to the world. You are loved. All is well. There's nothing to be done by you to earn this love. There's nothing you've done that will disqualify you from this love. The only thing standing in your way is your fear—fear to be embraced by *agape*, fear that smothers holy *eros*. Do not give up on the New Logic; don't extinguish the sexiness of the erotic quest for virtue, even in perplexing times such as ours.

Ceaseless Prayer

Thank you for coming this far on the expedition with me. To send you on your way, as trite or cliché as it may seem, I encourage you to take with you a commitment to prayer. Your prayer need not take a form or pattern that you find burdensome, boring, or unhelpful. But you need to set aside time for reflection, realignment, meditation, contemplation, repentance, and focus. You need to take time to listen and stay attuned to the New Logic. This is because, even if what we've discussed makes sense to you, it is all too easy to fall into Old Logic patterns of relationships. We must, therefore, pray without ceasing. I don't know where I heard it said, but I once heard a theologian say, "I don't believe in the power of prayer; I believe in the power of God, so I pray." I agree with that entirely, especially when it comes to erotic healing.

---

[21] Perhaps look up the concept of "universal objective justification" to understand the difference between what I'm saying here and the "decisional soteriology" common to many evangelical communities and the soteriology of Roman Catholicism.

How should we focus our prayers? I am fond of the stark form of the Lord's Prayer, found in Luke 11:2–4. Jesus provided this template after his disciples found him praying "in a certain place." He tells his followers to pray like this: "Father, hallowed be thy name. Thy kingdom come. Give us each day our daily bread; and forgive us our sins, for we ourselves forgive everyone who is indebted to us; and lead us not into temptation." I take this to mean that as we reset and refresh ourselves in prayer, we should focus on the following:

1. *Hallowed be thy name.* Align yourself and your thoughts to the infinite God, who offers infinite love. Without contemplating and calling out to this source of *agape*, the rest will be a waste of time.

2. *Thy kingdom come.* Stay focused on the kingdom. This is not about some future ethereal heaven. This is about God's New Logic taking hold of people in our world. Consider, therefore, all the people you can bring into life in the New Logic. Consider the healing you can help effect for all those around you who are hurting. Consider how you can live with others, not in a way that depends on moral bean counting and transactions. Rather, consider how you can cultivate a world of forgiveness and mutual gift giving. Start with a romantic partner if you can.

3. *Our daily bread.* Recognize that you need to have basic needs in place before you will have the strength and emotional energy to love others. Consider how financial stress might be hindering your relationships. Let go of the material desires that distract you, but ask God to help you establish a sane, stable financial life. All you really need is food in order to love and serve your neighbor. Don't let envy distract you from the infinite gift of loving and receiving love, for that is both the most valuable thing in the world and also something that has no monetary price tag.

4. *Forgive us our sins.* Don't become burdened by the need to list every infraction, navel gazing until you are overwhelmed by your failure. Rather, take a personal

inventory in order to reflect on the ways in which you have been blinded to your own selfishness and mistreatment of others. In the context of unconditional love and forgiveness, seek regular cleansing from the ways you've failed to surf the Tao.

5. *We ourselves forgive.* Practice letting go of your resentments, including in your relationships, even those that relate to betrayal and trauma. Clinging to wounds can sometimes tangle you up in a vicious cycle of anger and vindictiveness. Failure to let go hinders erotic virtue.

6. *Lead us not into temptation.* Of course, pray that you will be able to overcome sexual temptation and lust. But more important, pray that you will not be tempted by pettiness or anything that will distract you from the New Logic of grace. Pray that you will stay in the way of the Tao of Jesus, not the moral score keeping, the old karmic logic of religious and worldly people.

Since we're on the topic of prayer, let's begin to wrap up our expedition by turning to the source of all creation—the holy Name—Who is vitally important for our quest to erotic virtue. The following prayer from Søren Kierkegaard will serve our purposes nicely. This prayer is Trinitarian and reminds us that the nature of the Christian God is three persons with one essence; that is, God is by nature relational. This prayer inspires us to be thankful for the One who has sustained our love and inspired a way of deeper love that the world cannot offer. We can't overcome the pain of our romantic failures without the grace of the Lamb of God who takes away the sin—even the erotic sin—of the world. It invites the Spirit to empower us to spill out the love we have received to all those around us, including those who have failed us or acted as our enemies:

How could one speak properly about love if you were forgotten, you God of love, source of all love in heaven and on earth; you who spared nothing but in love gave everything; you who are love, so that one who loves is what he is only by being in you! How could one speak properly about love if you were forgotten, you who revealed what love is, you our Savior and Redeemer, who gave yourself in order to save all. How could one speak properly of love if you were forgotten, you Spirit of love, who take nothing of your own but remind us of that love-sacrifice, remind the believer to love as he is loved and his neighbor as himself![22]

When it comes to sexiness, prayer is about reminding ourselves daily about the love that has accomplished all, despite our failures. It returns us to the source of life, to peace, and to our calling to be the masks of God toward our neighbors. Prayer aligns us with the mission—that is, the *name* of Jesus. We contemplate, meditate, struggle, and weep in His name. Amen.

The Secret Chord amid the Noise

When we finally get to protect space for silence, we come closer to understanding the secret chord. I realized this one evening at a resort stay a student gave to Stacie and me. The gift came at the end of a hectic semester. Our family was living on campus in a special living-learning community. In our section of student housing, we hosted international students alongside American students who were interested in global issues, international business, and related conversations. After staying there for a few years, it became obvious that the family needed to get some space away from work. After all, I was living, working, and going to church on Sunday with the same people. Our living unit was generous and comfortable, as far as student-housing units go, but we lived most of our existence within the bubble.

Seeing this, one particular student who had been with us since the beginning became concerned for us. The resort stay was intended to give us a break and to restore our energy. Nonetheless, it's hard to force oneself to relax in a time of stress. Stacie and I set out for our stay knowing that finals week was around the corner, I had several small writing projects to complete before the year's end, and we were fighting more than usual. At one point, I needed to go sit out on the balcony of our room. There, I was annoyed that we were so close to

---

[22] Kierkegaard, *Works of Love*, 3.

a freeway that the sound of trucks and cars speeding by detracted from the natural beauty of the area. I had a Bluetooth speaker on the table, and I sat back to take it all in. After calming down a bit and praying, something changed about my perceptions of the place and the sounds I was hearing.

The noises around me started to come into harmony. I perceived that the wheels on the road were creating various notes. Indeed, it soon became clear that I was hearing the secret chord. What I had thought was just a bunch of ugly noise was something greater. It was the sound of life. Where were people headed? There's of course no way to know. But they were racing off somewhere: to live life.

Interspersed with the notes played by automobile tires was the song of a bird. It struck me that most of the time when birds are singing, I know how to translate their meaning rather literally. It's like this: "I'm here, ready for sex. Chirp-chirp. Sex, please. Whip-whip. I'm available for sex. Hoo-whip. I'd make a good mate. I'm a hunk. I'm also a good singer with healthy lungs. And I'm crooning just for you, girl." In other words, just as I heard the sound of life in the chords played by rubber on the highway, there was a call to pro-creation and to the instigation of new life; it was a sexy song, intoned from branches in the swaying tree outside my room. The final touch occurred when the song "Kyrie Eleison" (Lord Have Mercy) came on my Bluetooth speaker. The lyrics are in Greek and of ancient Christian origin. But behind it all was also a sort of *Om*. Tears flowed from my eyes as I finally heard the chord I was trying to understand. I started singing and humming in tune with the whole divine orches-tra. What from a limited perspective seemed to be discordant, ugly, and annoying was, from the right perspective, a beautiful harmo-nious chord. I went back in to the room. Stacie and I danced. All was joyful again. A glimpse of infinity returned to our time-bound drama. I think the sound and fury of the whole stage play signifies something eternal. That is the secret chord. And it is sexy.

For Further Reading

For bibliographic material, I'll leave you to the footnotes. Here I would like to share with you the most helpful books I've come across that can point us toward integration of divine and human love, *eros* and *agape*. I have intentionally kept this short, so you know I mean it when I say that each of these books might do you some good, depending on your situation in life. If you are entering into a relationship and thinking about marriage, consider reading some or all of these together and discussing your reactions before you get hitched. If you are currently struggling in a relationship, these can be good medicine.

Ansari, Aziz, and Eric Klinenberg, *Modern Romance*
This is a great collaboration between a witty comedian and a sociology professor. They explore the ways in which dating has changed drastically, and continues to change, in the wake of the exponential growth of new technology. This is a helpful read for older generations trying to understand the ways in which young adults date and think about sex and marriage.

Frykholm, Amy, *See Me Naked*
One of the most important things for a young adult or a parent to do before discussing issues of sexuality is to hear real stories from actual people who are free to share their stories honestly. You don't have to agree with the sentiments of the author or the people she interviews. But Amy is a great writer and does her work well. Listen before you speak, friends.

Gottman, John, *The Seven Principles for Making Marriage Work*
This is probably the only practical book on marriage you really need. This ain't no Dr. Phil hooey. This is researched and effective practical wisdom based on university-level research of the highest caliber. If you'd like, skip right to the relevant sections for your stage in life.

Grant, Jonathan, *Divine Sex*
This is more accessible than my book here but dances to the same melody. If you found my book too complicated or meandering but want to give something similar to a friend or relative, try this.

Hoffman, Bengt, *Theology of the Heart: The Role of Mysticism in the Theology of Martin Luther*
This is rather scholarly, but if you are interested in exploring the bold idea that Luther had a mystical side, check this out.

Keith, Scott, *Being Dad: Father as a Picture of God's Grace*
My longtime friend Scott, as I can attest from firsthand experience, is no permissive pushover as a parent. But he is able to explain the importance of graciousness within the vocation of fatherhood. Even if you aren't a father, or even a dude, some of the principles he addresses will be helpful for understanding the nature of a gracious family ethos in general.

Kierkegaard, Søren, *Works of Love*
Kierkegaard is often difficult to understand but always profound. This is one of his more accessible works, but it is one of his hardest to internalize in the long run. As far as the radical call of Christian love is concerned, there is hardly a better theologian-philosopher to struggle through.

Lao-Tzu, *Tao Te Ching*
I don't actually know any Taoists per se. As a religious phenomenon, Taoism has gone through various phases. Sometimes it's been focused on traditional healing, sometimes on talismanic magic, sometimes on sexual energy. But there are philosophical concepts contained here in this Chinese classic, which predates a lot of what might reasonably be called quackery (like the outer alchemy that

supposed toxic cinnabar could provide eternal life), can stimulate important thinking about the relationship between ultimate reality and ethical living. Don't think of it so much as a religious text as a philosophical exploration that can help stimulate good thinking and conversation about our lives and relationships.

Lemke, Rebecca, *The Scarlet Virgins: When Sex Replaces Salvation*
This short book will help anyone confused about the ethos and effects of the so-called purity movement. If Amy Frykholm's (see above) book is too edgy or liberal for your taste, Rebecca is a woman who knows and remains solidly within down-home American family culture. She was homeschooled in Oklahoma, remains an evangelical Christian, and has an unsettling but important story to tell.

Meilaender, Gilbert, *Faith and Faithfulness*
If you want to understand a Gospel-oriented and Lutheran approach to virtue ethics (whether or not you are a Lutheran is not important to enjoy this one), this is the go-to book. It is a relatively accessible work of philosophical ethics from a Christian perspective. His insights undergird much of what I do in this book.

van Voorhis, Daniel, *Monsters*
I didn't realize it when we started out, at roughly the same time, to write our books. Mine was ostensibly about sex, his about addiction and dating. But we discovered that we were really writing about the same spiritual reality, albeit from different perspectives. His is more of a memoir, so if you dig the concepts here but want something easier to digest and more artfully composed, check out his book.

Zahl, Paul, *Grace in Practice: A Theology of Everyday Life*
The Zahl family never disappoints. Here Paul gives the big picture and also fine-tunes the implications of the New Logic for daily life. If you want to explore grace as more than an abstract concept, this is for you.

Family Album

My future wife, Stacie, the night I first met her at a church youth group. We were in middle school.

With Stacie at her high school graduation.

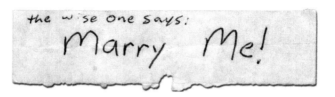

the wise one says:

Marry Me!

YOUR JUDGEMENT IS A LITTLE OFF AT THIS TIME	PUT UP WITH SMALL ANNOYANCES TO GAIN GREAT RESULTS

Proposal artifacts. I proposed to Stacie with a song I wrote for her, takeout Chinese food (in honor of our first date), and a fortune cookie I had modified. I removed the original fortune with tweezers and then inserted my own handwritten note: "Marry me!" Alas, there had originally been *two* fortunes in this particular cookie. When Stacie broke hers open, she got one of the remaining originals. It read, "Your judgment is a little off at this time." I've never been superstitious, but this made me momentarily think we should hit the snooze button on our engagement. In the end, we went through with it. Mine read, "Put up with small annoyances to gain great results."

Our first home in Bellflower, California. It was about five hundred square feet inside but with a big backyard. This is where we invented something we called the "love nest," which involves turning a sofa and love seat toward each other, making an almost fully enclosed cuddle space for late-night movie binging. The house felt smaller than the modest sailboat on which I wrote much of this book.

Our sons, Augustine and Aidan, outside our home in Evergreen, Colorado. We've lived in several places over the years, but sometimes I think the boys miss Colorado most of all.

Here I am with Augustine and Aidan, riding scooters through Yangshuo, China. We were, in fact, happy that day. Why the serious faces? We were pretending to be a biker club. Since I could never get any of my adult friends to ride motorcycles with me back home, the boys and Stacie helped me fulfill my dream of riding through winding mountain roads with a posse. Stacie took the shot.

The family in Hong Kong, where we were leading a group of recent college graduates, teaching virtue ethics and English. We ate like kings during that trip.

Here I am on the smoothest bike I've ever owned, a Triumph Speedmaster. I got it after my vintage Harley Ironhead gave up the ghost one too many times. One of my all-around favorite guys, Doug Klembara, took this shot. A note to the kids: use a full-face helmet (unless Doug is around with a camera).

With Stacie and Mana, a dear honorary member of the family, at the Grand Canyon. We had the chance to travel with international students to various American sites during the several years when the family lived on the Concordia University campus as leaders of the Global Village living and learning community.

Augustine and his girlfriend, Sydnie, going to a high school dance.

CPSIA information can be obtained
at www.ICGtesting.com
Printed in the USA
FFOW02n2118280817
39299FF